How to make great short feature films

Ghosthunter is the first carbon neutral® film.

Amulet Films is planting, with environmental task force Future Forests, over 30 natural indigenous trees to balance or 'offset' the carbon dioxide emissions produced in the making of *Ghosthunter*. The production produced 24.5 tonnes of CO_2, which equals 6.7 tonnes of carbon.

CO_2 is one of the main causes of global warming, trapping heat from the sun in the atmosphere. We can all help deal with this issue by reducing our CO_2 emissions at source, switching where possible to renewable sources of energy, such as wind and hydro, and offsetting – or absorbing – the non-reducible part of our CO_2 emissions by planting trees. Trees absorb CO_2 and produce something positive – oxygen and wood. Every tree planted not only helps protect the environment but also helps recreate indigenous woodland, new habitats for wildlife and local amenity space.

Future Forests works with the Edinburgh Centre for Carbon Management, world authorities on greenhouse gases, and with local authorities, the Wildlife Trust and Community Forests programmes to source planting sites all around the UK and abroad. If you would like to know more about Future Forests and its carbon offset initiative schemes, contact Future Forests at: Hill House, Castle Cary BA7 7JL (Tel: 0870 241 1932) or visit www.futureforests.com

Amulet Films is delighted to be working with Future Forests on this unique project and we hope that this initiative will become an integral part of the film industry.

FUTURE FORESTS

How to make great short feature films: the making of *Ghosthunter*

Ian Lewis

ELSEVIER

AMSTERDAM • BOSTON • HEIDELBERG • LONDON • NEW YORK • OXFORD
PARIS • SAN DIEGO • SAN FRANCISCO • SINGAPORE • SYDNEY • TOKYO

Focal
Press

Focal Press
An imprint of Elsevier
Linacre House, Jordan Hill, Oxford OX2 8DP
200 Wheeler Road, Burlington, MA 01803

First published 2001
Reprinted as paperback 2003
Reprinted 2004

British Library Cataloguing in Publication Data
A catalogue record for this book is available from the British Library

Library of Congress Cataloguing in Publication Data
A catalogue record for this book is available from the Library of Congress

ISBN 0 240 51945 0

For information on all Focal Press publications
visit our website at www.focalpress.com

Composition by Genesis Typesetting, Laser Quay, Rochester, Kent
Printed and bound in Great Britain by MPG Books Ltd, Bodmin, Cornwall

Contents

Foreword
by David Parfitt

Making a short film is one of the first, vital steps to becoming a filmmaker. Whether you're using a camcorder and friends or a 35 mm camera and a professional cast and crew, the experience will be a valuable one. Short films are an accessible way into a complex industry and a chance to create your own calling card. One of my first experiences as a producer was putting together the short film *Swan Song* directed by Kenneth Branagh, which I found an invaluable learning experience. Many of the contacts I made have remained part of my team for the past ten years.

This book and DVD set out to create a 'short-filmmaker's kit', which is something I would have valued when setting up *Swan Song*. It aims to provide advice and inspiration for aspiring filmmakers and some of the tools to help make their progress easier. It achieves this ambition by blending together general short-filmmaking advice with a case study of the short film *Ghosthunter*.

Ghosthunter was produced by Alison Reddihough and produced and directed by Simon Corris of Amulet Films. These two ambitious and resourceful filmmakers decided early on that *Ghosthunter* would be an exceptional film in many ways. Not only did they want to reproduce the high production values of a feature film but they also wanted the filmmaking process to be an educational experience for all involved. They quickly realized that the best way of learning was through hands-on experience. They enlisted the help and advice of some of the most respected members of the industry, including Freddie Francis, Frank Finlay, Peter Lamont and Barrington Pheloung, and were able to avoid many of the potential pitfalls of filmmaking. The result is an extremely well-made film that will hopefully launch their feature film careers.

As Alison and Simon hadn't gone to film school – they are both actors – their filmmaking research consisted of reading as much as they could about filmmaking; however, they found there were very few books specifically about making shorts. Along with the extensive knowledge of Ian Lewis, a writer with many years' experience of film and television production, they set out to create the book that they wished had been available when they first started out.

How to make great short feature films: the making of Ghosthunter contains sound advice, support and encouragement for short-filmmakers. It is a wonderful learning tool for those with ambitions to succeed in a very competitive industry.

Acknowledgements

Many thanks to all those people who not only helped with the movie, but also gave time to be interviewed for the book.

Amulet Films would like to thank all those people who encouraged us during the planning and production of *Ghosthunter*. To Kenneth Branagh, David Parfitt, Robin O'Donoghue and Jamie Payne for their invaluable advice and encouragement, to all our consultants for their continued support and especially to the entire crew for their time, energy and commitment to the film that made it all possible.

All photographs © Zoë Norfolk 2000.

Introduction

A lot of people feel that directing film is what they most want to do. Not everyone will succeed – just as people who feel that writing novels is what they want to do often never quite make it. But you can have a lot of fun trying.

To speak of having fun making movies doesn't mean that you're not treating it seriously. Almost the opposite, in fact. There are so many upheavals, worries, tensions and upsets in putting together even supposedly the simplest movie, that everyone involved needs to be enjoying themselves – or totally insane. But, if you intend (or dream of) a life in film, it's terribly important to take the activity seriously and to approach the film with a professional attitude, whether there's enough money available to pay everyone properly or whether cast and crew are working for experience, deferred fees or just to help out.

This is the story of the production of one film made in an entirely professional way – except that most of the cast and crew were working with very little pay – a short feature called *Ghosthunter*.

The crew

1 Beginnings

After many years of acting, Simon Corris and Alison Reddihough decided to make a short film with all the production values and working methods of a full-length feature film. They did a great deal of research before they started, looking for help, advice, tips and contacts. Nearly everything they found was concerned with making full-length feature films, whether with no money or with real finance. Advice for people starting out always began 'once you've made your short . . .'. There was almost nothing that talked about making that first short film.

Simon: *The books that deal with writing, producing, running a production tend to be* The Making of 'Titanic' *and the big budget Hollywood films, and they all seemed to be very American. Most of the stuff that we got was based on American writers writing about American films and American companies.*

Not only that, there are major differences in approach between making a full-length film and making a short film. Most of them are consequences of the difference in scale, it's true, but nonetheless, advice given for a full-length film lasting 90 minutes or more and involving filming for 4 weeks, 6 weeks or more is often not all that useful or relevant for something that has a production period of only a few days. Even advice on raising finance deals with a so much larger scale that the problems are quite different and the advice much less useful.

Simon: *Even when you read a book about a low-budget feature they're still talking about £200 000+ finance. The ideas don't quite relate. You read it and you think, well OK, that'll work for me when I start working on our feature, but in the meantime it's not quite what I need.*

Yet, traditionally, the short film has been an essential part of every filmmaker's development. The classic career structure (if something so haphazard can be described in that way) is to learn how films are made and try out that knowledge on one or more short films (let's say typically running for between 10 and 25 minutes), which can then be used as calling cards – as proof that you can handle a crew, a story and a budget.

This is the book that Alison and Simon felt they needed, but couldn't find. A means of short-cutting the learning process and helping them get it right first time.

Alison: *It's a book we would certainly have read, had it existed – a book about learning from other people's experiences.*

Why?

The first question to ask yourself is: why do you want to make a film? Silly question? Not really. The process of film production – technically speaking – is not actually that difficult. In essence: you point a camera at things – real people, actors, places – until you have the pictures you need. Then you put them together in the right order to tell your story, or create the atmosphere you want. Simple.

Very little involved in making a film is complicated or difficult on its own. Loading a magazine can be taught in a few minutes. Shouting a slate number and clapping the clap-stick is scarcely rocket science. Starting the tape on the recorder doesn't need a degree in physics. Nor does looking through the camera and starting the film rolling.

However, getting it right means that a number of different people (sometimes a very large number of different people) have to be doing their simple little things in the right order and in the right place at the right time. Arranging that so it works well can be quite difficult. The key all through the process, right from the very first decision even to make a film, is precision of thought. Filmmaking is not an activity for the ivory-tower artist. The results may be art, but the process most certainly isn't.

Oddly enough, this doesn't mean that anyone at all can make films. As with many other things in life, the important thing is not knowing which button to press but when to press it, and getting that timing right can take a lifetime of experience. Not everyone does learn.

Simon and Alison had been professional actors for ten years, working in theatre as well as television and movies, before they decided to make their own film.

Simon: *We have experience being on set as actors, but not actually running the production. It's very different. As an actor, you turn up, do your bit of filming, and you go away again. Which I found a bit frustrating because film is something I've always been fascinated by and I wanted to see how it works.*

And why make the move behind the camera now?

It has always been my ambition to get into film. There seem to be a lot of good opportunities for young filmmakers at the moment and I wanted to make the most of those opportunities. Alison has had a lot of producing experience – producing for the theatre – so we decided to pool our resources and give filmmaking our best shot.

Some people might think it a little too brave just to rush in to making a film straight away without learning a little more about how to do it. On the other hand, Alison and Simon did already have long experience of the industry in the real world, and:

Simon: *I didn't want to do too many courses, studying and doing 3 years in further education. I've always preferred the hands-on approach.*

There's no substitute for actually doing the work, under real-world conditions of pressure on time and budget. Those were the reasons that Simon and Alison decided to make their film. Other people will have gone through similar, but different, thought processes.

Be realistic

In the back of the minds of nearly all short-filmmakers runs something like the following scenario: 'I'll make this film now, for nothing, and it will be absolutely brilliant. I'll be famous, through screenings on the festival circuit around the world and through the Internet. The studios and financiers with real money will be falling over each other asking me to do their next big picture for them. Or, even if they don't call me, when I go to them with my full-length feature project (which will also be brilliant), they'll not hesitate in producing the chequebook from their pockets and writing out a cheque for the ten million I need.' The fact that – just very occasionally – it has happened in a way that looks a little like that, makes the idea even more alluring.

It's true that the film industry world-wide is always on the look-out for the next big thing. It's also true that risk-taking is not a concept that studio bosses and financiers are comfortable with. In this context it's very important to be quite clear about the fundamental difference between the Anglo-American industry model and the European film industry.

Generally, in most of Europe, cinema is considered an art form deserving of preservation and encouragement. Many countries consider it important to preserve a truly national film (or 'audio-visual' in the more general terms of European-Union-speak) industry as a way of helping fend off English-speaking attacks on their cultural existence. In practical terms this means that probably nearly all films made in this environment are partly or totally funded by various forms of government subsidy.

The criteria for funding in this kind of environment are obviously quite different from the environment we are dealing with here: Hollywood (and its English-speaking derivatives) is resolutely commercial. If a film doesn't stand at least a reasonable chance of making money, it doesn't get made.

Cinematographer and Director Freddie Francis, one of the consultants to *Ghosthunter*, is only one of many people to have said, 'We don't have a film industry in the UK. I always tell people to go to America. They have a real industry there.'

One can argue about the dates but, in many ways, the period beginning after the end of World War II and lasting well into the 1960s really was a kind of Golden Age for British Cinema. Lots of films were made. England was a cool place to be. The industry was large enough for people to have permanent jobs – or at least permanent work – so the grand tradition of apprenticeship, of learning on the job by doing the job, was able to thrive. And most people learnt their craft by working their way up from the bottom. The studios were mostly fully, permanently staffed. Production Designer Peter Lamont, another *Ghosthunter* consultant, began as a draughtsman in the Art Department at Pinewood. Those days are long gone.

The loss of permanently staffed studios isn't the only reason why it's so hard to get films made in the twenty-first century. Thriving though it was, the film industry of those days was very small. And it still is. Bluntly, there are too many people chasing too few opportunities.

What's it for?

The realities of making a long-term living in the film industry are depressing, but it's much better to know clearly from the beginning what it is you're getting yourself into, than to wonder later why the cheque for £10 million hasn't appeared.

The way the industry is at the dawn of the twenty-first century means there is often little alternative for people starting out in the business than to jump in and somehow get something made with whatever resources can be made available. The overall experience will be much more fruitful if the film's production has a clear goal, just as Simon and Alison were clear about why they made *Ghosthunter* and what they expected to get out of it.

Of course, anyone can get their friends together and make a film for fun, for the experience, and have a great time doing it, often producing some very good work. Amateur filmmaking can be an exciting and satisfying hobby. However, filmmakers who want to be professionals, mix with professionals and who ask for professional help, have to behave in a professional manner. And that was one of the things that distinguished *Ghosthunter* from many other, otherwise similar films. Everyone associated with it remarked on the professionalism of the whole operation.

Short films

Short films are, as their description states, short. They are easy to grasp in production terms and relatively cheap to produce. That's why so many of them are made. Unfortunately short-filmmaking is an activity that exists almost entirely by feeding off itself. There is no market for short films. Some shorts are sold to television; one or two every year manage to achieve the ultimate goal of any short film – to be distributed as support to a major movie. Thousands of them are seen by dozens of people on the Internet, or at one film festival after another. Practically every day there is a film festival of some sort somewhere in the world. But (in practical terms) short films never recover their production costs (unless they really were made for nothing) and cannot expect to make a profit. Exceptions only prove the rule. People don't make shorts in order to become rich and famous.

Jacqui Wetherill *Ghosthunter* Production Manager: *There's more of a market for a feature than there is for a short. Is it best to make a feature or short? It's a really really difficult issue. You can make a better-quality short because people are working shorter times and you can get better people but there's no market for shorts at the moment. You'll get £100 per minute for a short if you're lucky. If you've got a 10 minute film that's £1000, and it's cost you at least £15 000 to make. You're never, ever going to get your money back on a short. At least with a feature you've got a chance. But you have to be really really lucky, because a low-budget short is going to look like a low-budget short so it has to be a really cracking script and then you've got to be lucky enough to get the right people to see it.*

In the climate of today's industry, it's unlikely, too, that that £10 million will appear on the doormat, however brilliant the short film is. Not impossible, but unlikely. So what's the reason for making a short film at all? It's a very good question, and different people have different answers. For the same cost as the production budget of *Ghosthunter*, small though it was, some people have made full-length films, which stand a much better chance of being sold – to television, for video distribution or even getting theatrical distribution in cinemas.

Claire Moore, Unit Manager on *Ghosthunter*: *I don't get the point of shorts at all, because there's no market for them. This one is fascinating, because the production quality of this is so high – but you could have made a feature for the budget on this. Though it would have been very low budget and it wouldn't have had the production values I'm anticipating on this film. The difference is that they've actually planned what they're going to do with it – there's a whole series of events going alongside it, like the book, all part and parcel of* Ghosthunter, *which is very different from somebody just making a short in three days and then trying to sell it at short-film festivals.*

I know an exception to the rule – it's a horror film about dentists; it got picked up by 20th Century Fox and it went out in front of I Know What You Did Last Summer. *The reaction was that the short was scarier than the feature . . . It's very rare to have a short go out like that, because 20th Century Fox spent a lot of money on* I Know What You Did Last Summer, *and a lot of other people make their money on the trailers and the adverts, which of course is what the shorts would replace. And if you throw a short in there as well, you're going to lose one screening of the main picture.*

Luke Smith, *Ghosthunter* Production Designer: *Some people look at shorts as a promo or trailer or pilot – more like a calling card for the director, when in meetings with financiers for potential bigger projects they can show it. Like a show reel, rather than trying to tell a story that stands alone.*

The greater availability of technology – particularly digital production technology – has already had a massive influence on the short-film sector of the industry. People who were previously excluded from the filmmaking process simply because they couldn't afford the equipment are now able to make their own films. *The Blair Witch Project* is an oft-quoted example of the new low-cost technology democratizing the filmmaking process. In Denmark, the Dogme rules offer a certain kind of puritan justification for using minimal equipment. In some ways it's wonderfully liberating. But what it really means is that the importance of the film's content – the script – is even more obvious.

President of the Cannes Film Festival, Gilles Jacob, reacts to the growth of electronic cinema: *There is a risk that in the medium term we will be inundated with films shot digitally and made with small budgets by amateurs who take themselves to be the new Martin Scorsese, Ken Loach or Stephen Frears. Unfortunately a Loach or Frears only comes along once every 30 years. Meanwhile we see a lot of home movies in the hope of spotting some talent.*

And even if your short is recognized, what happens next – if anything – is far from guaranteed.

Freddie Francis: *I've never come across an example where people have made their own film and it's done them any good. The thing is you've got to get into the filmmaking* **business** *– unless you've got millions of your own money. I would say go to America. At least it's really going on there. If you're just trying to get a job in films*

DoP, Gavin Struthers (left), director, Simon Corris and camera operator, Rodrigo Gutierrez (right), set up the next shot. © Zoë Norfolk 2000

over here, I don't know where you'd go, and I think it's unfair, everybody working on films for nothing. I mean what will they get from it – even supposing the film is a great success? And I'm afraid people are going to take advantage of this. People are going try to remake Gone with the Wind *and nobody on the film will get any money.*

None of this means that you shouldn't make a film; but it's important that you've thought through the reasons why you're putting yourself – and all the people helping you – through a process that is never easy.

Anne Guidera, from Kodak, who helped with *Ghosthunter*, sees shorts as an important part of the industry: *About three years ago we realized at Kodak that there was a gap in the market place where we were very supportive of students at the film schools and supportive of low-budget features, TV commercials and main-stream features, but there was a whole area that wasn't supported and that was people on their own making short films. At the same time we realized that this area of short-filmmaking was becoming the training ground for filmmaking in this country, as fewer and fewer people were being taken on by the broadcasters and trained. More and more of these films were coming through and it was difficult for us because we didn't have a pricing policy and we weren't making contact with people working on short films, and we wanted to. So we set up a department just to look after short films and I now look after that area; I talk to people making short films and I've got 90 films on my book at the moment either being shot now or going to be shot in the next three months. It's an investment in the future. It's not profitable for us. We're investing in people for the future of filmmaking.*

Summary – the questions

Nobody makes a film by accident. Producing any film is too demanding a process for that. If you're cooking a meal you work out a menu that suits the people you're cooking for. Almost any activity is more successful for everyone involved if the goals are clear right from the beginning. Knowing from the start what you want to achieve from making a film is much more likely to lead to a happy result. Apart from anything else, people without goals can't know if they've achieved them or not. There are no right or wrong answers, but it's always worth considering a few questions.

- Are you making the film just to have a good time?
- Is the film intended for showing to real live audiences? If so, what is the audience? This is an important question to which we'll return.
  - Is it a public audience – if so, what kind of people: age group, interests and so on? An answer of 'everybody' is not normally sufficiently focused.

- Or is it a small professional audience of possible employers or financiers? If that's the case, don't forget that this audience, too, has a private life. They are 'ordinary people', too.
- What are you hoping to learn through the process of making the film?
- What kind of people are you planning to work with – and why? Will the cast and crew come from a small group of people you know well – or will you involve a wider group of participants? If so, will the other people be experienced professionals, gifted amateurs or beginners?
- What are you going to do with the film once it's finished? How is the intended audience to see it? Getting a film to festivals, financiers, executives is tough work. Making the film is easy.

Thinking through some of these questions not only helps to focus the film itself, it helps the film get made. Somehow you're going to have to raise the money to make the film and anybody asked to invest in a film will ask the same kind of questions. We'll return to this, too. 'Finance' is not just cash. Any cast or crew member who gives their time, any equipment company that loans equipment, is investing in the film. And every film, however small, needs a certain amount of cash, too, if only for parking meters, telephones, sandwiches and rail fares.

Ghosthunter

Alison and Simon decided that their own first film would be a short so that they could try things out over a short time scale. Through the experience of making a short film, they would learn what is involved in making a film whatever its length, and the whole process would be more easily kept under control. The whole exercise was intended as a training ground, not only for themselves, but for other less experienced members of the crew as well. Also they would come out of the experience with a calling card to show that they do know how to make films. It is a stepping stone to realizing the ambition of making full-length feature films.

First steps

Although Alison and Simon had been acting for 10 years, they knew that they had a lot to learn about the process of making a film since they had never been involved all the way through the process, from conception to delivery. They began doing research.

Simon: *We consider that we come from the Internet school of filmmaking. That's where we trained. The Internet has been an extremely valuable tool for us. We did all our research on it; we learned from filmmaking websites, we downloaded manuals and scripts, we ordered filmmaking books, we could search for anything we needed to learn about and find an answer easily and quickly. It provided us with all the information we needed.*

They were also very encouraged by the producers who wrote *The Guerilla Film Maker's Handbook* – filmmakers who just go out and make a film for whatever money they have at the time, whether it's £20 000 or £200 000.

The Essay

Their very first film was not actually *Ghosthunter*, but a short piece called *The Essay*. They were fortunate, of course, that they didn't have to go out looking for a cast. *The Essay* was written for Alison to perform. Simon was Director/Cameraman.

Alison: *Simon and I wanted to make a film – we'd been reading Robert Rodriguez's book* Rebel Without a Crew *and were inspired to get out there, get a camera and make a film – so we thought, 'let's just do it'. To drive ourselves along we set ourselves a day in the not too distant future to film our film and set about writing our first script. Simon booked himself on a basic filmmaking course for a weekend and we started to learn all the things we needed to make this short 5-minute film. So it was back onto the Internet for more research. I was digesting script-writing books and Simon was busy reading all he could find on the technical aspects of filming.*

Simon: *We actually wrote the script very quickly. We discussed a very simple idea, sat at the computer and within an hour, hot from the printer, we had our first script. To make sure that the story worked we spent a day filming it on Video 8 and I edited it on the home computer. This was a very useful dry run; we consequently made a few minor changes before we had our shot list for our production day. We'd decided to film on a Monday as this meant that we could pick up the equipment from the hire centre on the Saturday afternoon. That would give me the whole of Sunday to look at the equipment and become familiar with it, it also meant we'd still only be charged for a single day's hire.*

They hired an Arriflex 16 mm camera from a rental company. Simon had previously visited the Arriflex website and downloaded the camera's manual, which he had read from end to end – probably something very few cameramen have ever done! But he still didn't quite know what it all meant, since he had never actually held a camera in his hands.

Simon: *Once I'd hired all the equipment and paid the deposit I said to the girl on the desk, 'Now, can I talk to someone who can show me how all this works?' She looked a little surprised but found someone to help. This guy, Steve, came out from the back and asked when we were filming. I said 'Monday', he took a deep breath and said, 'Well, we'd better get on with it then.' He spent two hours with me and was very co-operative, he allowed me to ask the most mundane questions and answered them without patronizing me. I was able to experiment with the camera and the lenses and he gave me a brief overview on the lighting and sound equipment we'd ordered, then wished me the best of luck with the film.*

Then there was the problem of loading the camera. Film stock is not cheap. If it isn't loaded properly in the magazine, not only might it become fogged, it also might scratch or jam as it runs through the camera.

Simon: *I'd practised at the hire centre with exposed stock and I'd asked Steve to show me all the things that can go wrong when loading the film. I felt fairly confident but, when faced with our precious unexposed stock, I wanted to take no chances. I took the changing bag and film stock into a room that didn't have any windows and turned out the lights. Halfway through loading the magazine I realized I also had my eyes shut – like that would help – but I later discovered that camera assistants often load film with their eyes closed, they say it helps them to concentrate when they have to work by touch.*

We were up at the crack of dawn on the Monday, as we had to get everything back to the hire centre before 6 p.m. As we'd had the benefit of rehearsing the film on Video 8 we could be very tight on ourselves and make sure that we only did a single take on each shot. I was determined to get the film on a single roll on 400' stock. We almost made it; I spotted a light reflection in a picture on the wall that meant we had to go again on this particular shot. We actually went over by 30' so it was a good thing we decided to buy an extra roll, just in case.

Alison: *Simon was director, cameraman, DoP and sound mixer. I was taking care of the clapper, camera sheets and continuity sheets – then putting them all down quickly and acting when Simon called, 'Action'. We had a mike taped to a lighting stand and off we went. It was an exhausting day, because it wasn't just filming and getting all the shots in but also the unpacking and packing of all the equipment and moving it around; we were on the seventh floor of an apartment building. All the equipment was due back at 6 p.m., it was close but we just made it.*

The Essay is about a situation that's familiar to most people: an essay (or a script, or a book) has to be written. You've done all your thinking. You've sharpened all your pencils. It's time to start writing. So you get up and make a cup of coffee. Or read the paper. And make another cup of coffee; until it's the end of the day before the writing has begun.

Alison: *It was a story that was easy to film. We've had a good response to it – everybody says, 'Yeah, I've been there.'*

It was very exciting to get the rushes back from the lab. 'Did it come out? Was it in focus?' Our excitement was tempered, though, as we'd been sent the wrong tape. We ripped open the parcel, put the tape in the machine, pressed play and settled down to watch a Cadbury's Crème Egg competition film! Eventually, after an agonizing wait, we got our own rushes and were subsequently whooping around the room when we discovered it was exposed and in focus. We were very pleased. It's very basic, nothing like Ghosthunter, *but the experience was fantastic, not only from a learning point of view but also from appreciating the jobs of everyone on the set – from focus-puller to runner – how important they all are.*

A short world

With the very basic experience of their first film behind them, they began to think about what to do next. They continued to try to find their way around, both on the Internet and in the real world, researching Internet sites, books and writing letters to people asking for help and advice.

Simon: *There's a whole short-film philosophy. There are short-film rules, you condense your story. You keep it to a single location. You avoid special effects. You have one, maybe two, maybe three actors if you're really going to push the boat out, and it's a very conversational piece. So what you've got is a lot of short films which are all based around this philosophy and they're all quite similar.*

This 'philosophy' arises, of course, for fairly obvious reasons: most usually, simply the need to keep things cheap and simple. Whatever success some may have had in the traditional cinema circuits, most short films are made with tiny budgets in a few days. Large casts and multiple locations cost money and take time to organize and move around.

Short films are not just long films that are short, though. Even with unlimited time, money and other resources, a filmmaker might decide to make a short film because it's the right form in which to express what they want to say. If a conventional feature film is like a novel or a symphony, then a short is more like a short story – or even a poem, a song. A short story is not just a novel in 15 pages instead of 250. The form is quite different. The aims are quite different.

A great number of short films do end up having a similar kind of feel: two or three people in a restricted number of locations. A twist in the tail. It's hard to develop much of a story in 10 minutes or so; but still, audiences can often be forgiven for thinking that they've heard this story somewhere before. It doesn't always need to be like that. It depends on how you respond to the questions about why and how your film is being made.

Amongst others, Alison and Simon had written to David Parfitt, Oscar-winning Producer of *Shakespeare in Love*, who gave them a great deal of helpful advice; and to Kenneth Branagh, who agreed to see them to talk about filmmaking and give any advice he could. He had recently appeared in a short film for another young director, Jamie Payne. The film was called *Dance of Shiva*. Kenneth Branagh introduced Alison and Simon to Jamie Payne, and the experience of meeting him and of seeing *The Dance of Shiva* completely turned their ideas around.

The Dance of Shiva

Jamie Payne's answers to the questions about why he was making a short were different from most people's. Rather than making the traditional short-drama-with-a-twist in order to show off his technical abilities, Jamie Payne's film was a 24-minute drama-documentary telling the story of Indian soldiers during World War I. The film had its première 80 years after the end of the war, on 11 November 1998.

There was more that was unusual about this film. Jamie Payne had put together a cast including Kenneth Branagh, Sanjeev Bhaskar, Julian Glover and Paul McGann, and had involved the legendary cinematographer, Jack Cardiff – who celebrated 80 years in the industry in 1998.

Jamie Payne: *The first thing was that I wanted to celebrate the history of British film culture – some of the people who created some of the greatest films of all time, and they're still alive, and this country isn't very good at celebrating excellence in any shape or form. And I thought it's difficult for young filmmakers to serve an apprenticeship, to get an opportunity, so I thought I could pull some of my favourite filmmakers together, in my case Jack Cardiff, John Box, and John Mitchell, the Sound Consultant who's done hundreds of films from Powell and Pressburger onwards. I thought working with these people was the best way for me to learn and also create an opportunity for people who can't afford a film education. I was working in a video shop when I dreamt up this film. If I can do it then you can do it.*

And there was more than just the film itself. The complete package included an hour-long documentary on making a film, using *The Dance of Shiva* as its example. The two films were given away to schools and local education authorities, and shown in cinemas in screenings sponsored by the Rank Organization. The example of making a short film with high production values, and of constructing a whole package of other materials around the film, made a big impression on Alison and Simon.

Simon: *It's interesting that in the USA they're called 'short features', whereas over here they're called 'short films'. This concept was quite important to us. The*

Frank Finlay receiving direction from Simon Corris on his first scene of the film. © Zoë Norfolk 2000

intention was to set this up as much like a feature production as we possibly could. The idea grew from its initial concept, which was 'lets just make a short film and then we'll move on from there', and it became what it is now, with the names attached, the learning potential and the production values behind it.

Jamie Payne has a further reason for putting together his film in the way he did. The experience of handling a large crew is quite different from that of making a quick film with a few friends: *The filmmaking process is collaborative. As a director you have to learn to communicate with people and learn what different roles mean on a film set, and a short is a good way of learning how to communicate like that. So I set up an equivalent team to a feature film, so that I could learn how to do it.*

2 Putting the package together

A professional approach is important if you're playing with professionals. Even the smallest details are important. In some ways, the smallest details are more important than the big ones. The single thing that distinguishes this kind of filmmaking from the mainstream of feature film or television production is that there's no money. The producers have to ask favours of nearly everyone. And they have to convince the people that they're asking for help that their help is worth giving. Because there are plenty of other people out there asking for the same things.

It's often a tremendous – and very pleasant – surprise to people trying to establish themselves in film that, in general, experienced people are very willing to help. It's a way of giving back to the industry that has given them a living, and it's a way of helping to train new people in an industry where solid vocational training is very hard to find. But you have to ask right.

Realizing that the film industry, more than most, is all about front, Simon and Alison formed a company, Amulet Films. Starting a company is a sensible thing to do for all sorts of reasons. In the first place, a company is treated differently from an individual by nearly everyone, but particularly by other companies, bank managers, landlords, suppliers of any sort. This is true even if they know that the company they're dealing with is not, in fact, a mighty multinational empire but a couple of people who've just started a business on their kitchen table.

This is not quite as silly as it seems. In law a limited company has a legal existence quite apart from its directors. The directors of a company have high levels of responsibility, and starting a limited company should certainly not be seen as a way of avoiding paying your debts if it all goes horribly wrong. Company directors are also *personally* liable for their company's activities to a much greater degree than used to be the case. Should anyone you know be considering such a scenario, it's unlikely that they would get away with starting a company, running up massive debts in order to make a film and then putting the company into liquidation. People have tried that sort of thing (and the film business seems to be particularly attractive to certain kinds of aquatic creatures with large teeth), and have ended up personally bankrupt and disqualified from holding any company directorship in the UK ever again.

Nonetheless, the directors of a company are still only its officers. The directors may change, but the company continues. And, if nothing else, this puts a company's dealings in a different bracket from those of an individual. The downside of this effect is something often experienced in our business, too. You're working at the BBC, or Paramount, or Disney, and you call someone, saying, 'Hi, I'm Sam Bloggs from Paramount, I wonder if you could do something for me . . .' No problem. That distant thudding is nothing to worry about – it's the sound of people falling over themselves to help. Then you decide to set up on your own. You call the same person: 'Hi, it's Sam . . .', 'Who?', 'Sam Bloggs, remember me? Used to be at Paramount . . .', 'Oh, yeah', 'I need a small favour. I wonder if . . .?', 'Err, look I'm in a meeting right now. Let's do lunch. Call my secretary . . .' The way of the world.

Starting a limited company

It's not difficult. A private limited company needs at least one company director and a company secretary. A sole director cannot be secretary as well, but if there are two of you, one of you can be director and secretary. There's no minimum age, but Companies House doesn't like directors under 16 years.

You can either start a completely new company or (slightly cheaper) buy an existing 'off-the-shelf' company, changing its name if you like. The process can be done in a few days and really doesn't cost very much. You would, however, be wise to do it through a firm of solicitors or accountants who will help you make sure that you've done everything you need to do.

Companies House has most of the information you need on its website (www.companies-house.gov.uk), including the facility to search for basic details of all British companies, names of disqualified directors, FAQs on how to start a company and what it all means.

The limited liability of a company is real enough in a limited way, so companies often form separate limited companies (wholly owned or in partnership with co-producers of the film) in order to produce a film. This has two advantages. It insulates the fortunes of the movie from the fortunes of the parent companies, also making the business of who owes what to whom much easier to understand. And it makes the business of who *owns* what easy to understand. If two partners each have a half share in a third company, then it's quite clear when Third Company Ltd is in profit, and how much each of the partners gets. It can be very much harder to sort out when a movie's accounts are mixed up with those of a company doing other things, too.

So Simon and Alison founded Amulet Films Ltd (for the sake of convenience, they will be referred to as 'the Amulets' from here on, except in cases where either Simon or Alison did or said something) and went to considerable trouble to develop a professional-looking corporate identity, with well-designed stationery and a website through which people could follow their progress (www.amulet-films.com).

The package

However, there was more to it than cool notepaper. Interested investors and participants received a whole package (which grew as time went on and the project developed) containing a synopsis of the story; the script; a 'business plan' for the film – how and why it was being made and what it was intended should happen afterwards; biographies of Simon and Alison and of the consultants as they joined the project. A website was set up very early on, which contained all this and news about the film's progress as the project developed.

The film itself was only a part of a larger package, which it was not intended should stop with the film's production. Obviously, the film was the centrepiece, but a 'making of' documentary was set up; the plan being to put it on a DVD disk together with the film, stills from the shoot and other bits and pieces to expand the story. This book, of course, is also a part of the wider package.

A large part of the effort that goes into producing any film goes into putting together the finance. Every film, at any budget level, needs a presentation package of this sort to give to prospective financiers, distributors and major participants. The package answers the questions: What do they want to do? What's the film about? Who are they? What have they done before? How much money do they need? What do they want from me? What am I going to get out of it?

It's also useful to lay it out in such a way that the essentials can be grasped very quickly – in only a minute or so. People will read on if they're grabbed at the start. Make it easy for them, so that by the time they start to read the script, they're already in a 'want to help' frame of mind. Most of the people you're likely to be asking for help receive dozens, if not hundreds, of similar requests every year. If something is scruffy, badly thought out, hard to understand, however hard they try to be fair (and some of them won't bother) you'll be starting at a disadvantage to someone else (like the Amulets) whose presentation is clear and attractive. (But don't go too far the other way. There's a lot of hype in our business, and most people worth talking to have quite sensitive hype-detection apparatus!)

The professional approach is appreciated. John Rendall, from Panavision, who later became involved, helps many of the people who ask for support every year. Clearly, the projects that look most likely to succeed are the ones that get support.

John Rendall: *They came to see us and showed us the project. And we looked at it and we liked the idea of it, because we thought that their actual presentation was very good. It's important, isn't it, that you've got a well-thought-out marketing ploy? Sometimes you get people saying 'Well I think it's a good idea. I'll shoot it. I'll get my mates for two or three days and just go ahead and shoot it', and we help them, and two years later you think, 'where is that project we helped out on?', and it's probably on a shelf because the person hasn't thought it through, and hasn't got enough money for post-production work. It's not cheap. I mean, making a film and processing it and then editing it is not cheap. Making the final print on 35 mm, which we hope they'd go for, is not cheap. And it's part of the deal that they come and show it in our theatre at the end of the day.*

Anne Guidera, from Kodak, finds that the people coming to her for help fall into two groups: *On the one side the people who aren't really in the business at the moment. They've no budget. None of their crew members are established. They're planning a very tight shooting ratio, and they don't really know the business they're in at the moment. They're the ones who come on the phone to me and say 'I'm making a short and I haven't got any money.' But they're aspiring to make it on film. They could have made it on tape, but they decided to make it on film, so you want to help them as much as possible and help them get another step up in the industry.*

Then there are the people on the other side who are established, who have a budget, a realistic shooting ratio, and they probably want to shoot on 35 mm. The crew usually has experience from other short films or television, and the DoP will often be someone we know. These shorts will definitely have a higher profile, because they have enough money in the first place and this is the area that Ghosthunter *fell in – with the experience of the people on the crew – you knew they knew what they were doing. They were working within the parameters of their budget, things would happen when they were supposed to happen.*

And one of the reasons that Freddie Francis chose to help them was the professionalism of their approach: *Alison and Simon, they seemed to be very professional about it. They've got some showmanship about it. It sounds silly, I know, but they had nice covers to their script. They had nice headed notepaper. They go about it very professionally. So many people might be just as keen, but they don't have the show-business professional approach, which is very very necessary.*

Charlie (Frank Finlay) asks Sarah (Alison Reddihough) where she saw the symbol that she's sketched in her notebook. © Zoë Norfolk 2000

Professional help

The other major decision the Amulets made was not to attempt to go it alone. Although they were scarcely beginners, having considerable professional experience between them (or perhaps because they were professionals), they decided that the way to get the kind of film that they really wanted to make was to use it as an opportunity to learn from the best in the business. This would, of course, have a double benefit: not only would they be putting together a kind of Film School that money couldn't buy; the publicity value of the project would also be multiplied many times. Half the battle in this business is getting your name around.

During the shoot, Maurice Gillett, Consultant Gaffer, who has worked with Freddie Francis for half a century, was talking about the best way to gather experience: *Go and watch Manchester United play, not your local football team. That way you see the best people working. In this business you've got to do anything you can to get on any set and watch the Manchester United of the film industry so you can learn from them.*

Jamie Payne agrees: *Production values are important, and learning about production values is important and working with established filmmakers helps you learn lessons that they've spent 40 or 50 years learning – 80 years in Jack Cardiff's case. That's invaluable. Short films don't have to be small films. They can be 15 minutes long but they can really show your intentions for a feature film. What* Shiva *did, and* Ghosthunter, *is invaluable to help answer questions that usually cost a lot of time and money in finding out by your own mistakes – so learning by other people's journeys is a very good way to start.*

That's more or less what the Amulets decided to do. They called and wrote letters to lots of people, of course. Not everyone answered. Not everyone could help. But they did get to talk to a number of extraordinarily interesting and experienced people. Start at the top, why not?

Amulets: *Why not be ambitious with a short film? Let's see what we can do with it under the guidance of these guys.*

Gradually they assembled an impressive list of people they called 'Consultants' – big names with a great deal to teach, who were not expected to work on the film directly, but who had agreed to offer specific help and advice to the less experienced Heads of Department that the Amulets recruited to crew the film. Indeed, some of the crew members were introduced to the project by the Consultants. The four Consultants to the film in the end were:

1 Freddie Francis, distinguished cinematographer, who has been in the film industry for over 65 years. He has won two Oscars for Best Cinematog-

raphy for *Sons and Lovers* and for *Glory*. Other credits include *The French Lieutenant's Woman*, *The Elephant Man* and *Cape Fear*. He won the New York Critics' Award in 2000 for his work on *The Straight Story*, directed by David Lynch, with whom he had worked several times in the past.

2 Peter Lamont started his career as a draughtsman at Pinewood Studios and has since worked on all the *Bond* pictures except one. On the last few he has been Production Designer. Recent work that he found most satisfying was *Titanic* (for which he won the Oscar for Best Production Designer), with director James Cameron.

3 Composer Barrington Pheloung's CV includes an enormous body of work in film and television, including *Inspector Morse*, *Hilary and Jackie* and *Truly Madly Deeply*.

4 Mark Auguste is a leading Sound Editor whose work includes *Elizabeth*, *Tea with Mussolini* and *The Jackal*.

There are more detailed biographies of these eminences in Appendix H. They also assembled an 'Executive Crew' – highly experienced, working professionals, who generously gave their services and worked directly on *Ghosthunter*. These were:

- Rodrigo Gutierrez, Camera Operator, whose credits include *Gladiator*, *Greenwich Mean Time*, *The Match*, *Plunkett & Macleane*, *The Commissioner*, *Feast of July*, *Bliss*, *The Van*, *Split Second*, *The Turn of the Screw*, *Friendships Death* and *Out of Africa*.
- Trevor Coop, Camera Operator (Pinewood): *Star Wars: Episode I – The Phantom Menace*, *Anna and the King*, *Swept from the Sea*, *Feast of July*, *Frankenstein*, *Hamlet*, *In the Bleak Midwinter*, *Dealers*, *Ending Up*, *American Gothic*, *Santa Claus* and *Superman*.
- Maurice Gillett, who has over 40 years' experience as a Gaffer. His credits include *Princess Caraboo*, *Superman IV*, *Return to Oz*, *White Nights*, *The Bounty*, *Witness for the Prosecution*, *An American Werewolf in London*, *Flash Gordon*, *Superman*, *Revenge of the Pink Panther*, *Orca the Killer Whale* and *The Innocents*.
- Robin O'Donoghue, Dubbing Mixer on (amongst many others) *The Man Who Cried*, *Lost in Space*, *Shakespeare in Love*, *Hamlet*, *Michael Collins*, *The Madness of King George*, *The Fly*, *A Chorus Line*. Robin did the Final Mix of *Ghosthunter* in the Korda Theatre at Shepperton.

3 The script

It takes a little more than smart notepaper and persuasive talk to involve people of the Consultants' experience in a project of this sort. It takes a good script – one that people like (which doesn't always go hand in hand with it being good. I'm sure that you, too, know of works of art that you respect. You think they're good. But you don't *like* them).

Freddie Francis: *When I do a film – first of all I say 'Send in the script'. If I like the script, I'll go along and meet the Director, and I still won't agree to do the film until I know that I get along with the Director and I think he can benefit from any help I can give him.*

It is not possible to make a good film without a good script. It's possible to make a mediocre film with a mediocre script. Even a bad script can be rescued by brilliant filmmaking to produce a result that lifts it into mediocrity. It's certainly possible to take a good script and from it produce a bad film. But the only way to make a good film is with a good script.

It's very tempting to focus all the attention of making the film on the actual days of filming. You can't wait to get the toys out of the box because it feels so grown-up and real, and you're actually *doing it* not just talking about it. But it's nearly always a mistake. *Ghosthunter* involved 6½ days' filming. The Amulets spent months in preparation for those 6½ days, and months afterwards in post-production and promotion of the film. And underlying all that effort is the script. Time spent in preparation is *never* time wasted.

Choosing the subject

You want to make a movie. It's going to be a short feature. What's it going to be about? It could be about almost anything. In practice, once your thinking begins to turn towards the practical, the choices quickly become more constrained. But still they're limited mainly by the creativity of your imagination. Much of that creativity has to be directed towards problem solving. If money is no object, then the choices obviously are wider – but with this kind of film, the availability of money possibly makes less difference than you might think. The Strong Idea is the most important thing.

What distinguishes most British movies from the products of Hollywood? Hollywood thinks big. A truly theatrical film, whatever its length, just *feels* different from something whose true home is the television screen. And in the UK (possibly because of the relative strength of our television industry, particularly as a home for new dramatic writing) our cinema tends, in the main, to be too small in thought.

Luke Smith, *Ghosthunter* Production Designer: *Somebody who doesn't do any film work doesn't know what short films are about or for. Very few people outside the business ever get to see short films. They may see them on TV. They're certainly not going to go to any short-film festivals. Even people who are quite keen cinemagoers aren't going to see many shorts. People find them inaccessible, because it's only the very best shorts that are able to give the audience something that feels self-contained in that time, 10–15 minutes. Quite often you're left with the feeling that it's only a small bite at the story. You're left feeling a bit let down – it's not quite enough. If you're enjoying it you want more, and if it's something you don't relate to you think, 'Well what's the point in that?'*

Big ideas don't need to have big money and big casts. Big ideas are important, but you're going to have to compromise in the end. It's just that there's no point in starting small and then compromising, because you end up practically invisible. Start with a Big Idea and then make as much of it work as you can. But don't try to make things work when you know in your heart of hearts that they won't. That way leads to disappointment and wasted effort for everyone.

Any film has to be made with passion and enthusiasm. And that passion and enthusiasm is going to take a hefty battering between the time you start and the time you see your work complete on the screen. So you have to do something you believe in. 'Believe in' can mean anything from something a filmmaker is burning to say, to producing something really funny, intriguing, mysterious, scary. Whatever you can get enthusiastic about. But it has to be solid. If you have doubts to begin with, the whole enterprise will be doomed right from the start. In the end it was quite a small split that sank the *Titanic*.

Having said that a Big Idea is important, of course making it work is even more important. Filmmaking is a work of craft. It's a work of thousands of beautifully crafted details, slotting together in perfect form. It's a work of making magic, but the magic can only be made if your feet are firmly on the ground. You start with an idea, but it's a very concrete business making it real. So be practical, now you have your Big Idea, and look around you to see what there is close to hand that can help you make it work. Perhaps your story involves an isolated community. You might live hundreds of miles from the remote island you envisaged, but possibly something nearer to hand will serve. Is there a forest on your doorstep, for instance, or a lake whose shore could stand for your island? If you live by the seaside, perhaps you could borrow a boat for your film. Or set it on a big ship. You've an idea for a ghost story. Was it inspired by the romantic ruins down the road or can you use something more modern?

After the location, of course, comes the cast. A large cast is not only expensive (whether or not you're paying fees), it is also hard to handle in story terms. And hard to handle in performance terms. Good performances are more likely to be created by a few actors with meaty work to do, than by many with only the odd line.

The film can still avoid the short-film trap of two actors making tea in one room. That's just one of the things that the writer can think about with each line: 'Is this too easy? Can I make it more interesting within the practical constraints I have?'

The Amulets were lucky – but then you make your own luck. They live in part of a converted convent in the south of England. The nuns have built themselves new buildings very close by, and the rarely used chapel was an inspiration for their ghost story. A strong location can provide a focus for a whole film.

Story structure

Any film, of any length, has to be clear about what it is trying to achieve. If the filmmakers don't know what they are trying to say, then how can they expect an audience to understand the point of the film? Film is, after all, a medium of communication. This isn't to say that every film has to have the same traditional narrative structure of beginning, middle and sentimental Hollywood end. Or that every film has to be of the high-concept 'cyborg returns to rescue endangered leader from the future', or 'bus which explodes if speed drops below 50 mph' model. But it is important – and very helpful – for the filmmaker to keep in mind a single sentence that describes the film for them. Consider how it might be described in the programme of a short-film festival – or think about the tag line on the poster. If you can't say what it's about in one sentence, then maybe you haven't thought about it sufficiently thoroughly yet. And in the short passage of only 10–15 minutes, there's no room for anything that isn't essential.

Again, that's just as true of an apparently rambling atmosphere piece – a film that might depict a place or a group of people or an idea, by juxtaposing apparently random images and dialogue – as it is of a never-a-dull-moment action thriller. A piece of work might *appear* unstructured but, in reality, if it is to work at all, there must be a structure – a dynamic to move the audience from beginning to end – however well concealed that structure might be. In the end, film is a linear medium, whatever games you play with it. And for a film to work for an audience, the linear experience of having spent time travelling from one end of it to another has to leave them satisfied that something has been seen or learnt or considered, that would not have happened without the film.

So decide what the point of the enterprise is, and stick to it all the way through, from the time you put the first word on that vast empty page (or screen) to the time you finally accept the release print.

Audience

Why are you making this movie? The kind of story you decide to tell and the way you tell it need to be designed for the audience you hope to impress. If your ultimate ambition is to make action movies, then a contemplative piece about spring in Surbiton, however beautifully made, is unlikely to persuade action-movie financiers to part with their money. There is definitely a short-film, art-house style that exists nowhere else. If you're a filmmaker who treats films as poems, and desire nothing more than to be able to compose one after another, then something difficult, oblique and demanding is an ideal choice.

If you have any hopes at all of developing some kind of a career that earns money in the mainstream of film or television (and let's not be unrealistically rigorous about the boundaries – there were boundaries in the 1960s, they've largely broken down now), then a short film intended either as a calling card, or as a piece in itself, should consider its first duty to be entertaining. Give an audience something to enjoy, something to satisfy, something that has some kind of beginning, middle and end. At the end of the screening, you want the viewer to sigh deeply and say, 'That was nice. I'd like to see more of that. Let's help this filmmaker to do more work.' You don't want them to say, 'That was interesting. Very accomplished. Cold as ice. Such a shame.' Or do you?

Alison: *We wanted to do a ghost story – we thought that would be different. We were thinking of the chapel as we felt that it would be a really good location. We started researching ghost stories and were inspired by stories of ghosthunters. The script developed from there.*

It's crazy to ignore an obvious solution that's just sitting on your doorstep – in the case of the chapel around which the *Ghosthunter* story revolved, this was quite literally sitting on the Amulets' doorstep. On the other hand, it's important to be rigorous with yourself at every stage – particularly in the

Frank Finlay as Charlie, the Ghosthunter. © *Zoë Norfolk 2000*

early stages of working out what you're going to do. It's easy to tell yourself that you'll do this 'for now, and go back and sort it out properly later'. You won't. Decisions made early on tend to be the ones that you stay with. It's important to be sure about them.

There comes a point in any project when you can plan and talk and dream as much as you like, but then you have to get down and actually write something. That's the first of the very concrete activities that go into producing a film.

Alison: The way that we write is that first we'll sit down and discuss the story and the characters, making detailed notes. Then I'll take these notes and sit at the computer and hammer a script out.

However tough you are on yourself, yours is likely to be the kindest opinion you get, because you're the one that understands all the thinking and the assumptions behind the decisions you make, or the script you write. Things that are quite clear to you are not always apparent to others.

Alison: Then I hand it over to Simon and he sits there with his pencil while I nervously watch him make any adjustments. We then have a detailed script meeting going through it together, discussing the structure, character development, etc. and making any necessary changes. And of the first draft we probably kept about 5 per cent.

We started out at 30 minutes because we thought that would be a good length to sell to TV. Then we met Jamie (Payne) and he said 'No, no, no, make it 15 minutes; then you've got a better chance of getting it distributed with a feature.' So we started cutting it down and saw that it really needed it. We pared the dialogue back and tried to tell the story more in pictures and not in words. We wanted to make every single line relevant to what was going on in the action because in a short you don't have time to elaborate, so if there was a line that was repeated or wasn't relevant to the story or the character in some way, then it went. Eventually we ended up with a tight script.

A script is a blueprint or a musical score. It isn't a work of art that's complete in itself. Like a set of draughtsman's drawings for a set design, it should contain everything that's necessary to build the set, but nothing more.

Britain has a very strong tradition of stage, radio and television drama. There's less of a truly filmic tradition, with the result that many writers – and actors and directors – tend to approach the screen from a background of words, where text is king. They have little confidence in allowing the pictures to do the work and try to explain everything in dialogue. The result tends to be scenes that are wordy, too long, static and full of unnecessary clutter.

Alison: *Scriptwriting was something we did out of necessity rather than out of desire, but I quite enjoyed it in the end. I've been reading a lot of scripts recently and one of the things that strikes me is they often lack conciseness. Particularly with film the writing has to be concise. There are so many ways in which the story can be told – through the camera, the actors, the lighting and the music – and a lot of writers think you need to put everything down in the dialogue. Conciseness is the key. Ask yourself, 'Is this line relevant to the plot or the character?'*

Jamie Payne feels that writing a good short script is often harder than writing a full-length film: *What you would normally say in 5 minutes in a feature film, you have to say in perhaps two scenes in a short. It's a very good discipline.*

Alison: *You need good characters, too. If you get good characters it's very easy to write dialogue. In* Ghosthunter *there were some characters that were really easy and there were others that were difficult to get to grips with. Sarah, particularly, was very hard whereas Audrey I just found incredibly easy to write. She was a lovely character and I knew exactly what she would say in each circumstance. Get to know your characters and let them speak for you, so it's believable.*

It may sound an obvious thing to say, but the characters in a script have to be credible as people. If an audience doesn't like them, can't understand them or sees them only as cardboard cutouts or puppets, then the story isn't going to work.

Alison: *We developed (and threw out!) several plot permutations over the weeks – some of the more diverse ones included Charlie becoming the ghost, Charlie being Sarah's grandfather and the introduction of a little girl as a ghost character.*

Time spent working on the script is very rarely time wasted. We know that a good film depends on a good script. Particularly in the early stages of financing a film, the only thing you have to show is the script. Ideas, treatments, sales plans are all very well, but the project is unlikely to get anywhere until there's a script to look at.

Rodrigo Gutierrez, *Ghosthunter*'s very experienced camera operator, feels that scripts are often pushed out into the world before they're ready: *Develop your stories. Once you have an idea you have to develop it properly; but often everyone gets so involved in getting the film off the ground, when actually the script might not yet be ready. It will be easier if you develop the script further and take a little bit more time and hold yourself a little bit longer instead of pushing this project when it's not really ready. I often read scripts that are maybe 40 per cent there, but they need more work, and sometimes that's why they can't raise the money. So they get discouraged and complain that the money isn't around, when actually their project is not quite there. It doesn't shine. Just make sure your scripts have got to the point where they can be filmed.*

Paul Howson of the British Council sees a great number of short films: *One of the common problems that we see is people not really knowing how to end the film. You've got to pay as much attention to the ending as you do to the beginning. Often we see something ending and we turn to each other and say, 'Was that it?' – or we see it tailing off 3 minutes before the end.*

Alison: *We didn't want to send out a draft we weren't happy with, so we had a frustrating summer when we were desperate to get on with the filmmaking but we thought we can't do anything until we've got a script. So we spent about 6 weeks just trying to work through the holes in the story, writing it and getting a script we were happy with before showing it to people – and when we now look at that version we think, 'Oh my God, did we really send that out?'*

Of course, the script revision process continues even after there's a version you think fit to show other people.

Alison: *We probably went through about 20 drafts. Some of those were very minor changes to odd words or lines and some of them were quite major. About a month before shooting we had the final script. Apart from a few tweaks.*

Script and story checklist

You do need a good script to make a good film, whatever kind of film it is.

● Think about your intended audience: why are you making the film? For fun and festivals, and to impress your friends? Do what you like. As a calling card to try to persuade people to invest in you as a filmmaker? Then your film needs to be attractive to a mainstream audience.
● Think big first.
● Then be realistic about what you can really make work.

A script is a blueprint, not a thing in itself. The script should be a description of the movie you see unfolding in your head as you write. In general, if something is important to plot or character, then it should be in the script. If it isn't important, then don't put it in. In fact nothing should be in the script (or the film) if it doesn't move along plot or character, or both.

4 Finance and budgets

You can spend your whole life talking about making movies, if you like. That's as far as many people ever get. When you have a script (and a plan) – that's when a film begins to become a Thing; begins to take on a life of its own and begins its long, hard crawl towards an independent existence.

The Amulets had their idea, and they had their script. Knowing enough about filmmaking to realize that they didn't know all that much, they began to look for people who could advise them on the best way to go about getting their idea on the screen.

Kenneth Branagh agreed to meet them, and it was through his and Jamie Payne's stories of *The Dance of Shiva* that the Amulets completely turned around their ideas of what they wanted to achieve through their film. They went into the meeting expecting helpful advice on how to produce a quick and cheap short film for a bit of experience, with a later showing on the standard festival circuit, or perhaps even a television sale. They came out of the meeting knowing that they wanted to do something much more high profile. Much more professional. Much more akin to the real world of feature-film production. Because, in the end, while the essence of producing a film remains the same whether there are two of you and a camera, or 200 of you and a lot more gear, there is certainly a fundamental difference in the way you approach the work – and far more to learn simply in management terms – if you have 200 people working on a picture than if you have two.

Of course the underlying idea matters more than the technology – *The Blair Witch Project* is a brilliant example of the triumph of ideas over technology. *The Phantom Menace* is a brilliant example of the triumph of technology over ideas. Nonetheless, if you want to learn about making joined-up movies you need, eventually, to learn how to work with people who do it every day (or as often as they can manage). And that's what the Amulets decided to do as a result of the meetings with Kenneth Branagh and Jamie Payne. They called up other eminent people, sent them the script, invited them to lunch. It was a way of short-circuiting the learning process. If you don't know how to do something, ask the best people in the business for advice.

Simon: *We were trying to cut corners – we wanted advice to condense the learning curve so that we could get it right the first time round. We didn't want to experiment.*

Alison: *We got so much knowledge just from meeting people and talking to them. We learnt huge amounts.*

Now they had their script, they had their strategy, and they were free to embark on that most frustrating and heart breaking of all human endeavours – raising finance for a movie. It doesn't matter how difficult and complex the actual production process of a picture turns out to be, with very few exceptions, it is as nothing when compared with the long, drawn-out and generally appalling task of raising the finance in the first place. Richard Attenborough, famously, took either 18 or 20 years (depending on which story you hear) to get the funding together for his pet project *Gandhi*. Of course, he was doing other things in the meantime, but nonetheless you, too, should reckon that if you have a film financed in less than 12 months, you are doing well.

Drawing up a budget

You can't start raising money until you know how much money you need. Even if you don't know exactly where you're going to film, or exactly who is going to be involved in the movie, you can still draw up a quite detailed budget as soon as you have a script. With a little luck and realism, you'll find that you aren't very far from the end figure.

However, this is the point at which you need to make sure that your feet are firmly in contact with the ground, even if your head is in the clouds. Keep track of what you're doing at this stage – and from now on – and you stand a chance of bringing the whole enterprise to a successful and happy conclusion. The big danger is that you lose control and make promises that other people have to keep for you, or that can't be kept at all.

Everyone wants their filmmaking experience to be a happy and satisfying one for all involved – but it can matter more than you might think. Particularly if this picture is a way of working with some of the more experienced people in the industry, it's important that you don't make unreasonable demands on the people who are helping you. You want to begin establishing yourself as a professional and competent – not to say glitzy – filmmaker. If you upset people for whatever reason ... well, it is a very small industry, and people have very long memories. So it's important to be sensible about the way you plan both your budget and your schedule.

Sarah (Alison Reddihough) explores the abandoned church for the first time.
© *Zoë Norfolk 2000*

A high proportion of short films are so-called lo/no productions (low budget or no budget). In fact, because of the reasons that filmmakers decide to make short films in the first place, probably most short films are lo/no productions.

Nonetheless, even if you are intending (or hoping) to make the film for next to nothing, unless two of you really are just going out with a domestic camcorder and doing everything yourself, it's an important and valuable exercise to cost everything properly. What would this movie cost in the real world, if everything were properly paid for? If you do that, you'll not only learn more about the true cost of items on the movie-making budget form, but you'll appreciate the value of what you're asking people to give you when you ask them to help you for virtually no money.

Don't guess. Get hold of a standard budget form from somewhere and go through every item on it. If you don't need something, that's fine; but it's always worth thinking about it each time. There's a budget form in Appendix E. The rates might be out of date by the time you want to use it, but they'll give you a rough idea. It should be easy enough to check them once you start speaking to people.

Budget tips

A budget, however long, is just a shopping list. But it's also a checklist. There are some things that are absolutely necessary in making a film and which nearly always go forgotten – or at least underestimated. What are the things you really need to make a movie?

- a script
- a director
- cast
- equipment
- crew
- an editor with equipment
- music and general post-production procedures.

Script

Can you write it yourself? Well enough? If not, who is going to write it? And how are they to be paid? If you're adapting a short story (or even a whole novel), unless the author has been dead for more than 70 years, there will be payments (or persuasion) necessary for the rights to use the story. This may be a problem, or it may not. If an author feels that their work deserves to earn them some money, then they're unlikely to give the rights to you for nothing. On the other hand, a friend of mine did successfully persuade a well-known author to let him have non-exclusive rights in a story, providing the resulting short was only used as a show reel or at festivals – that is to say, it was not to be properly commercially exploited. Of course, hundreds of people (or so it will seem) will need copies of the script, too, the cost of which can add up surprisingly rapidly, and certainly shouldn't be forgotten.

Director

Presumably that will be you or your partner in the project.

Cast

The cast can affect the financing, too. 'Who's in it?' is often the first question people ask when being asked to give money. Even if you haven't been able to persuade a star name to join in, it isn't hard to find actors who are happy to help out with short films. It gives them experience and something for their own show reel – or they are happy to help people along in their career, and normally they're only giving a couple of days of their time. But they are still giving to you. There are a lot of aggrieved actors out there who have been very badly treated by short-filmmakers – taken for granted, largely ignored on set and they didn't even get the cassette copy of the film they were promised. Don't add to their ranks. At least if you cost in to your budget the fees that they should be getting (PACT/Equity minimum £650 per week at the time of writing (2000)) you'll better appreciate what it is you're getting. (Incidentally, there is special treatment for low-budget films in the PACT/Equity agreement.)

Equipment

This is a big decision. What format is the movie to be made on? If we're talking real money, you can *buy* a perfectly adequate digital camcorder for the rental price of 35 mm film equipment. But the decision is not just a budgetary one, because what you decide will affect the fortunes of the whole project from that point on. It may be true that *The Blair Witch Project* was shot on a number of domestic camcorders, but an enormous amount of money was spent on it by the distributors afterwards in tidying up the initial cut and making 35 mm prints from it. True, that money was not invested by the filmmakers; but they were lucky. The story of that production is one story out of thousands you've never heard. It's worth considering the various alternatives.

35 mm

35 mm is expensive, unwieldy and it's the medium of real grown-up movies. The picture quality is unsurpassed (except by 70 mm or IMAX, but if those are alternatives for you, you're reading the wrong book). The Amulets decided on 35 mm because it would give them, and everyone else who worked on *Ghosthunter*, the experience of working on a theatrical feature, but for a shorter period of time. If you make your film on 35 mm, then it can be shown anywhere at no great expense. But it's a more demanding and expensive project to get off the ground in the first place.

16 mm

16 mm was considered an amateur format until television embraced it during the 1960s. Obviously, it isn't as impressive as 35 mm, and you'll see the difference if you project 16 mm and 35 mm side by side, but 16 mm is most definitely a serious production format – particularly for television – and movies shot on 16 mm have often been blown up to 35 mm for theatrical distribution. This works very well for 'small' films, but wouldn't be so convincing if the *Bond* movies started doing it. That gloss just wouldn't be there.

If you're still hankering after 35 mm, but really can't afford it, then Super 16 has a larger picture area than standard 16 (and a wide-screen shape). Super 16 extends the picture into what would be the optical-track area of the film.

8 mm

Real 8 mm (or Super 8 mm) film is fine for learning and experimenting, but it has never been a professional medium and cannot really compete with other formats in that respect.

Those are the film formats to think about – you can decide whether and how to do wide-screen at a later stage.

Video

If the movie is intended for projection at festivals, or you're hoping to show it in cinemas accompanying a feature film, then don't think video. But on a television screen, video can look very good indeed. It can be tempting to take advantage of the ability of video equipment to produce a recognizable picture under very low-light conditions. Well, it's up to you. If you want it to look smart, you have to light video as carefully as you would 35 mm film. In fact, you have to light video even more carefully, because the exposure latitude of video is much less than that of film, so you have virtually no chance of rescuing bad lighting or exposure afterwards.

It is possible, of course, to transfer video masters to film. The results can be surprisingly good, but it's really only a serious option for subjects that are inherently 'gritty'. A gangster movie will probably look brilliant – even more 'real'. A glossy period drama is likely to suffer.

Formats

High-definition video

So far, high-definition video equipment is rare and expensive, and it is, in some ways, a solution looking for a problem. At the moment there are so few places to show high-definition video ('true' digital cinematography) at its best. There are hardly any TV sets. Transmission standards have yet to be agreed, although the situation is better in the USA.

However, if digital projection (and therefore distribution) of feature films in ordinary cinemas at last begins to be accepted, then the case for originating film digitally, too, becomes much stronger. It's certainly in the distributors' interests that it should. It would save them literally fortunes in print and shipping costs. In any case, since most special effects are now computer (digitally) generated and played out to film later, on films like the new *Star Wars* movies that consist largely of computer effects anyway, you could argue that the picture quality would actually improve.

It's worth considering high-definition video, even for a short, because the manufacturers of the equipment are often at the stage of looking for high-quality material with which to prove the whole system. If the script and profile of your project are right for them, you might be able to persuade them to help you by allowing you to use their gear. The same could be said of IMAX.

Broadcast standard video

The relatively recent appearance of the DV (digital video) formats has revolutionized and democratized this kind of filmmaking. All around the world, people have been leaping with glee on domestic DV camcorders, and using them to shoot short films and documentaries. Which is brilliant, so long as they know what they're doing. Using a domestic DV camcorder produces a certain look, which is fine if that's what you want, but can be a problem if it isn't. It looks rough, basically. Highlights burn out. There's little detail in the shadows. Under low-light conditions they perform wonders – but very grainy wonders.

This is because the cameras are rubbish. The tape formats (mini DV, Digital 8, DVCAM, DVCPRO – in practical terms they're identical) are capable of recording very high-quality pictures, certainly of true television broadcast standard. But the chips and the lenses in a camera costing less than £1000 can't be expected to compete with the chips and lenses of something like Digital Betacam, where you might easily spend £10 000 on the lens alone.

I recently made a short programme filmed on high-end DVCAM cameras (which are in themselves pretty good value for money, but not cheap). We had to use a few shots produced on a domestic DV camcorder. Although these shots looked quite impressive on their own, as soon as you put them next to the rest of the programme, you could see how awful they really were – and they were filmed in good daylight, under fairly low-contrast conditions, so it wasn't going to get any better.

With the digitization of television, it's now relatively easy to get hold of Betacam SP equipment at a good rate. Betacam SP was the workhorse of TV during the 1990s, and is a very good format. If you are going to shoot video, it's worth considering.

Stock

Stock might well be the element that makes the decision for you. Although video *equipment* costs more (typically) than film equipment, the stock costs of video are considerably less. Using film encourages good discipline when you shoot – because using more stock than you need will very quickly blow your budget. Not only does raw 16 mm stock cost around 30 times more per minute than a Digital Betacam tape; it still has to be processed and either printed or telecined before you can use it, whereas you can just pop the tape in the edit machine. Admittedly, you would normally want to make a copy of some sort, but you don't have to. Whatever you decide, make sure that you have the stock in time, and that you have enough of it.

Anne Guidera, Kodak: *Phone a couple of weeks before, because we might need to clear payments, and help you make a decision on exactly what you need. Make sure that your shooting ratio is realistic. 3:1 really isn't enough. In most situations anyone will shoot more than that. Secondly, if there's an inexperienced cast or crew, people will make mistakes, and other things will happen that are out of your control. Also, if you're shooting over the weekend and you run out of stock on a Sunday it's hard to find more stock. Much better to have bought an extra couple of rolls. You can always sell it back to one of the reselling companies. But if you're standing there and you've run out on a Sunday afternoon with 10, 15, 20 people standing around and you've not finished your shoot, it's much more expensive than the extra roll or two would have been.*

Crew

So far you have a handful of actors, and a pile of silver boxes containing equipment. Somebody has to get the gear out of the box and point it in the right direction. You can do this with lots of people, or with only a few. *Ghosthunter* had a large crew for two main reasons: firstly to make the experience as much like a real feature production as possible; and secondly to give that experience to as many people as possible. The whole *Ghosthunter* production was planned on such a scale that it would have been possible to have done it with a slightly smaller crew – but not with two men and a dog.

Quite early on, the fundamental decision has to be made – how are you going to crew the film? Are you going to pay everyone? Anyone? Are you going to use experienced professionals? Exclusively? At all? This all has an effect on the final cost of the film – but shouldn't really have much on the preliminary budget, because the whole point is that everything is costed realistically to begin with.

Pop goes the weasel

Now that all these people are gathered for the purposes of committing movie production, the hordes have to be fed and transported. This is where a lot of budgets fall apart completely, because no one has considered the catering. And in lo/no budget situations, even two people can seem like a horde. Cast and crew expect to be well fed and properly cared for on a film of any size and any budget. This isn't a matter of luxury. People are working very hard, often under very difficult circumstances. They deserve a bit of comfort from time to time.

If people are working for little or no pay, there's even more reason to look after them as well as you can. Certainly, there's no reason why they should be spending money in order to help your project, so all their travel, meals and accommodation expenses have to be paid somehow. In many lo/no budget films, this is where most of the cash goes.

Jacqui Wetherill, *Ghosthunter* Production Manager: *It's a very difficult thing to ask people to work for nothing. Nobody should be expected to work for nothing because we've all got to live at the end of the day. It is kind of wrong, but unfortunately it's the way the business works and the way the funding works. Shorts wouldn't get made at all otherwise, and it's a way of passing on experience. The time when it goes wrong is when people start taking the mickey. I always make sure that people get fed really well and their expenses get paid properly.*

Post-production

It's tempting to think that filmmaking is all about pointing a camera at things. As everyone *really* knows, the pointing-a-camera bit is only about one-third of the process. All of that glamour and activity is wasted without proper pre-production and proper post-production. You might remember how let down John Rendall at Panavision felt when those people he had helped with their filming had run out of money before they could edit the film. All that effort wasted.

There are various ways of cutting a picture, depending on how you filmed it and what editing equipment you have available to you. However you decide

Director, Simon Corris, with the actors Frank Finlay, Jacqueline Phillips (extreme left) and June Watson for the dining room scenes.
© *Zoë Norfolk 2000*

to do it (and we'll look at various possibilities later on) there will be a certain amount of money involved for copies of one sort or another. However, we now live in times when a desktop computer with a few add-ons is perfectly capable of being used to cut a film. There's no excuse for being unable to get to a stage when you have at least a pretty well final edit on VHS, which can then be used to raise the last bit of money for finishing if necessary.

That final stage of the production process, after all the edit decisions have been made, makes an enormous difference to the impact of the film as a whole. The difference between a not-bad copy on cassette, and a final, shiny, dubbed copy – even on cassette – is constantly surprising. Unfortunately, that final stage, often involving comparatively little creative input, can be very expensive. Particularly if you're producing a 35 mm show print.

Music

The penultimate budget-breaker. Unless you get your mates to compose and record your music track for nothing, music is expensive. You can't just use any old recordings from your personal collection. Rights have to be paid for, and musicians are not noted for being generous. More later.

Insurance

Finally, the production needs to be insured. There are various levels of insurance, of course, and it's up to you how much you decide to 'self-insure' – to take on yourself the risk and expense of sorting out things that might happen to delay the shoot, for instance. However, there are two kinds of insurance that you really do need. What happens if you've finished the film, done the rough cut and the negative goes up in smoke, or suffers an accident in the printer or telecine? Who pays for the reshoot?

Even if you decide to go without this negative insurance, you most certainly need liability insurance. You're working in public places, or in other people's houses. Someone trips over a cable and breaks their ankle, meaning they can't travel and lose the job they were just about to begin in Singapore. This person sues you for damages. Or you're filming in a stately home (or even an ordinary home) and some valuable antique is accidentally broken or damaged. Does your pocket money stretch to replacing it?

As Producer, you are also employing your cast and crew, and have employer's duties of care and liability towards them. If they are injured in the course of their employment with you, then you have a responsibility towards them. In everyday terms, this is not nearly as frightening (or as expensive) as it seems; but do not forget to talk to a specialist.

Jacqui Wetherill prepared exactly this kind of true-cost budget for *Ghosthunter* – it's included at the end of the book (Appendix E). The total came very close to £84 000.

Paying for it all

Now that there's a true-cost budget, you can try to find ways of making it happen. Obviously, the ideal would be that all the necessary cash could be found somewhere and you wouldn't have to ask people for free equipment or to work for nothing. But we all know that as a filmmaker somehow making a movie or two for nothing is the only way of being able to move on to a world where you can pay proper rates for everything. Still, there's no harm in trying.

Real money

In the UK, the British Film Institute (BFI) is probably the best place to start looking for real money for filmmaking. They publish a booklet called *Lowdown – The Low Budget Funding Guide* that offers lots of contacts and suggestions for places to go to find grants for low-budget and short-filmmaking. The BFI website is at *www.bfi.org.uk* And, let's be realistic, it's grants (gifts, in other words) that filmmakers are looking for. This kind of filmmaking can't honestly be described as an investment – except as an investment in the future of the film industry, which luckily is how a lot of the grant-giving bodies see it. The regional Arts Boards are among the sources of possible funding, and are fairly typical of the kind of finance available.

There are exceptions, but generally it's unlikely that any single source of finance will produce the whole budget for you. Levels of award vary typically between 25 per cent and 75 per cent of the budget. And the financiers will want to see and sometimes audit the budget, so you can't cheat by telling them it's going to cost twice as much as you intend to make it for, because they've thought of that one, too.

Other sources of cash

Assuming, for the time being, that you're still trying to raise the necessary finance as cash for the film, there are a number of other sources you can go to, even for this kind of (almost certainly) non-commercial production, to add to or replace anything you might get from Arts-type funding.

Nearly all of this type of finance will be 'funny money'. Contributions that people are making because they can afford it and because they like the idea of being involved in a movie. While it's not exactly recompense in commercial terms for any input they might make, it's often quite useful to offer them some direct involvement for their money. Individuals could be given parts as extras. Their names could appear in the movie's credits – it always makes a movie look more impressive if the credits are half as long as the film, in any case.

You could spend a little of the money on a couple of parties – a launch party before filming starts, to which the Press could be invited; and a wrap party when it's all over. All investors, whatever their involvement, would be invited to these parties. It might sound silly, but it's a way of making people feel involved. Building a family around a movie is something that can be of tremendous importance, and which can have reverberations for years to come. It's something that the Amulets certainly achieved with *Ghosthunter*.

Where can you find funny money? Well, you do have to be a little imaginative here. You might strike lucky and get to know a Very Rich Person who will give you all you need at one stroke. But it isn't very likely. More probable is that the finance will be accumulated from a lot of smaller sources. For this reason it's very important to know exactly how much you need, and to keep track of where it's all coming from. In the unlikely event of insufficient cash being raised to make the movie, you'll have to give all the little donations back to the right people. Friends and family might be a place to start. Even £20 or £50 at a time can add up if you can persuade enough people.

Sponsorship

Local companies might be persuaded to sponsor the project. Sponsorship does not normally mean just 'giving money', and an approach is more likely to be successful if you can show the company you're approaching that you've thought a little about what they can get out of it. Sponsorship of programmes, events, anything, normally comes out of a company's advertising budget. The company wants to put its name in front of the kind of people it wants to attract. It isn't normally necessary to push the product hard. Sponsorship is typically more of a soft sell, but it's still a sell. If you've thought clearly about the target audience for the movie (and you certainly should have done) then think about the companies that want to sell things to the same audience and approach them for sponsorship.

You might offer the sponsor their name on the film. You might offer special showings to which they can invite their guests. Even the première could be made more spectacular with the aid of the sponsor. Make it newsworthy and everyone gets more out of it. Editorials in newspapers and magazines – stories *about* the project – are far more powerful in attracting interest than paid advertising, and any likely sponsor will know that. Make it glitzy enough, and everyone will want to be part of it. And a sponsor will also know that, in order to get the most out of a sponsorship deal, they'll have to spend as much money again on telling people what they've done – otherwise it won't help them.

You could also offer the sponsor the right to send cassette copies of their film to their favoured clients, with the sponsor's name all over the cover. It all means more exposure for both of you.

Television

There are, occasionally, slots on television for short films, it's true. Honestly, except in these rare cases, television isn't a serious source of finance – or even sales – for short films. It's probably worth a stamp to approach your local television company for support in some form, but don't hold your breath. In general, television likes long series with which it can build an audience. One-offs of any sort are a problem, though a short film might be packaged in some kind of a short-film showcase with others. Also, as Jacqui Wetherell points out, licence fees from television for short films are very low. Even if a film gets a showing, the payment isn't going to go very far towards even a tiny budget.

Being kind – non-cash financing

Every production needs a certain amount of cash, but, in the real world, a major part of the funding for short films comes in kind – in the provision of facilities or time for nothing by people and companies.

It's a difficult business, asking people to help you in return for – well, nothing, really. It helps if you have done the budget properly, so that you are aware of the value of what you're asking for. It might indeed be possible to produce a film for a few hundred pounds cash, but the true cost of the film, if you include the value of contributed goods and services is much higher. The reason that budgets for full-length feature films start at £2 million even without expensive actors and special effects (and then continue upward to infinity, and beyond) is not because everyone is wasting time and being paid extraordinary amounts of money. It's because, in the real world, where people also have to make a living, that's what it costs.

The point of all this is to say that people and companies who invest time, equipment, services in short films, are just as much investors in the film as those who provide cash – and just as aware that they're unlikely to get any financial return. It's worth considering the reasons why they do help with short films and trying to ensure that they get the best return practicable.

Jamie Payne points out that this is one of the advantages of doing short films – you're asking less of the people you ask to help: *It means that you can ask people to come out for a day, rather than a week, and that's a big difference. Also when you're relying on people's generosity, you can only stretch it out so far. And that's not only people but companies, too. You can get support and sponsorship for shorts – equipment places, camera suppliers, laboratories, Kodak and so on are all very supportive – but filmmakers have to understand that those people are running a business and they can only give discount up to a certain point otherwise they're not running an effective business. And sometimes that's taken for granted. If you assume that kind of support for anything longer than a short it can undermine what you're trying to achieve. What people give you is more valuable than you can imagine.*

What are you going to get?

First of all, although your true-cost budget will probably have been put together from companies' rate cards, it's one of the open secrets of the industry that nobody pays the rate-card rate for anything – unless the amounts are very small. A fully paid-for feature going through a lab would expect a significant discount on the rate-card rate, as they would from all the equipment-hire companies. So perhaps you have been able to raise enough cash, after all.

As we've said, if you have persuaded people to give their time or facilities in order to help you, it isn't fair to expect them to pay for the privilege, too. So part – or even most – of the cash you've managed to get together will go in paying transport costs. You may have runners with their own cars to fetch and carry equipment and actors, but the production budget should expect to pay for their petrol. And make sure that the runners are insured to use their cars for that purpose. Otherwise, if anything goes wrong, the whole affair could become very much more expensive than planned.

The industry, generally, is a hospitable one that wants to help. If you ask nicely, and you create the impression that you know what you're doing, then you should be able to get some or all of the following, either free or at greatly reduced rates:

- camera and sound equipment
- lighting equipment
- film processing
- second-hand or short-end tape or film stock
- editing facilities.

However, it's likely that there will be strings attached. Companies exist to make money. Not necessarily a fortune, but a living for the people who work for them. It's likely that, while a company is willing to help you, for example with the free loan of equipment, quite reasonably they're not going take their most expensive and newest equipment away from revenue-earning work just for you. Either your film must wait until the equipment has nothing to do; or you'll get cheaper, older equipment that doesn't get out much any more.

Jacqui Wetherill, *Ghosthunter* Production Manager: *But people do under-stand the problems when you're starting out. If you're genuine, they do help you out. But they won't help if you push your luck. Play fair. People are usually really helpful if they know that you're trying.*

Similarly with editing, facilities are likely to be offered during down time – at weekends or overnight. And there's always the chance that the timing will change and leave you without something you had counted on having – like a camera. *Ghosthunter* was relatively lucky in this respect, but did have problems getting started with the edit, which was delayed some weeks in the end. Not ideal, but there was nothing that could be done without money.

From the News section of the *Ghosthunter* website: *MARCH 15th. The first assembly of the film was ready for viewing last night. Due to our editor's commitments to the feature he's working on it has taken until now to put the film together. We can now begin to fine cut the film and release the effects sequences to Quantel, the fine cut will take place at evenings and weekends over the next few weeks. After such a long delay it was wonderful to actually start work on the post production of the film. There is a lot of work ahead.*

Cast and crew

The hardest thing, though, is to find experienced people who are able and willing to help. It has to be said that it is much easier to achieve this with a short film, than for a lo/no budget feature – simply because the length of time for which the production needs people is much shorter. If the script is good and the production feels right, it isn't that difficult to find people who will agree to work on the film. But they will all say that if an offer of paid work comes along, they will have to take it – which is not unreasonable.

Jacqui Wetherill: *When you're trying to do something like this with no money you can never plan absolutely. For example, we went through about seven grips because they all got paid work somewhere else. When you're asking somebody to do something for free, it's their perfect right when they get paid work to drop out. I think it's always really really difficult. And your expectations of the crew, as well. You always have to be a little bit guarded and aware that these people are working for free, whereas you might push a bit harder if people were getting paid. But people who are in film tend to push themselves hard anyway, so it's not often an issue.*

Deal structures

People who give their time for nothing are investing in the film. One thing that is quite important whether the cast and crew totals four people or

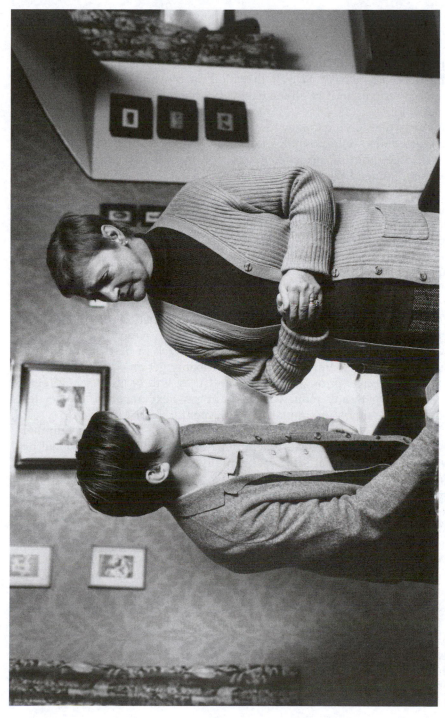

Anne (Jacqueline Phillips, left) and Audrey (June Watson) in the guest house. © Zoë Norfolk 2000

100, is to be quite clear of the basis on which people are making their contribution.

1 If the film does make money after all, what happens to it?
2 Ensure that you have the right to exploit the film and all the performances and copyrights in it in all media, everywhere you might want to.

Nobody likes giving money to lawyers, but you need to be able to answer these questions – and possibly others, too. The most efficient way of doing this is to get hold of formal contracts, or contracts that other productions have used, amend them to fit your own film and then get a lawyer to look them over.

(Disclaimer: what follows it not legal advice, but personal suggestions for approaches to the problems. Consult a legal expert for advice on any given production.)

If the film does earn money after all, what happens to it? You can say 'thank you very much' and keep it – perhaps putting it towards your next picture. Or you can divide it up amongst your investors. How you do this depends on what you've agreed with them in the first place. Also, there are two stages to the process of covering the true production cost of the movie: repayment of investment and payment of deferred fees.

Cash investors normally expect to be paid back in first position. If you have a number of them, then they will probably get an equal share of each pound that comes through the door, and they will be fully repaid before anyone else gets any money. What happens next depends on the deals you've done with your suppliers – equipment, cast and crew.

Since there is a true-cost budget, one way of handling equipment, cast and crew is to suggest to them that you agree the same notional deal that you would agree if they were actually being paid, and they will then agree to defer those fees. The money won't be payable until it is earned from sales of the film. Any money which does come in is divided amongst the crew in proportion to the fees they would have got, until their fees have been paid. Alternatively, you could make everyone equal. It's up to you.

You may want to offer a small share of so-called 'net profits', too. Any money coming in after the film's production and distribution costs have been paid is 'net profit' and financiers would normally expect a share of that – although the producers obviously try to keep as much as they can.

This may seem overkill for a short film, where everyone knows there isn't going to be any money; but it's just as well to have everything thought out clearly (just in case there is), and it will be necessary for a longer picture, when you will be asking far more of the people who help you. The attitude behind *Ghosthunter* has always been that everyone should treat it as a feature. The only difference is that it is shorter.

But the most important thing, silly though it seems, is – if you make promises, keep them. Everyone gets carried away in the enthusiasm of getting a film together. It's easy to forget that you promised to send copies to people, or to write thank you letters to people who have allowed you to film in their houses, but it matters. Not only to you, because you might want to go back there later on, but also to other filmmakers who come after you.

Ghosthunter *finance*

Ghosthunter was financed, as most films are, through enthusiasm. The Amulets did try to raise finance from 'official' sources – the various funding bodies.

Simon: *We looked at getting finance from some of the funding bodies and we found it very difficult in a bureaucratic way. It's something that Alison had experienced as well when she was raising funding for her theatre company. A lot of effort went into putting applications in and sitting waiting for responses. We were spending most of our time researching and developing application forms rather than researching and developing scripts and we were not very enthusiastic about it because we wanted to get on making our films.*

The amounts of money available from these official sources are typically very small, too – sometimes only a few hundred pounds, which often doesn't even pay the catering bill. Of course, in some ways, that's really what this kind of support is intended for, to provide some kind of assistance with the inescapable cash costs that every project has to deal with, even if all the equipment and the people involved are contributed without charge.

Of course, movie-making is a world-wide activity, and a world-wide business. Some people find that the climate of encouragement is much greater outside the UK.

Simon: *The Guerilla Filmmaking people funded their film through foreign money. If you can get the money privately, then do that. Kenneth Branagh said the same. It's not very encouraging for filmmaking in this country really that most of the advice we got was to forget the funding bodies and get the money together privately.*

In the end they managed to raise around £30 000 cash from a number of private sources – the largest of which was their own resources; and in the end the movie needed a further £10 000 to finish it.

Simon: *The money mainly came from private investment. We were very lucky. We got a big investment from somebody who believed in the project and to whom we'd been talking for a long time, so we decided to go for it. We also got small amounts from other people who knew us, and we put in a large amount ourselves – it was about one-third.*

When you're trying to make a movie with a budget really down at the limits of the possible, it's very hard to be realistic about how much cash you really need. It can be very tempting to be over-optimistic, and say to yourself, 'OK, we've got this much money. It'll be fine. We can do it for that.' If the budget is a real one, you won't be able to do it for less, however much you try to convince yourself that you can.

Simon: *It cost more money than we planned. And we're supporting ourselves with the money we've earned over the last few years. It's important not to have to worry about where your next bit of income is coming from. We're very grateful for all the commercials we've made over the last few years.*

And inevitably it's more time-consuming than you expect. You think you can have a life outside the movie. Then you find that you can't – not unless you want the whole process to drag on for years.

Alison: *We're currently working full-time on it. It would have been terribly difficult if we were out there trying to earn a living as well – it's one of those things with filmmaking, if you're serious you have to do it full-time. Eventually we hope it'll all come back to us threefold – tenfold. At the moment, we're longing for the day when we can pay ourselves something from Amulet Films, even if it's only £50 a month.*

Simon: *We hope that once we've got through the post-production period we can get back to earning some money again. The Guerilla Filmmakers found that that was their experience, too. There are a lot of people in the business trying to scrape a living by it, and they're all achieving it, somehow.*

5 Lining up the ducks – pre-production

Scheduling

All the elements of pre-production are interdependent. None of them exist in isolation, but let's pretend they do, for a while.

The first thing is to decide when the shoot is going to take place. A lot of the financing – specially the availability of cast, crew and equipment – depends on timing, as the Amulets discovered. The second thing is to decide how long you need in order to shoot the film, and what – and who – you need to achieve what you want to achieve. All this can be changed as things develop, but you can see that quite a lot of detailed planning should really be done very early on.

A long and sufficiently detailed pre-production process is absolutely necessary to the success of the film. If it isn't properly planned the whole experience will be purgatory for everyone involved. If it is properly planned, with everything and everybody where they should be, then everyone will have a great time and the results will be the best they can be. Proper planning frees everybody to concentrate on putting their best artistic work into the project.

Claire Moore, *Ghosthunter* Unit Manager: *Organization is important. The most important thing is to get the script absolutely right – absolutely the best you can do. Work out how to shoot it, like you can afford to shoot for this many days. Make sure you can fit your movie into it, and if you can't, then look again.*

Ghosthunter was fine. I would have liked another day on the shoot. But the script is what's really important – and that goes for features as well. The skeleton of the whole thing is the script, and if it's wrong, if there are any problems with it, that's going to send problems all the way down the line.

What kind of planning?

Well, you can't really decide how long the movie will take to film until you know how you intend to do it. The director needs to sit down with the script

Freddie Francis and Maurice Gillett at Pinewood Studios. They have worked together over the past 50 years, having started their careers together in the army, stationed at Wembley. © Zoë Norfolk 2000

and more or less go through the whole film on paper. How is each scene to be covered? Produce a shooting script with each shot detailed, either in words or using a storyboard. Once that's done, you still have to decide exactly how you're going to shoot it. How many set-ups? How long do you think you need for each one? Much of this will change, but if the production process is to flow smoothly, it's work that needs to be done.

Simon: *The production office wanted a shot list and I'd never done this before. For* The Essay *I'd been able to experiment by rehearsing my shot list on Video 8 and editing the film together to see if it would work – it was also a simpler film to visualize.* Ghosthunter *was much more complex and it wasn't like I could go out and rehearse the shots on the trusty old camcorder. The thing was, I dreaded doing it and I kept putting it off because I thought that I might not be able to visualize the story – that I might just be met with a blank, a kind of director's block. I had certain thoughts about the film and certain sequences of the story I had strong ideas for. There were also parts of the script that I was unsure about. So I set aside a weekend to go through it, word by word, building the film in my mind and then broke this down and built my shot list.*

I'd start work on page one and Alison would go upstairs – she'd come down a couple of hours later and I'd be halfway down page two. It was a slow process but extremely valuable and it did speed up as I went along. I came away with a complete visual image of the film that I was able to develop and which has developed since. Now I'm going through it with Gavin (the Director of Photography) so that when we get in there on the day the two of us will be pin sharp as to where to put and move the camera. Also the camcorder has evolved itself back into the picture – as we worked through each location we were able to rehearse shots with one of us walking through the action and even to experiment with new shots. I was able to review this footage and see how it fitted with my thoughts on the film. My main problem with all this was that the actors would probably have their own ideas and suggestions on the day as to how they'd like to move within the scene. I now had an idea as to the overall look and pacing of the film, the mood of each scene and even how I could use music to enhance the drama. By working with the actors on the day I hoped to make any adjustments necessary, with all this in mind, without compromising this visual image that I was becoming very attached to.

Whichever way I approached the film the production office needed a shot list so that they could start to build a detailed schedule for production. The important thing to remember is that this preparation gives the director a starting point from which to develop the film and any suggestions are a bonus, or otherwise, to his visualization.

The work done on the shooting script can always be amended – and undoubtedly will be amended; but fundamental decisions about how the film is going to be produced are made at this stage, if they haven't been already. The character of the whole film is set at this stage, and everyone else who has pre-production work to do takes the basic information they need from this shooting script.

Simon: *Our first AD took a look at what I'd done and said 'wow, you're really shooting the hell out of this script'. But I didn't want to do lots of simple shots. I wanted to put lots of camera moves in and develop the shots and blocking with the actors.*

Don't underestimate the time it takes to set things up. Within reason, it's nearly always better to take slightly longer than you think you need in pre-production.

Peter Lamont, Production Design Consultant: *On Titanic, we started work in the design department in November, and we started shooting in September the following year. It wasn't actually a very long time because we didn't even have a site for the ship to start with. We ended up in Mexico, which is good because there's a good pool of labour there, and it's only a short drive from LA.*

Originally, *Ghosthunter* was due to shoot in the last week before the Christmas break. In the end it just wasn't possible to get everything together in time. Actors wouldn't commit. Crew were unsure; so the filming was postponed until the second week of January.

John Rendall, Panavision: *The time factor looked incredibly short on prep time, but in fact it was put back because of artists' availability and it all worked out all right. I think they would have found it really hard to have started when they originally planned to start. And because it was delayed, we were able to give them one or two items that weren't available earlier on.*

Simon: *It was difficult. We'd spent the whole year working towards that point, and we were looking forward to relaxing at Christmas with it all over; and then we had to delay. We still had no cast. We were determined to get the best possible cast for Ghosthunter. However, nobody was prepared to commit so close to Christmas, so rather than compromise we postponed shooting.*

Alison: *But it worked out really well. As soon as we said we were going to put it off, almost everyone started coming up to us and saying, 'that's so much better for us'.*

Casting

Getting the right cast can make or break a script – and a whole film. We're lucky in the UK in having huge numbers of very talented actors available. Unfortunately, in the real world it isn't enough that the cast of a film (or a stage production, for that matter) be good at their job. Particularly if a film is without a star writer or director – where the story is not even from a famous bestseller – then it's through the cast that the film is sold. 'Who's in it?'

So casting has to be undertaken – or undergone – at two levels: finding the right people for the roles, and finding at least one person with a name that's sufficiently well known to give the film a spark of recognition right from the very beginning. So how to go about it?

The very first thing you need is a cast breakdown – a list of all the parts you need to fill. Simple. Go through the script and list all the characters appearing in each scene – not forgetting the ones who don't say anything. This can be a very useful exercise in more ways than one. Not only do you end up with a cast breakdown to form the basis of the schedule (you may find that you need to group together all the scenes with your star, for instance), but sometimes you find that some parts are smaller (or bigger) than you thought. Characters often live in your mind in quite a different way from the amount of time they actually spend on the screen.

(For example, as an aside: in *Much Ado about Nothing*, the character of Hero, the wronged daughter, seems to have nearly as much to do as Beatrice. In fact, the part is quite small, and Hero appears in surprisingly little of the play. Still, it's a lively part, and the play ostensibly revolves around her fate, so she has a much bigger impact than the time she spends on stage would suggest.)

Conventionally there are two levels of artist activity: 'cast' – actors, who are then described as 'leading' or 'supporting'; and extras, who are either 'extras' or 'walk-ons'. Extras are crowd artists. Bodies who occupy the set; people who are just there. Walk-ons are extras with one or two lines to say, where the content of the lines might be important, but the actual words used are not. These might seem very fine distinctions, but they make sense to agents and the unions you will have to deal with sooner or later: Equity (the actors' union), and the FAA (the Film Artistes Association) who deal with extras and walk-ons within a 40 mile radius of Charing Cross in London.

Children

A quick word of warning about working with children. There are very strict rules about how and where children are allowed to work. The following is a very brief summary of the main points as they affect filming at the time of writing.

● All children aged under 16 years need a licence to work from the Local Education Authority. So does anyone under 18 years if you're taking them abroad. It's your responsibility (the Producer/Employer) to get the licence, and you need to apply for it at least 21 days in advance. If you're filming an event that would be happening anyway, you don't have to worry about licences. If any are needed, it will be up to the event organizers to sort them out.

- The hours that children are allowed to work in any given period of time are strictly controlled – you can't work them all day.
- They have to be accompanied by a parent, a teacher or a matron approved by the Education Authority (who is allowed to look after a maximum of 12 children).

These rules are not about payment, but about working hours. They affect you whether or not your cast members are being paid. All this can make working with children a real pain. However, although filmmakers like to feel as if they are outlaws, you probably don't actually want to *be* one. You can do deals on a personal level with anyone. You don't need to stick to union agreements, though they're quite useful to give you an idea of what's expected in the 'real' world; but exploiting kids is not a good idea. Your Local Education Authority will be able to tell you what the current rules are, of course.

Finding cast

You've done the cast breakdown by scene, so you know how many people you want, who they are and roughly how long you need them for. The next thing is to write a short but clear description of each of the roles you're trying to cast. It's a bit like describing the house you're looking for to an estate agent. For example:

Ross: middle 20s, tall, blond. Spoilt little rich kid who's never done a serious day's work in his life. Loves driving fast cars – so must be able to drive.

Samantha: mid-30s, brassy, very self-confident. Archetypal pub landlady.

So far, so good. However, theatrical agents and estate agents have a lot in common. You can tell an estate agent until you're blue in the face that you're looking for a country cottage for under £100 000; you'll still be offered city flats at £250 000. It doesn't matter that you ask for a Rutger Hauer look-alike, you'll still be offered Bob Hoskins' hitherto undiscovered twin. At least you'll have thought properly about who it is you really want.

If something like the ability to drive is important, then say so. I'm told by a friend who worked on a picture called *Loose Connections*, a British road-movie of 1983, it was only discovered on the first day that neither of the lead actors could drive. Practically the whole movie was filmed on a trailer, which was towed along while the actors sat in a car pretending to drive. Now that's acting.

It has also happened to me that an actor said he could ride a horse at the casting session, but when he found out that he was expected to gallop across the fields with others, he admitted that what he meant was that he had actually sat on a horse once, and that was about the limit of his riding experience.

Particularly if you're asking people to work for little or nothing, it's always better if you can get them to offer themselves to you, so that you're not asking them for favours. And the best way to achieve that is to announce your project in the daily or weekly casting bulletins that most actors and agents subscribe to. An entry in these bulletins typically describes the film and its story, and then lists the roles to be cast with short descriptions in the manner of those above. Some of these lists distribute via e-mail and the Internet. The following isn't an exhaustive list, and it will inevitably date, but you can find others by doing an Internet search for expressions such as 'cast actors film UK' or something similar:

- www.castcall.demon.co.uk
- www.castweb.co.uk
- http://home.btconnect.com/bdw/
- www.uktw.co.uk/casting.html has links to loads of others
- Equity also has a Job Information Service.

These lists also have the advantage of producing quick responses: 99 per cent of the reaction that you're going to get at all will be in the week following the announcement going out. It's worth doing this as a first step, because if you make the project sound appealing enough, just sometimes you might find an agent offering you an actor with a name big enough to help give the film a higher profile – and that can save a lot of work chasing after name actors. If you're not that lucky, then nothing has been lost, and you continue with stage two. Chasing names.

You would have thought that two actors, as the Amulets are, would have had no problem in casting their movie. To begin with, that's what they thought, too. As things developed, though, casting turned out to be a long process – although it all worked out well in the end. This is Alison's summary of How To Do It, written as the *Ghosthunter* experience was concluded:

Agents and how to deal with them when casting a low-budget short film

Step 1. If you can afford it, employ a casting director! Early on we did approach a couple of casting directors, who were very helpful, but unfortunately they were either too busy to commit to our project or too expensive. (Note: casting directors work either for a fixed fee, or, more usually, for a percentage of the final fee they agree for each role cast on your behalf. You may find a (smaller) agent who will act as casting director for you for a small fee, particularly if some of their clients are cast. In any case, if you cast one part from an agent, it's often worth asking who else they have that might fit your requirements. Let them do the work for you.)

Step 2. So assuming that it's up to you, firstly find out who represents your potential actor. You can do this easily by looking your actor up in the Spotlight directories (available to buy – expensive new, very reasonable a year old) or by calling Spotlight directly. Spotlight should also give you the agent's phone number, or you can get it from Contacts (also published by Spotlight).

Step 3. When you call the agent, make sure that you ask for the person who represents the actor you are interested in. Don't just assume that because it's 'Joe Bloggs Agency' that Joe Bloggs is who you need to speak to because it's likely that Joe Bloggs either a) died 10 years ago (I made this mistake) or b) is a cover name for several different agents.

Step 4. When you (hopefully) get through to the right agent, the first thing to do is to check the actor's availability. There is no point spending precious moments of their and your time selling the project if the actor is already working.

Step 5. If the actor is available, the agent will want to know something about the film, so sell the project, sell it well and sell it quickly. Make sure that you're prepared for this beforehand (write it down if necessary). Be prepared to be asked about the director, the film company, the story, the part the actor is up for, where it's being filmed, who else is cast and what the actors fee is. Be positive, make the film sound EXCITING and something that their client would LOVE to do – but be honest (agents can sniff a lie instantly). One other thing, if you're approaching a famous actor, approach the agent with an offer – they will not be impressed if you want the actor to audition.

Step 6. Get straight to the point – 'is this the sort of project that Alan Actor would be interested in?' A good agent knows their clients well, and should be able to give you an indication of whether it's worth sending the script to them.

Step 7. Get the script to the agent (or straight to the actor if you're lucky) as quickly as you can. Fax or e-mail it if possible and then, most importantly, **check that they received it and have passed it on to the actor**. I wasted five precious days because a script I'd faxed through had been put in a pile by an assistant and forgotten about.

Step 8. Chase them up every day. You may not get through, and they may occasionally get a bit snotty, but at least you're showing them you're there and you're not going away until you get a response. Be polite, professional and friendly at all times though, even if you want to wring their neck.

Step 9. Pray, and pray hard.

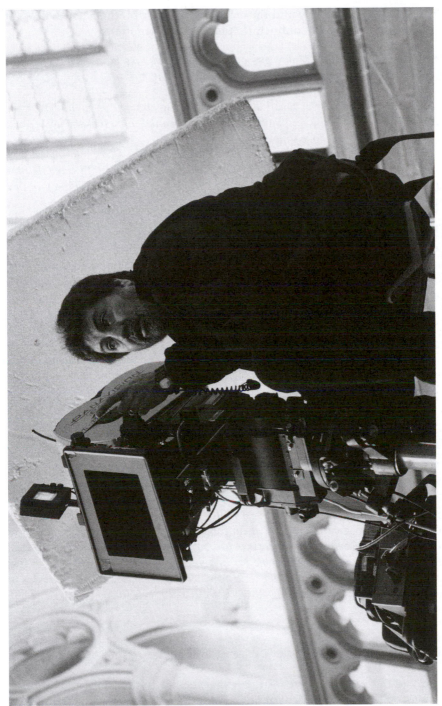

Camera operator, Rodrigo Gutierrez, on the Cinejib rehearsing the next shot. © *Zoë Norfolk 2000*

Step 10. If you're lucky and the actor likes the script, the agent will want to discuss their fee and contract. Be prepared to negotiate.

Simon: *Getting Frank Finlay was a major landmark. We thought then that the whole cast was going to fall together quite simply; but, no.*

Alison: *At the end of the day, it doesn't matter who else you've got on board, the actors are interested in the script and in their part. Frank Finlay took the job because he loved the script and loved the part.*

Simon: *When approaching agents all we wanted was a fair shot, to know that the actors had had a chance to look at the script. We often felt that they hadn't and that it was the agent who had rejected us.*

Having achieved the major result of getting Frank Finlay for the part of the Ghosthunter – and already being sure of having Alison, who was to play Sarah – they still needed to cast the part of Audrey. They had come very close with a couple of actresses, but in the end it had come to nothing. Time was running out.

Simon: *And then we found June Watson 10 days before filming started. We've known her for a long time and we had previously thought of her, but we hadn't asked her because we thought she was too busy. So we phoned her husband, Chris Dunham, who's a director that we've both worked with, to ask him for casting advice and he suggested June. It was that straightforward in the end.*

Alison: *And likewise Jacqueline Phillips, who played Anne, was an actress Simon knew from drama school.*

Simon: *Yes we had to wait with that part because we had to know who the mother was before casting the daughter.*

Alison: *And then we still hadn't cast Emily four days before filming started. Bea, the costume designer was pulling her hair out because everyone was being cast at the last minute. Eventually we turned to Chris (our stand-in casting director!) again and he gave us a list of people he thought might be right. One of them was Josie Kidd who, luckily, was available. It was very hair-raising casting like this at the last minute, but thankfully it all worked out very well in the end.*

Auditions

In the end the Amulets were fortunate that they didn't have to hold audition sessions, but most producers of any kind of drama have to go through the process at one time or another. Auditions are about finding the right people for the job – and that means, not only whether they look right, but whether they will fit in to the production team, too. Consequently, people handle auditions in different ways. A few things to think about:

- The photographs sent out by agents, or contained in *Spotlight*, give only the vaguest idea of what the person actually looks like. Don't *ever* cast from a photograph and CV.
- When you're looking at the CV, be aware that working for the camera is quite different from acting on stage. It wouldn't be fair to make this a general rule, but you might like to consider whether you're making life difficult for yourself if you cast someone who has only ever worked on stage.
- As Alison says, you really can't audition Famous People. What you could do (particularly with experienced but Less Famous People) is ask to borrow a tape of something they've done recently – or at least find out the title so you can get a copy for yourself.
- It's a shame, but you can't give everyone a job. You'll see a few people, maybe more, for each part. You won't remember them all later on, so take a Polaroid shot, or run a video camera to help you put the face and the name back together later.
- Often you'll like some of them a lot, but they're not right for what you need at the moment. That's OK. Keep their details in your book, and you can work with them later – on your next project perhaps. Doing this can also save a lot of auditioning as time goes on.
- Whatever happens, treat people well. The only people who really enjoy auditions are those producers and directors who like proving how powerful they are. For normal people, they're a necessary evil which has to be endured.

What do you do in the audition? You look for someone who fits your vision of the character as closely as possible. You talk to people, try to get them to relax, find out a bit about them and you work with them on some of the script. The idea is to find someone you can work with who can do the job.

Some actors are very good at auditions, but disappointing when it comes to the real thing. They'll give a wonderful sight-reading of the part in the audition – and stick with it absolutely all the way through the filming, not responding to anything going on around them. What you had in those first moments is the best you'll ever get. Others are the other way round – uncertain at auditions, but a generous and imaginative pleasure to work with. Finding which is which is a problem with no easy solution.

The most important thing to get out of an audition is to find out whether you can work together. Not so much a perfect performance – there'll be time to develop that later – as the ability to respond to suggestion and direction, and to *change*. So try playing a scene three or four different ways. None of them may be right for the film, but if they do all come out different, then you have the basis of a working relationship that can grow. If the acting is always the same whatever you try, then you're likely to have problems later on.

Once you have your cast, treat them well – particularly if they're working for little or nothing. After all, your film depends on them. The principal cast of *Ghosthunter* were given rooms in the Amulets' house where they could wait in comfort, and all the cast were provided with transport to and from the locations. In the end it took quite a large chunk of the budget, but it was worth it.

Pre-production – by department

Of course, every part of a unit depends on and works closely with every other – or should do. Nonetheless, each department has its own concerns and its own desire to do its particular job in the best way possible. Occasionally the needs and desires of one department conflict with those of others.

The production department

The production department is the part of the film's unit that makes things happen. Filmmaking might well centre around a camera pointing at some actors, but it's the production department that makes it appear so matter-of-fact that camera, actors, crew and everyone else is in the same place at the same time. And it's a task full of detail and pitfalls.

Probably the first thing the department does is to work out a schedule. Directors are always complaining that the production department expects too much of them, and Producers and Production Managers always feel that the Director should be working faster, with fewer people and less kit. Invariably everyone is right.

The schedule is inevitably a compromise, a juggling act, that attempts to get the best out of all kinds of conflicting needs. The most important thing is to be realistic about how long it is going to take to shoot each scene. It might seem unnecessary to say so but, although you can reckon on roughly 1 minute per page of screen time for a conventionally laid-out script, this is only an average. A car chase or a fight scene, described in two or three lines, could take a day or more to film. Six pages of well-rehearsed dialogue might be done in an hour.

The single most important job of a good schedule is to minimize movement. That applies equally to movement across the world as to movement within a room (to which we'll return later) because moving a crew, cast, camera, lights, takes time. Especially if you have a large crew, even moving half a mile down the road can take half a day. Even moving into the next room takes 30–45 minutes by the time the scene is lit and you are ready to go again. It doesn't take very many moves like that to make a big hole in any schedule.

In anything but the simplest film, the ideal, consolidated schedule might not be possible. There are other things to juggle. Some of them are to do with budget. For example, if you have hired some expensive piece of equipment, as *Ghosthunter* did with the Cinejib, it makes sense to schedule the scenes that it will be used in as close together as possible, so that you don't pay hire charges for gear you're not using.

Another problem might be artist availability. If you have been lucky enough to have secured the services of a prominent actor for your picture, you are likely to be at his or her mercy as far as their availability is concerned. On the other hand, once they have agreed to something, you're probably less likely to lose them because a paying job comes along, which is a risk you have to take into account with any member of cast or crew who isn't being paid the going rate for the job.

Naturally, there will be any number of other scheduling problems, all of which are peculiar to your film, but all of which crop up again and again in one form or another. Every film is a prototype, but the same kind of problems go round and round wearing different disguises. A location might only be available at certain times. A set might need more preparation time. If you have locations in two main centres that are a long way apart, obviously you'll only want to travel once.

Then there's the weather. Having juggled everything and managed to get it all working to everyone's satisfaction, the weather – especially in Northern Europe – is more than likely to turn the whole house of cards into a soggy mess. How to cope with weather? Well, there are several options. The safest is to have no exteriors at all. If you need a desert island, build it in a studio. Hugh Hudson's Tarzan film, *Greystoke*, alledgedly built a whole jungle at Pinewood. Or you buy weather insurance to pay for extra shooting time if weather forces you to cancel a day or days. But that's expensive. Or you film anyway, wind or rain. It's surprising how much water there has to be falling from the sky before it shows up on camera. You see puddles on the ground and wet streets long before you see falling rain. However, you can help yourself along by structuring the schedule sensibly so that you put all your exteriors as early as practicable in the schedule. If it rains or snows or hurricanes and you can't film the cricket match after all, you can simply move another scene up (since it will already have been prepared to provide precisely this kind of weather cover) and swap it with the cricket match. So, along with everything else, you can save yourself a lot of grief if you build a degree of flexibility into the schedule.

Camera operator, Rodrigo Gutierrez, on the Cinejib for a shot of Charlie and Sarah in the main body of the church. © *Zoë Norfolk 2000*

Jacqui Wetherill: *I mean, if you schedule right and get your pre-production right there should never be any need to work those sort of hours more than one day. Of course if you get a problem you need to get it done, but not more than one day in the shoot. The film I'm on now is a nightmare because they didn't do any pre-production. The week before should always be left to check that everything is coming together at the right time and the right day and there haven't been any changes – because there are always changes. Always book the equipment as early as you can and think of details – like what do I need to make this thing work? Like, if you get a crane, do you need an operator? And how are you going to get the crane there? The way to go forward is to get your basic deals and then fill in the details. As you go further towards the shoot day details like how you get there: do I have to help the cast? Do I need two drivers? Every single project is different. You need a good schedule – and a good First Assistant Director.*

A good schedule makes everything flow easily on the set; so that you keep changing locations to a minimum; so you stick in one place because moving the crew and the set always uses up the most amount of time. So keep it so you shoot everything in one place before you move on to the next. And a good First AD to keep it cracking along.

Claire Moore, Unit Manager: *If it's low budget – as this is – generally keep the cast and locations to an absolute minimum – if you can do it with the script, keep it all in the same room – but make sure the room is big enough to have space round everyone. We're lucky here on* Ghosthunter *because all three locations are within a few minutes of each other. Have a production base that's an absolute base – one of the hiccups that we've discovered is that because the production office is split, some mistakes have happened. Nothing drastic, but it's so much better if there's only one contact number. Keep it under control.*

Sam Jones, Second Assistant Director: *This film is different. It all comes down to the pre-production. On this film it seemed to be a lot more organized, with schedules and everything. And we had a drinks meeting in London last week so they'd made the effort to introduce people to each other. When a group of people have never worked together before, it can all go horribly wrong – make sure that it doesn't. Preparation makes a big difference.*

Getting it together

Once you've sorted out an ideal schedule, you can get down to the real work – making it happen. Some things can be done a long way in advance. Others can really only be done at the last minute:

Claire Moore, Unit Manager: *Practically all of my job I had to do the week before. I couldn't do anything in advance – like booking rooms and food, because I had to know who all the crew was first, so I was kind of stuck. They put the shoot back – I was just beginning to get going then I had to stop.*

In the end, practically all of *Ghosthunter* was filmed in the grounds of the old convent in Sussex where the Amulets live. Claire, the Unit Manager, was responsible for getting everyone to the location and looking after them while they were there.

Claire: *I had to make myself known to everyone at the convent. Food had to be ordered a week before. Another crew member was added and we were in a permanent state of flux. We had a couple of scheduling hiccups and suddenly there was a bit of equipment coming with a specialized crew – a Cinejib that had to be sorted out and its crew fed and accommodated.*

Once you can't get everyone in the same car, transport becomes something that needs careful planning. How do you get everyone to the right place at the right time? Do they know where they're going? Have you organized somewhere for all the vehicles to park? All the vehicles involved in transporting even a small film's worth of cast and crew can take up an appreciable amount of space. What about the people who don't have their own transport? Is it practicable to use public transport? Certainly, if people (such as prominent actors or consultant technicians) are doing your film a favour by becoming involved, you can't ask them to get up at 5.30 a.m. and slog it to wherever you are by train.

Jacqui Wetherill: *We had three actors in different parts of London and Maurice (the 85-year-old Gaffer) to pick up and return when required. Transport is one of the hardest things. And on a film like this it's hard to get drivers who are over 25 years, so they're insurable. Then you need cars available to go and get things. We needed extra radios – we were hoping to manage with three but with this size of crew and the huge amount of gear, we needed more. There was a bit of drama when they had shot more stock than they thought so we had to get more stock urgently. And the simplest things happen. We lost the key for the bike chain that was locking a ladder up. At the end of a long day we still had to get the rushes from Sussex to Technicolor. You just have to be understanding with the people on the crew.*

Parking and transport can be an important influence on a choice of location. It isn't easy to find enough places to park in city centres – and at least some vehicles have to be parked right at the location because you can't carry the gear a mile along the road. Apart from wearing everyone out before the real work starts, it wastes an enormous amount of time. Also, if someone has to run back to the vehicles to get that forgotten battery or another roll of stock, you want the vehicle to be downstairs, not 15 minutes' run away.

If you speak nicely to the local authority it's often possible to arrange street parking where it's normally restricted – or to have a parking meter bay suspended while you park the unit truck there. But ask carefully about fees. One council very helpfully suspended a couple of meter bays for us for a week, very good. But then we were sent a bill for all the money that the meters would have taken had they been continuously fed all week. We were given parking permission, but at a price. This was one London borough. Others (even in London) have been known to be helpful without charging.

Street filming

While we're on the subject of working in the streets, there's a lot of confusion about what filming can or can't be done in the streets. In general, in places that are not private property (such as most streets), in most parts of the world, you don't have to ask permission to film, and nobody can prevent you from carrying out your lawful activities. However, you have to be careful that you're not infringing some other law, rule or by-law. In the case of filming, the one that concerns us most is that we must be careful not to cause any obstruction. So, in the real world, documentary filming (particularly if you're not using a tripod) is likely not to be a problem. Equally, a full feature-film crew is not something you can just put down in the middle of the road expecting to remain unnoticed.

While it's sensible to inform the police that you're going to be filming – and they can be very helpful – they can't actually grant permission. If you're planning on closing roads and generally making a nuisance of yourself in public, it's essential to talk to the police and the local authority and find out from them what they need you to do.

Private property

On private property, you can do what you like, providing that it's arranged and agreed with the property's owner. Obvious. Not always so obvious is that a number of places you might have thought of as public places are not, in fact, public places, even though the public are granted access to them. For example, shopping centres and malls are almost always private property – as the big and burly security guard will tell you as soon as you produce a camera inside them. Station forecourts, and the roads leading in and out of them usually belong to Railtrack, and are not public roads. Likewise, airports, airfields and car parks are all privately owned.

This kind of thing might or might not be a problem for your film; but it's always important to think of possible problems and confront them early on in the pre-production stage. If something turns out not to be a problem, then it's out of the way early on. If it isn't so straightforward, then you have a sensible amount of time in which to do something about it.

Crew

The film and television industry is still a predominantly freelance world. People are used to being offered a few days' or weeks' work at very short notice. So there's rarely any real difficulty in finding a crew for a production. But finding the really good people you want might turn out to be a bit less easy. And finding the right people to work for little or nothing is a whole new can of worms.

Philip Shaw, *Ghosthunter* First Assistant Director: *People aren't being trained properly in this industry, so a lot of learning is done on short films, where lots of people are working one step up. A camera assistant working as a camera operator; an Assistant Art Director working as Production Designer. So it all takes a bit longer, and sometimes it's difficult to get a cohesive crew because the crew isn't full of people who've done it a thousand times before.*

Alison: *We found a lot of the crew through Jacqui, our Production Manager. So much of it is word of mouth – like we found Philip, the First AD, through Bea, the Costume Designer, since they'd just been working together, and he brought along Sam, our Second AD. We chiefly wanted people who worked happily together. We didn't want people who behaved as if they were doing us a big favour.*

Simon: *It was always meant to be something with high production values. We didn't want the experience of making a short that was 16 mm with very little equipment – we'd done that with* **The Essay**. *We wanted our experience to be such that when we move into features all the elements are the same.*

Unfortunately, we couldn't pay the crew very much at all – expenses and a token payment. We couldn't pay the going rates but we deliberately set some money aside in the budget to pay a flat rate for everyone. So they all earned the same money and stayed in the same accommodation at the end of the road. It was a fair project.

Jacqui Wetherill: *The best way to do it is to get heads of department and give them the choice of their own crew and fill in the gaps. Bring in people you know are going to get on because it's so stressful. It's really important to get the right team together – get people who are keen to do it. Get good key people who know what they're doing. Whatever the budget is. We lost some people because they got paid work, but we had a cracking crew. Mostly they're people that I knew. But it's a really closed thing – it's all word of mouth. The wardrobe lady I'd worked with before said, 'Oh there's a really nice make-up girl I worked with the other day.' And Rodrigo, I asked him if he knew anyone, and he said 'I'll do it.' I couldn't believe my luck. And he wanted to bring in his crew. It's always cool if a team brings in its own people. But it's a long time not to work – for people of this calibre especially.*

Claire Moore: *I'd rather have too many crew than too few, because if there aren't enough things get forgotten and lost.*

Charlie (Frank Finlay) is overwhelmed by the spirits in the church as Sarah (Alison Reddihough) looks on. © Zoë Norfolk 2000

The delay to the *Ghosthunter* shoot was one of those things that seemed terribly frustrating at the time, but which turned out better for everyone in the end.

Simon: *There's always a temptation to cling to what was already in place – we'd ticked it off the list, and when it falls through, you think 'Oh no, another problem.' But it happened several times that the solution was better than the original. It does add to the stress level, though.*

Alison: *But you become aware if anything is not working, if it's bringing bad energy – it's better to cut it out than bring yourself more grief. Like we lost a location, but the one we replaced it with was ultimately better.*

Simon: *We had a month pre-production. A month ahead was the earliest that people were prepared to commit and I felt it wasn't enough time. The postponement gave us more pre-production time, so it was very valuable in the end. It was another example of a problem working for us, not against us.*

Jacqui: *The biggest thing is to think ahead and try and foresee problems, that's the key to my job – What's happening tomorrow, what if . . .? It's just looking ahead.*
There were lots of problems getting gear within budget – It was hard to convince people to give for nothing or to help us out. It took three or four weeks of phone calls. After all, they're all businesses – why should they give for nothing, or little? And then the transport for the gear, that has to cost, because otherwise they'll be laying out money on your behalf and they won't do that.

Art department

The story so far has an excellent crew (with gear and transport) and a knockout cast – but nowhere to put them. This is where the departments of art and location begin to work together.

Luke Smith, *Ghosthunter* Production Designer: *It's easy to think of our work as being artistic – and that's very important; but the organizational side is very important, too, and it's surprising how much time that takes up. You've got all the logistics of prop hiring and transport and dressing locations in advance so the art department's often the first one to turn up and then when the rest of the crew have gone the art department are clearing up, so you have to do all the planning about how to fit it all in.*

Luke had been the Production Designer on Jamie Payne's film, *The Dance of Shiva*, which is how he had become involved with *Ghosthunter*. He had already designed a number of low-budget films, and was well established in that particular part of the industry.

Luke: *At the start it was meetings with the Director and having a look at the script and deciding whether it was something I was going to get something positive from, rather than just furniture removing.*

'Furniture removal' is the way Luke describes work on a film where there's nothing for the designer to do but change things around in a room, because there's no scope, or money, for any real design input.

Luke: *Quite early on I asked them if they wanted to do any studio sets. There was one scene in Sarah's bedroom that seemed to be a good opportunity to do something big because we could then play with the fabric of the room – the haunting takes place in that scene, which if we used the original location, was rather limited. So I started putting together proposals for what format the studio set might take. It was only going to be a very simple design because of restrictions of money and time. I knew there wasn't going to be much time to do more than a simple box set.*

Ideally, Luke would probably have liked to do everything in the studio, because there the Designer rules; but even if the necessary resources are available, an all-studio shoot might not be the best for the picture. In practical terms, very few low-budget films will have the opportunity even to consider an all-studio production. Though it needn't necessarily be completely impossible. If a studio is having a quiet period, and they have the sets you need in store, then even a studio film becomes a possibility on a very low budget. The problem is that in the UK, studios don't normally keep sets in storage any more.

Peter Lamont, Consultant Production Designer: *If you go into studio now you've got to build a set. Pinewood used to have a great scene dock, so you could just reuse a set but you can't do that any more. In the USA you can just rent stock sets. But they have a big industry over there, a real industry. And they have good weather so things can be stored outside. Sets fall apart outside here. In California they don't use tube and scaffolding like they use here, they use timber, and if you go into the desert around Albuquerque you can find plywood western towns, and if you add to them it just makes them better.*

Meanwhile, back in Sussex, *Ghosthunter* had to find its locations.

Luke Smith: *The script was written based on the chapel in Sussex, but they didn't assume that that would be the right place, so we did look around for other places – other chapels, the bed and breakfast and Charlie's study – and that was something I was involved with very early on. That was happening alongside the production department's pulling things together and transport and things. It's all very well me finding a wonderful chapel somewhere but it's no good if it's miles from anywhere. The aesthetic value is outweighed by the problems. There are so many things you have to bear in mind.*

What makes a good location is much more than whether it looks right or not. You already know not to forget parking problems. One other aspect that's nearly always forgotten about (until it's too late) is what the place *sounds* like. You can't film a period drama next to a motorway, however beautiful the garden (or cottage, or stately home) is to look at. In fact, you wouldn't really want to film anything next to a motorway unless the motorway were part of the scene. Even features of the aural landscape that are in keeping with a period can make work impossible – a noisy river or mill-race, for example. And intermittent or continually variable noises are just as bad, because they make editing very difficult. Silence is golden. You can always add extra noises in the dub; but it's very hard to remove the sounds you don't want.

Other things? Access is always important. Remember that heavy equipment (and quite a lot of it) has to be brought in from the vehicles that you've found all that parking space for. Maybe it is necessary to film in the attic bedroom, but better not to if it can be avoided, because it's going to take lot of time and grumbling crew to set up, and nearly as much again to wrap everything afterwards.

Communications. Are there telephones the crew can use? Or do mobile phones work properly? And is it going to be a real problem when you need extra stock or gear?

Finally (well, not finally, but these are some of the things that often get forgotten), power. Lighting needs a lot of power. Are you going to use the mains power in your location? If so, is the wiring in good condition, and does it have enough capacity to give you the number of lamps you need? Are there sockets where you need them? 13 A will give you just over 3 kW of light. If the house has a total capacity of 30 A, that's still only around 7.5 kW. Fine for a small room, but not once you start thinking of creating sunshine with that 10 kW lamp out there. So you'll need a (probably blimped) generator, somewhere to park it and time to rig it with all its cabling.

In the case of *Ghosthunter*, it eventually became obvious that the convent complex provided virtually everything they needed, including parking. And it was easy to get the crew there, too.

Luke Smith: *So then I started surveying the locations to see what was there and what needed to be made, and I made accurate plans of them. In the past I've prepared measured drawings of locations – directors find it very useful – and whoever's looking after the locations can plan access. It's useful for a number of reasons. In this case, because we were doing period sequences, we had to hide a few modern things in the chapel and come up with reasonable solutions for hiding modern lighting – come up with hanging banners and things – and I was also putting together an art department team because it's important to have people with various skills to be on set and preparing stuff too.*

I did a lot of calling around and you end up following chains of contacts. It's good when you find someone who fits the bill and is keen to find out more and learn on it. I was very happy in the end that we had lots of people who realize that it's an interesting thing to do and who got something out of it. It was certainly an enjoyable atmosphere.

No part of a film crew, however large, can work in isolation from everyone else. So many things are interdependent – the perfect solution to a problem on one film might not work at all on a different picture, because something simple will be different. Maybe something as simple as having the necessary time or the extra person or the room. In the end, the whole crew (including the director) is there to do one single task: to effect the transfer of the story from script to screen in the best way possible.

Peter Lamont, Consultant Production Designer: *A good production designer listens to what the director wants, reads the script and knows that what the script wants, you can supply. For instance, walk through the set reading the script – that tells you how big it has to be. In effect, you've got to direct the film. How do I see it in my mind?*

Like most jobs to do with film, it's a job that mixes the artistic and the intensely practical; and like in every other job on a film, the script is important.

Peter Lamont: *If the script says there are two windows, don't put one or three. And if there's someone coming in one door and out the other put in two doors, not one. One film I worked on, the construction people had built a huge set for a tiny little scene and the director said to me 'All I needed was the corner.' There was no need to build the whole room.*

On the other hand, if something is mentioned in the script, then it's the art department's job to make sure that it's there, however tiny it might seem.

Philip Shaw, First Assistant Director: *Every teaspoon needs to be there. I worked recently on another film when we needed to shoot a meal and nothing was ready: no plates, no knives and forks. The whole film was like that. I'm not going to do another film with that designer.*

And there's no substitute for getting to know people. Everyone is different. Every team is different.

Peter Lamont: *If the script says the character comes in one door and walks across the room, usually I'd put the door on the right, so the actor would walk right to left; but working with James Cameron I'd put the door on the other side, because Jim's left-handed and he'll think of the actor walking the other way.*

Peter Lamont's approach is often to build a rough model of a set very early on, because he finds it's easier to discuss a model – something that everyone can see in three dimensions – than sketches, which need interpretation.

Peter Lamont: *On the last Bond picture I built models of the oil rigs, because a model is better than a sketch, and becomes a talking point. If you do a sketch you've got to do it from all angles. So we all looked at the model, and Vic Armstrong, the Second Unit Director, said 'Could you add a bit here, put a stairway in there?' and that was very useful for everyone so that by the time we were ready to build it, we knew it wouldn't alter much.*

In the magic world of the movies, surprising effects are often achieved in the most unlikely ways. On his way home from Pinewood one night, Peter Lamont noticed that the telegraph poles along the road were being replaced, so he got his assistant to get in touch with the contractor and find out how much they wanted for the old ones. They were told £10 each, but they bought so many they got them for £8 each – and they were the basis for the uprights on all the oil platforms built in the tank at Pinewood on the Bond film. Also, in the distance, behind the telegraph-pole oil platforms, they put fibre-optic lights with twinkle-wheels in front of them to give the effect of flickering lights in the distance. Imagination and simplicity can often go further than throwing money at a problem. Which is just as well if you're trying to make a film without any.

Ghosthunter

Right from the start, *Ghosthunter* was intended to have a very particular look to it. The story takes place in two different time periods, and the Amulets spent a long time discussing ways of differentiating the two periods with Luke, the Designer, and Gavin, the Director of Photography. Part of the effect was to be created by the look of sets and costume; and some of the effect would be created in the camera.

Luke Smith: *We spent a lot of time discussing things like colour schemes and the effect of the camera process to make a distinction between the flashback sequences and the contemporary sequences. It was very useful that they did camera tests, which we all went to have a look at. And that was very useful for me because I threw in a few colour swatches and looked at how they were affected by the process and that affected the way we decorated the set.*

Simon wanted the flashbacks to have a very saturated colour scheme. We decided on deep reds and golds, and most of the scenes were going to be lit primarily with candle light, which exaggerated the colours. And the contemporary scenes were going to be colder and more autumnal and more washed out. In order to enhance that I tried to be strict about not letting some of the colours like red and gold from

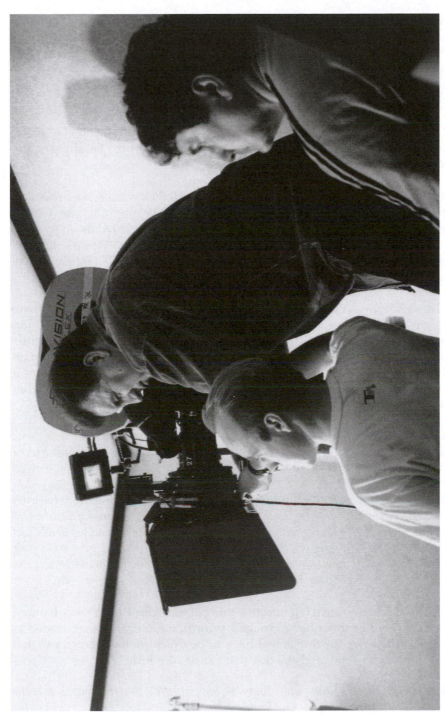

Trevor Coop, camera operator at Pinewood, in action. © *Zoë Norfolk 2000*

sneaking into the contemporary scenes. In fact it wasn't all possible because the dining room was decorated in very rich red wallpaper, but I did my best.

I found the bit of the process that's most enjoyable (because it's the least pressured) is the brainstorming sessions with the Director early on where you're both immersed in the script. You both know it inside out and you can throw ideas backward and forward.

Luke found that Peter Lamont's help, as Consultant Production Designer, was extremely useful. Not just in the big things, but in the handling of the details of the work.

Luke: *For example, for the studio set at Pinewood, Simon and I had discussions with Peter and he gave us examples of his experience with James Cameron. He said that James Cameron always asks for a fixed ceiling, quite a low ceiling, to persuade the audience that it's not a film set. His advice was to make sure there's a ceiling and make sure it's low so that it discourages the DoP from trying to light it from the top, and it looks more natural.*

Ghosthunter was mainly shot at the Amulet's convent in Sussex, but there was one day at Pinewood, immediately following the main shoot. Nothing out of the ordinary, but a particular problem for a short film with little money, because Luke really needed two crews – one to work on the main shoot and a separate construction crew for the set at Pinewood. It became a particular problem because, to be realistic, few people who make their living building sets can afford the luxury of working for nothing.

Luke: *I had to be down on location in Sussex and the set had to be built at the same time at Pinewood so I did need a separate construction crew, and I found it very difficult to find people who were prepared to help with the project on a very low budget.*

Peter Lamont visited the studio while the set was being prepared: *Luke did very well. When I went down to the studios on Monday it seemed a little bit in disarray – he'd had problems with work people, I believe. He was on his hands and knees with a saw. Anyway you don't want to get in there and interfere – it's their show. So I just made a few comments – I felt that maybe a fresh look from someone else could save them a bit of time. By the next morning he'd done it all very well.*

One of the many small but effective things Luke learnt from Peter Lamont was something he described as triage – prioritizing the work that needed to be done into three: the things that have to be done immediately; those that have to be done soon; and the rest that can wait a little.

Luke: *One piece of advice was about a flying flat. We'd designed one wall of the set to float out. Peter suggested we leave work on that until last, because most of the time it won't be there. In any case, they won't need it until later in the day. It's another way of prioritizing the order of doing things.*

When Peter came down to the studio he found us painting a door before it was hung. He thought that was a mistake, because then you've got to wait for it to dry before you can hang it, and you get thumb-prints all over it. He said 'Get the door up. Then if they need to shoot it they've got a door, and you can still paint it and it can be drying in place.'

Peter Lamont: *I can understand it. Sometimes it's a temptation just to keep people working. It seems like a good idea at the time, but it isn't always the best thing to do.*

If you find that you're really up against it, as long as you know in which order shots are going to be covered, then you can make sure that the set-ups planned for early in the day are ready first, and continue working while filming begins. On *Aliens*, Peter Lamont's crew were still dressing the last of the props seconds before James Cameron walked onto the set. It can happen to the best. But that doesn't mean that it should.

The camera department

It's possible, but unwise, to organize a shoot so that the cameraman turns up with the gear on the first day of production without having been involved in pre-production work. If everything is to go as smoothly as it should, the Director of Photography needs to be involved on several counts during the pre-production period – though not necessarily for the whole of the time.

The DoP on *Ghosthunter*, Gavin Struthers, became involved through Freddie Francis. The leading members of the British Society of Cinematographers each sponsor a student at the National Film School. Gavin was Freddie Francis's sponsored student at the time that the Amulets asked him to help with *Ghosthunter*.

Gavin Struthers: *Normally the DoP isn't involved until close to shooting. But we talked a lot about effects and we did lighting and film tests and talked to costume and design because that affects the colour, too, and we looked at locations. It was good fun. I did it for the experience of working with such a professional team. And it was nice to work with a different director.*

Because it's a ghost story, it gave me some leeway in using lighting and photography to break away from reality – I could experiment in ways that I can't in realistic drama. And the scale of it is very exciting. In the past I've shot a number of shorts and I produced them. It's nice to be able to just concentrate on being DoP.

As Luke said, Simon wanted to use not only the colours of the set, costume and props, but also the way the film was shot to differentiate between the story's two time periods. He had decided to make the present-day scenes appear very muted, and to fill the scenes set in the past with rich, vibrant colours.

Gavin: *We decided that the past was going to be lit practically by candlelight, and the present by daylight or practicals or whatever. We needed to find a way of dulling the colours in the present, and we opted for a combination of flashing the negative and bleach-bypassing the print.*

Normally, in the final stage of processing in the lab, the print is bleached to remove all the unused silver halide from the film, leaving only the silver that has been exposed to the light. Technicolor's variable bleach bypass process allows the amount of bleaching to be controlled.

Gavin: *Bypassing the bleaching process reduces the colour saturation. The more you do, the less colour you get. We chose 30 per cent bypass.*

The other side of the effect is that the shadow areas become very solid and inky, because the silver still left on the negative clogs the blacks and takes details out. In order to counteract that effect in the present-day scenes, Gavin and Simon decided to use a Varicon in the camera – a process known as flashing – which has the opposite effect, of effectively adding a stop of fill light, making the blacks slightly greyer.

Gavin: *From tests, we worked out that flashing roughly an eighth on the Varicon compensates roughly for the 30 per cent of bypass which takes out a stop. For the flashback sequences we chose not to flash, so we got that inky black and slightly richer colours. The effect is quite popular. It was used on* Evita, Saving Private Ryan *and several other pictures, mainly with two specific DoPs – and Freddie uses it all the time. On the set it means adjusting fill light – you put a bit more lighting in the shadows that you might not otherwise do – and you can do with less lighting overall which can be an advantage. But in this case we were really using it to mute the colours.*

Like many things in movies, it's not necessarily all that difficult to do this kind of thing, but what it does need is a high degree of precision – and confidence – on a number of successive steps, each of which is relatively straightforward in itself. Gavin and Simon did a number of camera and lab tests before the shoot began, so that they could be absolutely sure that they would get what they wanted when it mattered.

Of course, not every picture has such a need for a complex, particular look, but every picture needs the same care and effort put into preparation, so that when production starts, everyone is clear what they're doing and

Sarah examines a mysterious symbol etched onto the wall of the Retro-Chapel in the church. © Zoë Norfolk 2000

how they plan to do it. It's always completely different from the way you imagined, but if everything is properly planned to begin with, everyone will be in a position to solve problems from a position of knowledge, rather than from one of panic.

The format you decide to shoot can make a big difference to the equipment you need, and to the way you treat the cast and locations. This is true of both meanings of 'format': whether 35 mm or DV (or something in between); and whether 4:3 or widescreen.

Gavin: Choose a format early on and always go on recces – go on two: one with the director and then one with the gaffer. Be aware of the format when you do the recce and choose your lens set accordingly, so if you've got a smaller location and you're going to be doing lots of wide shots you're not going to be using tight lenses. And be aware of how much room the camera's going to take up. Go to the equipment place and make sure you know the camera and so you're aware of what your crew are having to do.

Freddie Francis, Consultant Cinematographer: I don't see how you can really act as a DoP unless you understand the job of everybody beneath you. It's not a highly technical job. It's a creative job where you've got to get into the director's mind. What you see on the screen is a combination of both their work, so if they're not as one it could be a bit of a mess.

You shouldn't have a style. I read the script and, while I'm reading it I've photographed it. But if I do it in my style it's not going to be right for the director. I get the style when I'm talking to the director and put his ideas into what I do, but if I thought we were way out, I wouldn't do the picture. It's no fun to do a picture if you always do it in the same old style or if you do it the way someone else wants. The people are as important as the script. The script is important, but all the people involved have to feel the same way about the script. I let Gordon (Freddie Francis's regular Camera Operator) *choose the camera equipment, and Maurice* (the Gaffer) *choose the lamps and I just supplied the ideas. Obviously, given the length of time we've been working together, we all understand each other. For instance a lot of DoPs operate themselves. I wouldn't dream of doing it because the time I spend operating, I can't spend with the director.*

Whether or not the director of photography chooses to operate the camera themselves is entirely up to them, and their relationship with the director – not how good it is, but whether they feel they need to be with each other all the time. Whatever the DoP decides, it mustn't be allowed to lead to neglect of the other part of the job. A DoP close to a director must not neglect the camera crew, and vice versa.

Lighting, of course, is something that needs to be very thoroughly thought out before the shoot begins. If only to make sure that you have ordered the lamps you need and you have the power to use them.

Gavin: *I'm used to lighting with large light sources. I've never gone down the avenue of lighting with lots of small sources. Now on this film I used a lot of large soft sources because it suited the film. Also because the process we're going through – the bleach bypass – lends itself to aggressive soft sources, an overall look. It doesn't respond well to hard light on faces and so on. The softer the light, the nicer the look. It's a distinct way of lighting. You've always got spill, so everything has soft edges. It's something I want to work on in my repertoire.*

Gavin found a number of other things to think about during the pre-production period: *Then there's choosing a stock – two aspects: one is what length of time you're going to be filming for and whether interior or exterior, and the other is what your lighting budget is.*

It's all a kind of domino effect once you've got the script and the visual style – and the visual style should be locked. If the script is locked, then the visual style is not something that changes. Lines change and blocking of actors change, but the visual style stays pretty much the same. And communication. Let production know what you're doing. Talk to make-up and production design.

Communication between departments is increasingly important as the project progresses. Most locations, for example, have only a certain amount of space. It might be easy for the designer and for the director of photography to decide that they were going to fill it all up on their own. There's no point in building a beautiful set if there's nowhere for the cameras to see whatever action is taking place on it. Any number of problems are caused by people not telling each other what they're doing. Also as the filming comes closer – and as it goes on – everyone is likely to feel under more and more pressure to do their own job well, and less and less likely to think of what everyone else needs. That's when things really start to crumble.

Gavin: *Having a good idea of the script, a visual landscape of the film in your head and communication are the three most important things – and don't get distracted, because that's when things go wrong.*

DV

Possibly you're planning to shoot on DV, so all this talk of heavy planning, big crews and film processing techniques might seem overkill. Well, maybe. In the end, all filmmaking is very similar, and something can be learnt from every experience. The level of care and thought in preparation put into *Ghosthunter* is absolutely necessary for every production if it is to run smoothly, if all the effort is to produce good results on the screen and not wasted on panic and rescuing a situation gone wrong because it was badly prepared.

DV is dangerous. Fast film is dangerous. Because you can practically see in the dark, the temptation is not to bother with lighting – to go with available light or a couple of big lights bounced off the ceiling. Well, fine, if you want that very particular, rough look; but lighting in film and TV is not done to purely provide a level of illumination – you can usually get some kind of exposure almost anywhere – but to make things look good to help create a world. 'Painting with light' is a phrase most often heard ironically when a single big lamp is blasting across a room; but it is still, whatever the acquisition medium, the primary job of the director of cinematography. That's why DoPs often don't operate the camera – so they can concentrate on the lighting. The most beautifully framed shot can be worthless if the lovingly prepared cast and set can't be seen properly on the screen.

Special effects

Special effects might be described in two ways: those that happen in 'real life' and those that happen in post-production. But in practice it's very rare for any effect that happens in 'real life' not to have further work done on it later. Equally, most post-production effects can be made a great deal more convincing and/or more cost-effective if they are properly planned before the shoot begins, so that material can be shot in the best way for the effect. Yes, a telegraph pole can be physically removed, frame by frame, but it certainly costs a lot of money.

Quantel and the Computer Film Company (CFC) were also sponsors of *Ghosthunter* and involved Matthew Twyford, a special effects expert, in the project as part of the Visual FX crew. Matthew points out that special effects are more common than most people realize.

Matthew Twyford: *I'd say now that around 90 per cent of movies have effects in them – but a good 70 per cent of effects are invisible – such as putting clouds in where there weren't any on the day.*

As ever, it comes down to thinking the movie through as thoroughly as possible before the toys come out of the box. Does the script call for special effects? Are you sure? It may be that something you'd planned to sort out during the edit could be achieved a lot more easily if you think about it before the shoot, so that you have material that's right for the effect, rather than having to work with what you happen to have. The simple rule is to ask sooner rather than later.

Matthew: *I can help the director directly to realize what he or she wants; tell them whether it's possible, maybe enhance it with little tricks. After all, my experience of effects is broader than most directors', because I do it all the time. And there are a lot of things I can do to help the producers save money. Digital FX are very expensive, so you need to make sure you get the right elements, because a day's post-production can be almost as much as a day's shoot. And I can also say 'We can do this, so we don't need to do that . . .' – if we're involved early we can save money. Usually the producer says digital effects cost too much when we only become involved after the shoot. We can also help the cameraman with lighting for the effect – and the editor, with transitions and so on. It's a very good idea to get the effects people involved early. Effects that are planned properly are generally cheaper in the long run – and there are a lot of things that can be done completely in the computer so you don't need to shoot at all.*

With the power available on desktop computers now, it's perfectly possible to do a lot of effects work on a home PC that would not so long ago have needed equipment costing hundreds of thousands of pounds. But it will take you a lot longer than it takes the guys on the top-end equipment – both because they do it all day and because the top-end gear is still a lot faster than a home PC. One thing you certainly can't do is scan your computer effects work back to film, so if you're working on film, you'll still need the expensive stuff for that. Still, as all-digital production from camera to projection spreads, this will change.

Sound department

Sound is often seen as being taken for granted throughout film and television – ask any sound recordist. When everyone else has set things up for themselves, the sound recordist is somehow expected to get perfect sound, without boom shadows, from half a mile away. And should he or she dare to ask for a retake when the pictures were OK . . .! Well, either it doesn't happen (it's only sound) or everybody scowls at the poor old recordist, trying to stir up as big a feeling of guilt as possible. There are two things to say on this issue.

Firstly, imagine a dialogue scene with no significant physical action. They happen a lot. Now consider this: what if something happens to the negative, so you have no pictures? It might not be ideal, but the scene could almost certainly be rescued by running the dialogue over other shots. What happens if the sound is NG (no good), but the pictures are perfect? Yes, you can post-sync the dialogue, but that only goes to prove how important the sound is. Whatever happens, you certainly need to recover the sound, but you might be able to get away without reshooting the pictures.

Secondly, as a single, general, rule you need to get the microphone as close to the edge of the frame as you can. That will usually also take care of the sound perspective – you get close-up sound in close-up shots and wider sound in wider shots.

DV very quickly developed a reputation for being a medium with inherently poor sound quality. This is wrong (particularly with the professional/broadcast variants of DV, where the sound quality of the system is capable of being better than CD). DV acquired this reputation because people were using the camera microphones on domestic equipment. By definition, microphones were being placed in probably the worst possible position – a long way from the source of the sound they were being expected to record and very close to all the whirring whining mechanical and electronic noise that even small digital cameras make. Never use the camera microphone unless the alternative is a mute shot.

Pre-production for the sound department need not be very prolonged but here, too, it's important that the script is read and that sound, camera and design are all sensitive to each other's requirements. Every set-up has to have somewhere for the microphone to go and the sound recordist needs to make sure that they have the right equipment – and the right number of people. A sound assistant/boom swinger will almost always immensely improve the quality of sound, because the microphone can be put in the right place while the recordist worries about the levels and the recording quality.

Ghosthunter – the documentary

The final piece of fixing for *Ghosthunter* was to set up the 'making-of' documentary, which the Amulets hoped was going to be an important part of the total package. They knew that they wouldn't have any time or thought to spare for the documentary once the main filming had started, so they set it up as a completely separate production, with its own experienced director, Charles Sharman-Cox, and a crew of two cameramen and a sound recordist, who would shoot for three days – one day on location in and around the chapel, another in the studio at Pinewood, and a third during post-production.

Finally, a stills photographer, Zoë Norfolk, agreed to cover the whole shoot. Good production stills can be an important part of any film's selling package, and they have to be done properly. Don't expect someone with spare time on the crew to take a few snaps. First of all, if the crew is well organized, there won't be much spare time. Secondly, you have to be sure that the results are going to be good, not just good enough. Zoë's stills are featured throughout the book.

Executive gaffer, Maurice Gillett, proves just why he's the executive gaffer as he places himself by the best available light for a photo opportunity with Producer, Alison Reddihough. © *Zoë Norfolk 2000*

Pre-production checklist

This can actually be quite a short checklist.

- Know the script inside out.
- Each department should know exactly what it is expected to achieve.
- Think through the whole process to ensure that everything you need is in place.
- Predict as many problems as possible. The unexpected will always come along, but if everyone has worked out how they might solve the expected problems, then there's a better chance of survival when something comes along that wasn't predicted.

6 The shoot

So, after months of preparation and fundraising, *Ghosthunter* finally makes it to production – after a last minute delay that moves the shoot from mid-December to mid-January. Just when you think everything's in place, there's always one other thing to change it all again. All those months of work now depend on the results of 6½ days of work.

Doing it

You've spent weeks in preparation – getting the project financed, crewed, cast; finding locations; organizing the catering – all the thousand tiny details. You, the producer – and, more especially, the director and the DoP now need to stop, be calm and focused before it all starts.

Everyone who is any good has stage fright – the worry that they'll mess up big time: if you're not worried, you probably will; if you've done all your homework, you probably won't.

Simon: *The weekend before the shoot our house filled up with a huge amount of camera gear and we started to get tense, so I just tried to take my mind off the film.*

However big the machine of the picture is – however many there are in the crew, and the cast – the whole operation is designed to concentrate on one area: the director, the DoP, and the action. Everyone else is there to make sure that the really important things have room to breathe and grow to their best advantage. And the traditional working methods of the film industry, developed over a period of more than a century, are a pretty good way of making sure that the vital effort is concentrated in the right area.

It doesn't matter whether the film is being made on 35 mm with an enormous crew or on DV with a tiny one, in the end, a performance has to be recorded and the machine of the production is there solely to serve that function. The attitude of the director is, of course, crucial.

Luke Smith, *Ghosthunter* Production Designer: *The happy atmosphere was down to a combination of personalities – it's pot luck whether it tends to gel or not. A lot of it stems from how a director is on set and how they interact with the crew members they directly have to deal with. If a director is relaxed and gives the impression they're getting what they want then everyone is more relaxed. Simon seemed relaxed and knew what he wanted and seemed organized. The worst thing is when a director hasn't quite thought it through and is hoping for inspiration on the day.*

Sam Jones, Second AD: *The director has to really feel like he's making the movie. The director has to take the lead. It sounds obvious, but with so many other people working for you, you have to. On a film I was on recently, the director was quite lazy and I thought, 'You've written it, do you want to direct it or not?' This film was really different.*

Maurice: *There are some directors who wouldn't know how to make a bad film – like Fred Zinneman. He worked rather differently from a lot of directors. When we were doing* A Man for All Seasons, *he called us into his office and he had four Rembrandts on his wall. Rembrandt always painted by north light. No shadows. And he said, 'That's what we're going to do.' At the beginning of the day he'd say to everyone, 'Go and have tea. Give me artists and continuity and I'll call you when I need you.' Then he'd rehearse and when he was ready he'd send for the cameraman and the operator and he'd say, 'We'll do a long shot and five close-ups.' Then he'd send the actors away to get dressed-up, frocks on and get made up, and that was it. We all knew it was going to be an LS and five CUs, so we didn't get out equipment we didn't need.*

Filmmaking is not a democratic process – it's too expensive for that. Discussions can last (and should have) for the weeks and months before the shoot. They can continue in the evenings after the shoot but on the set, everything needs to be concentrated on keeping to the schedule, and the director must direct. This is not to say that all directors must be autocratic dictators. On a happy shoot, there should always be room for people to make suggestions – whoever they are. But in the end, it's the director's job to invite, accept or reject suggestions. And get on with the shoot. Two things (and, really, only two things) need to be in the back of everyone's mind during the whole shoot: performance and edit.

Performance

First and always: the performance. Yes, the way the camera is used and the way shots are set up affects the way the story is told, of course. But it doesn't matter how brilliant the camera-work is, if the actors' performance is rubbish then the film will be rubbish. Some actors are brilliant technicians and know instinctively where the camera is and what it's doing. Others may be less comfortable and perhaps intimidated by the whole machinery of film. It's one of the jobs of the director (and, to an extent, of the DoP) to create a bubble around the performers, such that they don't have to worry too much about the technology. Let them do their job while the technicians do theirs. This can be hard for a director to achieve, because there is so much that needs to be thought about and the technology can easily dominate if it's allowed to. The answer is trust. And confidence. Both difficult at times but, in the end, essential. Everyone on the crew needs to have confidence in their own knowledge and trust that everyone else will do their job well, too.

Most people working in the business tend to form around themselves a group of people they know and trust, and enjoy working with. To outsiders it can make the industry appear like an exclusive club but, in fact, everyone is just trying to create for themselves a situation where they have the confidence that they can do the best for themselves – because if they can't, they may not work again. You'll be the same.

Edit

Secondly, always be aware of how the stunning material you're shooting is going to go together. You may have heard tales of Old Hollywood Directors who practically cut stuff in the camera; who say, 'it'll only cut one way' and how brilliant they were. Well, it's a good trick if you can really do it. But remember, these Old Directors were people who made several pictures a year, year in year out. And I bet they made mistakes, too.

In the real world you have to give yourself a few alternatives, without running the risk of blowing the budget and the schedule by shooting everything that moves (and a few things that don't) because you haven't the faintest idea of how you're going to cut it together afterwards. What the camera crew do here is clearly important – little things that the director shouldn't even have to think about. It can be very instructive for camera-people/operators to be asked to cut their own material. Sometimes they think quite differently afterwards. For example: some camera-people have a tendency to 'snatch' shots. Even static cutaways need to be static (without any focus, stop, framing adjustments) for at least 10 seconds. Even though the shot is basically a moving one, it's surprising how useful a 10-second hold at the front – and at the end – of the move can be. Often it can be used as a separate or even alternative shot. Close-ups and cutaways are always useful (providing they're relevant). Generally speaking, it's hard to cut between wide shots, but you can always cut between close shots.

Remember that if you're shooting film you can only use a piece of footage once (unless you make a duplicate negative). If you're shooting tape you can, of course, use a shot as many times as you want. Whether it's a good idea or not is a different question. A relevant example might be an establishing shot of a building to which the story often returns. It might be fine to use the same shot. If you're shooting film you need to make sure you have enough of it.

Shooting a scene all the way through for each camera angle can have several benefits.

- The actors have room to develop a performance, rather than being asked to work one line at a time.
- By the time you've stopped and started the camera, reset the scene and put a clapper on the front, it's often quicker just to keep running. The shot can even be adjusted halfway through.
- You give yourself lots of alternative ways of cutting the scene.
- Single close shots for dialogue have reaction shots built in to them, so they don't have to be shot separately.

There will always be extra lines or reactions to pick up, but most of a scene can be covered quite quickly like this.

Thirdly (of the two things to remember), just as the schedule has been constructed to minimize travel between locations (even if the locations are in neighbouring rooms), so it's just as important to avoid moving around too much within each location. Even if you have several scenes to shoot in a room, if you can do it without completely scrambling your brain, you could shoot all the scenes from one angle before moving the lamps or changing the camera position to shoot them all the other way around. That way you only have to move and relight once, instead of continually going backwards and forwards.

This is one of the cases where the director is probably the only person who can get their heads around what is supposed to be happening in each particular set-up. But then, that's part of the job. If you can hack it, it will save a lot of time. As we've said before, moving lamps and reversing angles might only take 10 minutes but if you do it six times, you've cost yourself an hour; and it's surprising how short a normal working day can become. By 'normal' working day I mean 10 hours, not 7.

I don't think you should plan to work more than a 10-hour day. If that goes over, it's not too much of a tragedy. If you plan 14 hours, not only does it make unreasonable demands on your cast and crew, but if you over-run you begin to drive people into the ground – and nobody works well in that condition. Quite apart from the fact that most of them are probably doing you a favour in the first place.

Ghosthunter had one long day and one other day that went one hour over the scheduled 12-hour wrap time. In fact, discussion about whether the schedule was realistic or not went on long after it was all over – with the not uncommon tension between what the director really wants and what the production department know they can afford.

Inside the main body of the church during a break in filming. © *Zoë Norfolk 2000*

Finally, log everything. Whether you're shooting tape or film, there should be logs from production, camera and sound departments, with time codes or slate and take numbers, any comments – and the good takes clearly marked. You can't have too much information.

The shoot – Director's diary

Simon's diary begins with the read-through, the Saturday before filming began.

Saturday 8 January

Saturday morning at Ealing Studios was the venue for the read-through with the cast. I'd talked on several occasions with the various cast members individually but this was the first time we'd all met. I'd asked several crew members to be present to help break the ice and act as an audience for the actors. After a nervous start (I introduced Frank to everyone as Freddie – I think he's since forgiven me), we got on with the reading. The script read extremely well and afterwards we had a long discussion about the story and the characters. We read the script again and I went home happy that we were all thinking along the same lines.

We arrived home to find our house full of camera gear. Our main location for the film was in an old convent. We needed an abandoned church for the main scenes in the film and we lived very close to one. Consequently our house was to become the production office for the week. Also, for insurance purposes, we had to keep all the camera gear in our house overnight. A lounge full of 35 mm camera equipment doesn't leave much room for anything, let alone anyone, else. Fortunately all the grip equipment and props could be left in the church. We'd also set up a crew room in the church (heated, the only warm room in the whole building) and that was now full of drinks and snacks. All morning Jacqui (Production Manager) had been receiving these deliveries and the art department was hard at work preparing the main body of the church for our first interior scenes on Tuesday. Gavin (DoP) and I spent the evening at work on the shot list for the film.

Sunday 9 January

We'd hired a conference centre 100 yards from our location that would accommodate the crew during the week and people arrived throughout the day to check in. The centre was also to provide our catering for the shoot and the meals they served us were excellent.

Monday 10 January

The first day. I'd slept better than I'd anticipated and awoke to the perfect day for our exteriors. I'd been hoping for a sunny winter's morning with a hard frost on the ground and this is exactly what we got. Gavin bounded over with a huge grin across his face. We'd discussed the weather for the exteriors many times and so to be given exactly what we'd wanted was more than we'd hoped.

Unit call for the morning was 11 a.m. but most of the crew had arrived the night before and they were up and about from 9 a.m. The 32 feet combined lighting and generator truck arrived and we began to look like a film set.

Rod (Camera Operator) arrived and I took him over to our first location. Luke (Production Designer) had already dressed the scene with various gravestones and Rod, Gavin and I talked through the first tracking shot that would establish the character Sarah and her entrance into the abandoned churchyard. All was coming together nicely and it was looking more and more likely that we were to turn over well ahead of schedule – this wasn't to be.

All was in place, the camera was set, the crew standing by, Alison (playing Sarah) rehearsed and ready. We'd had a little welcome and introduction for the crew. When it was found that the Varicon, a device that fits in front of the camera lens and pre-flashes the negative, wasn't working. There are two bulbs in the Varicon and one of them had blown, the same was true for the spare. Whilst a new spare was biked down from London, the camera crew and sparks got together to see what they could do. They actually managed to fix the bulb but didn't have confidence in it to use it. Whilst we waited for the spares to arrive, time ticked on and we had yet to turn over on the film. We had to do something. We decided to go ahead without the Varicon and look at the shots when the rushes returned. If we had to film these shots again, so be it.

The rest of the day went extremely well and we only dropped one shot because of failing light. I'd wanted a point-of-view of the exterior of the church silhouetted against the night sky; we had a narrow window to get this shot and we missed it by minutes. When your DoP tells you the light is going fast, believe him. Owing to our late start we only got two shots without the Varicon before the spare bulbs turned up; how those shots would work we'd have to wait and see.

Tuesday 11 January

Matt Twyford, our digital effects supervisor, was with us for the day to supervise the first of the effects sequences in the film. Also with us were our documentary team. They spent the day snatching interviews and filming behind the scenes. They managed to get an interview with Maurice Gillett, our executive Gaffer. Maurice has been in the business for over 40 years and has worked with Freddie Francis, our Cinematography Consultant. The material the documentary team got from Maurice is worth a programme all by itself.

We got the shots for the effects sequence and these will be worked on in post-production in Newbury at the headquarters of Quantel, our effects sponsors. The effect I wanted was to animate a shadow that we establish behind Sarah, when she's inside the church.

During lunch Gavin and I were able to watch the previous day's rushes. There is always a moment of anxiety just before the first rushes are viewed but we were very excited to see that all had gone well. We were particularly interested in the non-Varicon shots and we were happy that the two shots concerned could be graded later, so saving us a reshoot in an already busy schedule. We could report back that the rushes were looking good.

The afternoon was spent shooting the flashback sequences for the film. The church we use for the main location was built over 130 years ago and is almost completely empty inside. During cold weather it seems to refrigerate and always feels a couple of degrees colder than the ambient temperature – we were to spend a further 2 days inside this location. We used all of our scheduled time for these flashbacks, big set-ups for what will amount to small moments in the film. However, we were unable to shoot the fire and destruction flashbacks that Frank's character, Charlie, sees at the end of the film. We hope to pick up these shots when we go back to the church, on Thursday. The crew worked very hard and we wrapped on time. To thoroughly thaw out we ended the day in the local Indian restaurant.

Wednesday 12 January

9 a.m. unit call for the first day of warm interiors. The crew have settled into Neale House, the conference centre, and have been enjoying late nights in what have become known as the kitchen parties. After our 8.30 a.m. breakfast and production meeting it was into the guest house location to talk through the first set-up.

We were to spend the whole day shooting the lounge scenes of the guest house. Once rehearsed, the actors were released for costume and make-up and the sparks set about lighting the set. We didn't turnover until close to 12 o'clock as Gavin was keen to light the entire lounge to save set-up time later. I was getting nervous that so much time was being spent setting up for the first shot. The previous two days were relatively light compared with what was scheduled for the next 3 days, also Frank Finlay was with us for the first time and I couldn't afford to drop shots that included him.

There were other problems. Later in the afternoon we ran into a potential stock problem. I'd shot far more on the flashback sequences than anticipated and we were running a little low. More had been ordered but wouldn't be with us until the next morning. It was at this moment that things seemed to conspire against us. The floor of the lounge was wooden and it was proving difficult to get the camera to run silently on this creaky surface. The local train station seemed far more busy than usual, which was strange given that they were in the middle of an industrial action and were in fact cancelling most services. It also felt as if Gatwick had suddenly diverted all aircraft to our vicinity. One particular shot was to be confronted with all of the above issues, a slow track into Frank during one of his speeches. We couldn't afford to keep running this long sequence and there was a moment when the entire crew turned to look at me for a decision.

Before we started shooting Alison and I had visited all our consultants and asked them what they'd like from us. Mark Auguste (Consultant Sound Editor) had asked us to try and wildtrack all dialogue. An unusual request, as most people would assume there would be syncing problems with the wildtrack and the picture, but he was confident that as long as the dialogue was clean then they could work with it. Brian (Sound Mixer) was about 75 per cent happy with Frank's dialogue on this shot but requested another take; we couldn't afford the stock. I was very happy with the take: Frank was excellent and the track into him just right, the crew waited for the decision. I decided to wildtrack Frank's dialogue. I asked Frank to run through the scene in his mind. He closed his eyes and ran the speech again; it sounded great and the dialogue this time was clean. We moved on confident that the shot was covered in all aspects. I was very grateful for that meeting as it saved us time on set and will save time and money in post-production and a potential looping session.

Despite all this we ended the day on schedule, having dropped one shot but added several others. Gavin's plan to light the entire set had caused us some grief in the morning but helped us speed through the set-ups later. There is inevitably some tweaking of the lighting for each shot but the general and major lighting set-up for the room was already in place. A fine plan, but it didn't do the heart rates of the Director and First AD, Philip Shaw, much good.

Thursday 13 January

Back to the guest house location for the dining room scenes. Frank was again with us for the whole day, as was June Watson (Audrey) and Jacqueline Phillips (Anne). I was particularly pleased with the casting of June and Jacqui in the mother and daughter roles. Everyone said how alike they were and they quickly established themselves on set as 'The Bookends'.

I was confident that today would go smoothly. I felt that today's schedule was lighter than yesterday's and we'd be out of the guest house location and into the next location, the Retro-Chapel of the church, in good time. Yesterday and today were to be Frank's heaviest days and we were all concerned to get what we needed and release him as soon as possible.

We also started to receive the first of our VIP visitors: John Rendall from Panavision and Anne Guidera from Kodak. Both spent much of the day with us and we were able to show them rushes from the previous days and talk to them more about the project. Both were impressed with the footage we had so far and it was lovely to spend some time with them on set after the help and support they had given us in setting up this film. That they were encouraged meant a great deal and was another indication that the film was actually coming together.

This wasn't to mean that the dining room scenes lived up to my earlier optimism. By 5 p.m. we had to wrap this location for the day and, in so doing, drop two whole scenes and the fire and destruction pickups from the day's schedule. The two scenes involved were set up as one-shot scenes, which is why the decision was made; they would be easier to pick up, possibly tomorrow. June and Jacqui were released and we moved over to the chilly church. We had just the one scene here but, again, a noisy tracking shot helped put us slightly behind. It was nobody's fault; it was just that the scene was a quiet moment between Frank (Charlie) and Alison (Sarah). We were crammed into this reverberating room and the tiniest sound echoed around the walls. We were now under pressure to release Frank and so concentrated on getting his shots in first. We also delayed supper for the crew to enable us to do this. Once Frank was released we broke for supper. We were also at official wrap time but the crew were happy to continue to finish this scene. It was an anxious moment. I didn't want to take advantage of a crew that had worked particularly hard during the week. The support in the crew for the film was a great comfort. We shot the reverses on Alison and I read Frank's lines, this is not an ideal situation for the actor concerned. I asked Zoë Norfolk, our stills photographer, to stand in for Frank for his eyeline, as she was closest to his height. I also asked her not to look at Alison. She needed to play the scene with the memory of Frank still fresh in her mind, asking Zoë to look away gave Alison that opportunity without having someone stare blankly back as the lines are read off-camera. We got the scene and wrapped for the evening and Zoë subsequently became Frank's stand-in for the rest of the shoot.

One of the scenes that we dropped from the day was a Cinejib shot in the main body of the church. This gave us greater concern. We'd set up the shot earlier in the day and the equipment and track were already in place. I'd also asked the art department to set up an area in the main body for the pickups of the fire and destruction flashback sequences. They had done an excellent job and had an area ready, containing burnt beams, debris and a burnt body we had managed to get hold of, that was used in the beach scenes of *Saving Private Ryan* (the body became known as 'Crispy Kevin'). It was also all set up, lit and ready to go. We just didn't manage the time and now they were both going to interfere with tomorrow's shots, scheduled for the same location. Gavin and I went away to think of a way round this problem. I wasn't about to instruct the art department to clear away all their work or the Cinejib grips to take apart the crane. We still needed these shots so it seemed appropriate that we should look to work around the problem before making a hasty decision.

Friday 14 January

The solution to yesterday's conflict of set-ups actually helped us out with the day's schedule. We just needed the time and space away from the set to be practical about it. I asked the art department to somehow include the fire and destruction set-up in the abandoned church scene we were to shoot that morning. With the help of various dustsheets, a chair and some leaves, the area became as much a part of the scene as if it had been planned all along. It was also a simple task to return the area to the original set-up for the pickups. The Cinejib was also worked around. That we now intended to keep it in its place for the whole day enabled us to add two unscheduled shots for the crane. I'd been up late the previous night with Gavin and we'd amended Friday's shot list. By shooting around the crane we were well ahead by lunchtime and the Cinejib was still in place to pick up on the dropped scene from yesterday.

We were also visited on set by Peter Lamont (Consultant Production Designer). Luke and I had a meeting with him prior to production so it was good to have him on set to see our work come to fruition. Ian and Focal Press were also present and Peter gave us an interview for the book. The art department were thrilled with his visit and were able to talk to him about many of the films he has designed.

The afternoon was, perhaps, the busiest part of the whole shoot. We were to film the biggest scene of the film and were to go on long after our official wrap time. For this I have to honour the entire crew. The whole scene was to be shot in 12 set-ups. Within these set-ups were lighting changes as the ghosts appeared, the extras themselves, the blocking of our two main actors and the individual effects shots. Philip Shaw (First AD) handled the extras wonderfully, leaving me free to discuss the effects shots with Matt Twyford (Digital Effects Supervisor) and make sure we got all that we needed. That we achieved all this is tribute to the crew and the spirit within the project. Once wrapped we arranged beer and wine at Neale House. It was almost the end of the location filming and the party that evening went on till about 3 a.m.

DoP, Gavin Struthers (left), script supervisor, Claire Eades (middle) and director, Simon Corris, around the monitor as the camera crew and extras prepare to shoot a flashback sequence by the altar of the church. © Zoë Norfolk 2000

Saturday 15 January

After the late night all the crew were on time and ready to work by the unit call of 9 a.m. We had only half a day scheduled today, with only two scenes (Charlie's house), and the pickup in the dining room of the guest house. The scenes went without problem, including the final effect shot for the film. We wrapped just after 12 o'clock. After lunch the last piece of business was the crew photograph. I gave Maurice Gillett the honour of holding the clapper, he'd been with us the whole week and offered much advice to the lighting department. He was very active around the set and the source of many anecdotes. Not bad for a man in his 80s.

The afternoon was spent on the fire and destruction pickups that had been dropped earlier in the week. We were able to set up a small camera unit that consisted of Gavin, Adam White, our camera assistant, Harriet (Gavin's girlfriend), Alison and myself. The art department had re-established the pickup area in the church and we got various shots for the end sequence in the film. We were also able to pick up the shot of the church silhouetted against the sky that was dropped from the first day's schedule.

Sunday 16 January

The cleanup of the location began today. The camera gear and grip equipment will remain with us until tomorrow. The crew room in the chapel and the church itself is in much need of a good clean.

Monday 17 January

The Panavision truck arrived to pick up all the gear. As all of the crew left us on Saturday there was only Alison, Claire (Unit Manager), myself and the truck driver available to load all the equipment. Once done, I needed to get to Pinewood and go over the shot list for tomorrow's shoot with Gavin. Alison, Claire and Tanya (Runner) got on with the cleanup.

On arrival at Pinewood there was much activity. It appears that 1½ days were lost in the build of the set (Sarah's bedroom) and there wasn't much to look at. Philip Shaw was now construction manager, not what he'd expected on his day off, but he got on with the job. His help during the build really saved the day. Luke was looking at an all-night stay to get the set dressed in time as all the art department worked late into the evening. Peter Lamont visited the set in the morning and again in the afternoon. I reviewed the scenes with Gavin and left to put together the shots for tomorrow.

Tuesday 18 January

Alison and I were up at 5.30 a.m. to get to Pinewood for the unit call of 8 a.m. We arrived just after 7 a.m. Luke had been there all night and the transformation from the previous day was amazing. We now had a set, wallpapered, painted and dressed. We also had Trevor Coop as our camera operator for the day. Rodrigo had started a feature this week and so was unavailable. Trevor was approached and was happy to help us out.

The day went extremely well. There was a complicated set-up that I was worried about, involving symbols that mysteriously glow through the walls of Sarah's bedroom, but all went smoothly and we got all we needed. We also had various visitors to the set throughout the day. Maurice Gillett was again with us, as was Freddie Francis. Freddie had been away in New York during last week picking up an award for his latest film, *The Straight Story*, and so was unable to spend any time on location. Peter Lamont arrived again in the afternoon. Jenny Welham from Focal Press and our documentary team interviewed all our visitors about the project. Illumina TV were also there for their own documentary on the film and will be following us through post-production. They plan to feature the film in a series called *Short Attention Span Cinema* for FilmFour. They also interviewed our consultants as well as the key crew. Quantel were on set to see out the final day's shooting and Gordon Hayman, camera operator on many of Freddie's films, also dropped by. As the day progressed, Luke was to be found sat on various camera boxes fighting to stay awake. Once wrapped it was decided he needed a lift home for fear that he may fall asleep and awake 2 days later in a remote part of England. He did make it home for a good night's sleep but was still at Pinewood early the next day to break up the set.

It was a lovely atmosphere at Pinewood and everyone was very relaxed. I felt much more at ease despite the attention from the documentaries, the book and our visitors. That it had all come together was very rewarding. We'd had some problems but in retrospect they now seem minor. As the whole project has developed over the last 8 months the solution to all our problems was always better than the original plan. We'd had a real mix of levels of experience on this production, from some of the industry's most respected filmmakers to those who'd never set foot on a film set before. There was a great spirit of openness and co-operation and this was summed up for me on the second day of the shoot when I turned round to see the camera crew instructing two of our runners. Tanya and Vicki were being taught focus pulling and camera operation and tracked up and down on the dolly whilst the scene was being lit. All of us took something from the project and, for me, it was the privilege of working alongside Rodrigo and Trevor; these two have worked with some of the great directors in the business and what I learned from them is worth years in the classroom. Post-production is the next phase and I can't wait.

Experience from *Ghosthunter*

There is something to be learnt from every film experience. *Ghosthunter* was a well-planned, enjoyable production. Given a rerun of the shoot, much would stay unchanged. Some things, however, would be done differently.

Simon: *I expected to be more nervous, more unsure of myself. I expected more pressures from everywhere else – to be challenged about the shots I wanted to do. What I actually found was that Rod was very co-operative. He was so helpful – a lovely guy to work with. He understood that it was my first time, but he didn't try to force his ideas on me. He listened to what I had to say and to how the actors were blocked and how the shot was set up and then he'd make his own suggestions. I found that by the end of the week the three of us – Rod, Gavin and I – had a nice rhythm going. We'd discuss the shot and if necessary make any adjustments. Having that level of co-operation was a great bonus – it was something I thrived on and I quickly felt very comfortable. Of course, it was down to the crew around me that I felt so relaxed and confident.*

The only real problem was with the schedule. That was one of the biggest things I've learnt – that I'd give the planning of the schedule much greater emphasis. What else? Be prepared. I didn't want to be unprepared for any scene and that paid off. It was something that allowed that co-operation during the shoot.

I was a little in awe of the camera team to start with – because they were the most experienced people on the set; as the week went on and I found out more about what they'd done, the more in awe I became. It was probably a good thing that I didn't know too much about them when we started.

The work we did in pre-production – with Gavin and Luke in particular – was very valuable. I felt very at home with the script, very comfortable. Knew it very well. And the other thing is to allow yourself time to think about things properly, even if you're running behind schedule. Otherwise you just waste time.

The director wants more time. Production say he's taking too long.

Claire Moore, Unit Manager: *Enjoy it? Yes I did. It was so fast. I'm used to features, where they go on and on. Yes I was fine with it. I like the people. I met a lot of people I'd like to work with again. Everybody was just so nice. There really wasn't anybody who wasn't. Normally there's one or two people that nobody quite gets on with – apart from the First AD, but then it's his job that nobody likes him!*

I liked the fact that although the place was a bit strange – Neale House was just like a school and people just behaved like that, everybody regressed, and that was surreal. There was a kitchenette with a kettle and bread, and that became the place to hang out. Everybody piled in there. Runners, art department assistants and Rodrigo. And he sat and cracked jokes and it was just surreal to look at him and think, 'You did Gladiator, *and you're sitting there at home with us.'*

It definitely seemed to be considerably less stressed than usual on a film like this. There was only one evening where it all went slightly crazy.

Well, in the real world there are always things that you want to change. The real question is not whether you make mistakes once but whether you make them again the next time. As long as you can learn from your own mistakes and, even better, from other people's because that's much cheaper, then 'every day in every way you can get better and better'.

Jacqui Wetherill, Production Manager: *I think it went really well. Productions always have their ups and downs. It was a very ambitious project, which got more ambitious towards the end and it came in for a little bit more than they thought it would, with the extras they added in at the end, but it came out really well.*

What Jacqui means is that they went over budget. So, what would she have done differently?

Jacqui: *Maybe I would have pinned Simon and Ali down to a few more details before we started but it was difficult in that we were against the clock with casting and things weren't really fixed until the last week, and then we had rehearsals so we were closed in for time.*

I'm thinking of transport for the actors; we were originally only going to provide transport for Frank Finlay but it ended up being all of them. So that was a huge hassle – we'd planned on only having one driver, but then we had to get all the actors home at the same time.

Given more time I would have gone through everything and said 'Are you sure?' But, all in all, the crew were great and I think they've come out with something really quite special.

The length of the days was an issue that came up during the shooting – a couple of days were too long and I wasn't happy about that, when people are working for nothing. But they were asked if they would do it and they could have said no. It's a difficult question. I wasn't happy about it, but it was down to a series of problems. Again it comes down to scheduling when you've got to be so careful – and you need a really good support team for the director as well. You know for a first film it's a big film. It's a big responsibility. All in all it was OK.

Simon: *One of the biggest things I learnt about was with the preparation of the schedule. We'd put together a preliminary schedule before Christmas and this was to remain unchanged up until production. We did intend another meeting to review the schedule but this meeting never took place – for a number of reasons. Having never experienced scheduling for a production of this size I was initially unsure of how long it would take to film. We were advised to allow ourselves between 5 and 10 days, depending on who we talked to, to shoot the film; I instinctively felt 7–8 days would have been ideal. However, as time went* on we were advised to squeeze production into 6 days. I was always unhappy with this but put my feelings down to my own inexperience. The compromise was 6½, 10-hour days, including lunch and tea breaks. It quickly became clear that this was not nearly enough time and the days were extended to a standard 12-hour day, including breaks. Alison and I both felt very bad about changing the schedule so close to the production but we were very conscientious about talking to the crew and getting their approval. To their credit they were all 100 per cent behind the project and happy to accommodate this change. Although this extra 2 hours on each day meant we were closer to getting all the scheduled shots it still meant that we had little manoeuvrability for any dropped shots. We now had to get everything we needed or start thinking about pickup days sometime in the future, something our budget could not afford to contemplate.

What would I have done differently? Well, for a start, given more preparation time to the planning of the schedule. I'd also like all the heads of department present at all the schedule meetings and to start planning it as soon as the shot list is made available. That the schedule is assessed throughout pre-production and that time is made available for pickups. As the director I want to be the most familiar with the schedule so as to be able to adapt quickly on the day should any problems arise. The more familiar all of the key crew are with the schedule the smoother the running of the production and the better the communication channels function.

So all was well in the end? Not really, as we did have to adapt and make some compromises. One scene in particular suffered more than most and will therefore be cut from the film. To try and catch up I cut down the coverage I'd planned and covered the scene in one shot. The result is a morning's work that went for nothing. What is the point of the cast and crew's work if you don't give full value to the scene being shot? A scene should be cut from the film for valid reasons. What we got on the day is single coverage, zero editing options with no way to try and make it work. In our haste to catch up we actually wasted more time and money. Had we had the space in the schedule we wouldn't be cutting a scene simply because it looks rushed and sits at odds with the film. The pressure of the moment was greater than my objectivity and will be a valuable lesson for me to take forward.

Having subsequently spent a long time in the edit suite with our film, there are only a couple of scenes that give Simon (editor) and myself several editing options. Most of what we shot was my visualization of the scenes before moving on. In an ideal world I'd love the time to shoot what was intended and then shoot a few alternatives. I remember listening to Sam Mendes talking about his experience on the set of American Beauty, he worked the scene with the actors, shot as planned and was then able to try something different. This kind of production relies on a well-planned schedule and is something I'd certainly like to aim for.

Freddie Francis, Consultant Cinematographer: *I wasn't there on the shoot, but I talked to Maurice. He said they had a lot to learn, which is obviously going to happen in these situations, but they wanted to learn. They were keen to learn and they were going in the right direction – they're showing signs of professionalism and not, as one comes across so often in these situations, signs of people trying to run before they can walk.*

A lot of professional filmmakers are way out but they know how to make films before they go way out. I think filmmakers really have to know their craft. I did it by starting as a clapper boy and by learning from other people's mistakes.

Maurice was on the set all the time and was comparing the *Ghosthunter* crew with the best in the business.

Maurice Gillett: *I think they do too many rehearsals. If you're doing a film like this, all you need is two quick rehearsals and then turn over. And sometimes they're doing five or six takes and they can't really afford it. You don't need it. Basic question of confidence.*

Simon: *During one pre-production meeting we discussed the issue of rehearsing. I said at this time that I'd probably rehearse more than usual until I was comfortable and the actors were comfortable so that we wouldn't be stretching the stock budget to the limit. Actors will often complain that there is precious little rehearsing on a film set. Coming from an acting background I was very aware of this. I was also aware that anything caught on film is potentially useful but we didn't have the stock or the budget to commit to film until the action was ready. On one day we were so short that we didn't have any stock available for the following day – we rehearsed a lot that particular morning whilst waiting for the courier to arrive, it's also a scene that assembled very easily in the edit suite – does this relate? I'm not sure. Actually, outside of the tricky technical shots, we averaged two to three rehearsals, over 110 slates we averaged 2½ takes, very few by most filmmakers' standards, and we shot a stock ratio of 7:1 – that's 14 000 feet for a 20-minute film.*

Alison: *As an actor on set for 70 per cent of the shoot, I felt that time was tight and I would have ideally liked more rehearsal. The main reason for delays on set came from technical hiccups – a shot was changed, lighting was fiddled around with etc., which is to be expected on any film set! Of course as the week went on everyone tightened up and less time was wasted but, on the whole, I think we were reasonably organized, considering it was our first project of this size.*

Of course it's a question of confidence. You can't expect people just starting out to work in the same way as people who have been doing the job for years. It's very good that people were demanding of themselves, but it was a very ambitious project and everyone learnt a lot as they went along.

Gavin Struthers, DoP: *Creatively I think we achieved what we needed to achieve. There were a couple of things that were not as well done because of the time constraints – we were up against it at the end of the day. One particular scene, Simon's not happy with the performances and I'm not happy with the lighting, and*

Maurice Gillett entertains DoP Gavin Struthers and director Simon Corris, with another anecdote. © Zoë Norfolk 2000

the camera-work's not perfect; but generally I think it went fine and I'm hoping that everything I did as far as balancing the lighting and getting the colour schemes and so on that Simon wanted has worked. He seems quite happy with that. We were running really well up to that point and one of the biggest lessons I've learnt is scheduling, allowing a lot of time and making sure that Production liaises with me early on so that we get a realistic timetable. We tried to cut shots down every day, but on that one we couldn't.

It's organization and communication. I guess on the shoot, as far as within the department was concerned, the organization and communication were quite good, but with other departments there's a knock-on effect and, definitely as far as producing and scheduling are concerned, it knocks on to my department. A lot of the time we were on the money but certain times we felt a bit pressured and, because I was pressured, the communication in my department then lapsed because I was too busy. So it became a vicious circle. But we got there and I'm really pleased with it, and it was quite a relaxing shoot compared with a lot of the shoots I've been on.

One of the few things that didn't quite work was an attempt to grab a twilight shot during filming of exterior scenes. Light drops very quickly towards sunset. By the time the camera was set up for the shot, the light had gone.

Gavin: *I learnt a tremendous amount. I learnt stacks from everyone: Rod the operator, Dean the focus puller and Jason the clapper loader – they were just fast and efficient, adding another creative aspect to the movie and that was good, and tested what we were trying to achieve and how we were going to achieve it. Also we set up an atmosphere where they felt they could put in ideas, which was good. On the last day Dean came up to me and said, 'I think you should stand next to the camera a lot more', which was something I'd been aware of through the whole shoot but I'd been spending a lot of time with Simon, and he was at the monitor. He directs from the monitor, which was fair enough – you get directors who do either. He needed to communicate with me more readily; the monitor was often off-set and he liked me near the monitor, I was happy there because that's where I normally am – but I'm normally there because a lot of the operators are not as good as Rod is and I like to keep an eye on what's being framed, but I didn't really need to, because Rod got it spot on all the time. So I could have been nearer the camera and watching how the lighting and performance were going from right next to the lens, which is definitely an ideal position for the DoP. So I should have done that.*

On *Ghosthunter*, Simon decided to use a monitor attached to the camera so that he could see what the camera was seeing; but not to record the output.

Simon: *Other filmmakers who've done it advised that it could be dangerous on a low-budget set. The reasons are that it encourages everyone to gather around, during playback, to offer their opinions and that it encourages retakes to iron out that tiny camera shake . . . deliver that line better . . . set that vase . . . comb the hair . . . adjust the lighting . . . fix the lipstick . . . I did want a monitor as it was important to me that I watched the action as the camera sees it. I had my own image of the film in my mind playing on screen and I wanted to compare both images. What I would recommend is to get the monitor as close as possible to the action; sometimes this isn't possible because of the space available, but when it was close by it certainly saved on time and shoe leather and you don't feel isolated from the production. Having the monitor also highlighted a problem that I should have fixed on the day. We were filming a reaction shot of one of the actors and this was set up whilst I was dealing with something else. We didn't need to rehearse the shot and I came back to the monitor when it was ready. I was worried about the eye-line that had been given to June, playing Audrey, but let the shot go ahead. When I looked at the rushes of this shot it still looked wrong and when we got into the edit suite and tried the shot it was obviously wrong. My own inexperience let me down on the day but the monitor is a useful tool when you can't always be looking through the camera itself.*

As Gavin says, where director and DoP stand on the set is a matter of preference. Not that it happened in this case, but a lot of people rely mightily on the video assist, and stay glued to the monitor in the corner. There is the danger in this that director and DoP, while they're in touch with what's on the screen, are out of touch with the real work that's going on on the floor – because they're watching it on television. Taken to an extreme, this 'watching on television' detachment has seen several news cameramen filming their own demise as they somehow didn't understand that those guns were shooting at them. Well, movie-making doesn't usually expose you to that kind of risk, but it is worth considering whether a director who sits in a corner and stares at a screen is putting a barrier between themselves and their cast and crew – you can't *feel* what's going on as well as if you were watching for real. It's worth trying both ways, to see which works best.

Before video assist became widely used. The only person who could see through the camera was the operator. So people trusted good operators more, and didn't work with less good people.

A useful trick, and one that's not that hard to learn, is that you can tell pretty well what the camera is seeing by looking at the focal length of the lens (whether zoom or prime lens). You know (or can learn) what a 50 mm or a 25 mm lens will see. If you don't know, try it out with a 35 mm stills camera. The lenses will give you more or less the same view at the same focal length. And 16 mm is roughly half – a 'standard' lens (neither wide nor telephoto) is 25 mm rather than 50 mm. You can also tell by keeping an eye on the camera as it moves whether a track or a zoom is smooth, and whether the timing is roughly right. In this way it's perfectly possible to work without relying entirely on a monitor, and by trusting the operator and your own knowledge.

Gavin: *I was learning to light faster with fewer lamps by the end of the shoot. The rushes were being shown on VHS every day and I sort of gauged how the stock was going with flashing and what I needed to see and what it was seeing in the blacks and the highlights and so on, so by the end of the shoot I was able to light a lot faster because I knew what would match and what wouldn't.*

Maurice Gillett: *Self-confidence. It was Gavin's first picture on this scale, and he was obviously sweating on it turning out properly. But he's forever taking his meter out. He goes and reads everything. I said, 'Gavin, Ted Moore (A Man for All Seasons) used to take his meter out at 10 o'clock in the morning and never took it out again. You've got to trust your eyes.'*

Gavin: *The great thing about Maurice is he knows where to put lights and he knew how to achieve a look. If I got into a situation where I was little bit stuck I would go to Maurice and ask or he would suggest something to me. There were moments when I started questioning whether I was doing the right thing or not, which was healthy. I was glad Maurice was there, because he wasn't pushy. If you wanted to ask him he was there; and if not, he just sat and watched; he would come up with suggestions and you could take them or not and he wasn't offended if you didn't.*

A good gaffer can do far more for a cameraman than just put lights where he's told to.

Maurice: *I used to make a point of learning all the different cameraman's styles, so that I could do a rig scenes ahead for them. That was what they wanted. On Princess Caraboo, we were in a stately home, and we knew we were going to be in the next room, so I went off with the sparks, and left him with the Best Boy, so when they arrived they didn't have much lighting to do. I remember* Orca the Killer Whale. *We had to do a night shoot in a harbour. Now the great thing about lighting water is you light it twice for every light you set because you get the reflections, too. So Ted said 'Get three Brutes, that's all we need.' Confidence.*

One of the other things that Gavin learnt was how to work with other departments. It's very easy to get buried in your own concerns and to forget that everybody is supposed to be making the same movie. As usual it's very often the little details that make the most difference.

Gavin: *Working with Luke was a big learning experience – again scheduling-wise, because we were trying to pick up shots through the film, so liaising with Luke about what was happening there and talking about colour schemes and talking about dressing into the frame and working with his stand-by props department was good experience.*

Sometimes it's surprising how many ways you can use the same room.

Luke: *At one time, to keep up with the schedule, there were four different set-ups in the chapel at the same time. If you looked in different directions the processional entrance for the hooded figures was set up at one end and, at the other end, the contemporary scene where the chapel was in mothballs – dust-sheets – was set up, and so on. It was lucky that we could do things that way because we were in that location the whole week. And we could go back and pick things up later in the week, which we couldn't have done if we were moving locations.*

If I did it again – having said that I like making props I'd actually resist doing it because it used up a lot of time in preparation – and that's not the best use of my time. They worked well, but it took too much of my time.

There are two kinds of things you can learn from a film. One is just the confidence you get from having done something. The other is the dozens of little details that eventually you forget you ever had to learn but which, together, shape the way you work.

Gavin: *Next time I would definitely take more notice of the lead characters' faces and how to light them. One particular shot, I didn't twig until too late: Frank has quite a protuberant skull shape by his eyebrows, which caused a line of shadow across his forehead because he was lit from below. I'd definitely light him differently if I were to do it again. It looks like the light's coming from a lamp – the light was where the lamp was – but that's not good enough. It would have been kinder to have put it somewhere else.*

Learning to work with named actors is another big learning curve. Being aware that they are very aware of what the camera's doing and how you're lighting them. And making sure they're comfortable and none of the equipment is in the way for them and they feel that we're covering them from the right angles and making them feel comfortable, really.

Some people go through their entire career without encountering special effects. Not if they worked on *Ghosthunter*.

Gavin: *The Quantel stuff was a massive learning curve, too. Something I'd never even thought of was the depth of field. I ended up shooting the whole film at 2.8 – that was just the way it came out – but it was good for Dean (the Focus Puller), because it gave him something to play with. But Quantel really wanted a bit more depth of field because of the way they were plating the shot – we had to do several plates. We had a ghost in the background and Sarah in the foreground, and Sarah was sharp, but then as soon as we took her away, we couldn't rack focus to the ghost because it would have changed the focus of the rest of the room. I should have thought about it before.*

The effect was going to be produced by dividing the shot into a number of separate planes, from foreground to background, so that areas of the scene could be separately manipulated digitally. In order to get more depth of field, more light was really needed.

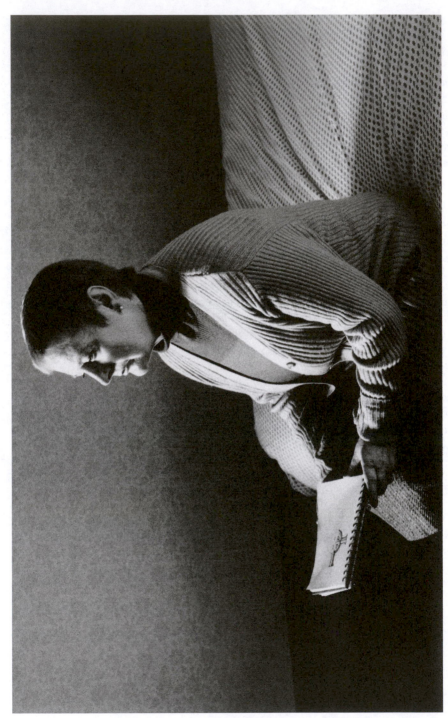

Audrey (June Watson) alone in Sarah's bedroom after her disappearance. © *Zoë Norfolk 2000*

Gavin: *We needed to light up but we just didn't have the equipment. If you're doing that sort of thing you really need to know in advance. In general the chats between Matt Twyford and myself and Simon were really positive and Matt was a god to me, it sounded very complicated and he explained it and it all came crystal clear.*

I feel much more confident now, yes. It was the first thing I'd shot on 35. I'd use the same lenses again. The lenses were brilliant. Lots of things I learnt on this film – they're all tiny but they're really important. Things like story telling; motivation of camera movement; frame sizes; thinking about editing on set; cheating lights to look as if they're coming from a source; how fast you can work with a crew that know what they're doing and what you can achieve; lighting lap-top screens; faking lantern light whilst an artist is on the move. All little things but, when they all come together, all really important. I know how to light certain scenarios now.

The most important thing was that I learnt to trust my eye – that was a big learning curve – basically because I didn't have time to take out the meter and meter everything. All I did was run in and make sure artists' faces were lit and you could see them, and then judge everything else by eye – like I found I knew whether we had to see into a corner and how much we were going see.

It's great to work on a short because you get to work with new directors. All directors work differently, some are more creative visually than others. It was good to try out new things – Simon was very happy for me to do that on this film and trusted me. So I was able to experiment trying new lights and new techniques. The challenge of telling a story in a very short space of time and being concise but not predictable. Trying to make it look interesting and something that people haven't seen before – that's always a challenge – and getting the visuals to follow the character curve of a single character. It's a testing ground for everything. It's one of the hardest things to do, making a good short – or a memorable short.

Rodrigo Gutierrez: *Gavin was great; very good. I'm very glad that the film schools are turning out people who are mature in their approach to filmmaking. I'd definitely work with Gavin again. And it's good that people are doing their homework so they go out there knowing what they want to do. Half the battle is doing your homework. You can always look back and say, 'we could have done this better' but the film set out to involve experienced people with inexperienced people; everyone enjoyed themselves; everyone had a good experience – and we achieved what we set out to do. Even when things went wrong it was a learning experience for everyone involved and that was useful.*

How to get it right – a summary

Quite rightly, most of the tremendous effort required to get any movie made is concentrated on the shoot. It's the time when most people are working and the time when most of the money is spent. It also typically occupies only 25 per cent or less of the total production period from the beginning of pre-production to the delivery of the final print. It's a demanding time for everyone – it is, after all, the time when the film is actually being manufactured, if you like. You can't undo the things that you have done during the shoot. Choose to drop them, yes; change them, no.

Partly because of all these things – the pressures of concentrating all that effort and expense in the most useful way possible – the filmmaking machine is usually a bit of a juggernaut. In short, decisions made before filming begins usually stick. It's tempting to throw something together quickly and to tell yourself, 'We'll sort out the details later.' You won't. If you haven't sorted it before the shoot begins, you won't change anything once the machine has started up. In the case of *Ghosthunter*, this led to the problems over the schedule, which had never really been properly discussed.

So: **thought (and preferably time) spent in preparation is never wasted, and will make more difference than anything else to the success and quality of the film.**

If your crew and cast are brilliant, then good preparation will give them room to breathe and allow their brilliance to shine, rather than soaking up all their technical skills in getting the film out of a hole. If your cast and crew are less experienced, then good preparation gives everyone as much time as possible to do the best they can.

Secondly, don't get yourself into a 'blind leading the blind' situation. It's often tempting just to go out and shoot it yourself, and get it cut together by a mate, using 'real people' – that attractive person from the pub – as cast. It's all under your control that way. It's much quicker to get together. Sometimes it works out really well. But usually things would work out even better if you had some help. Hollywood movies have stars, not only because stars are the best actors (often they're not) but because they bring people in to see the movie. Every project could do with some extra help: if you can't get stars, then you can at least persuade some experienced actors to take part. If you can't get a member of the British Society of Cinematographers to shoot the picture, at least you can put together a crew that includes some experienced members of the industry.

Don't try to do it all alone.

Experienced crew can save you a lot of time. They know how things are supposed to be; and they've often been through these problems before, so they can suggest a solution straight away, without having to go through alternatives they know are not going to work.

Don't get blinded by technology.

The movie-making machine can be very impressive and seductive – particularly if you have a large crew and lots of gear. But always, always, always, all those people and all that gear are there for one reason, to cover a performance. What counts in the end is what's on screen, not what it took to get it there.

Finally, **don't forget the edit**.

To mix a few metaphors, if the script is a musical score – a description of the film as it will be – then the rushes are the bricks and mortar from which you will ultimately build the palace of your story. With the possible exception of special effects, if you haven't shot it, then you can't put it in the film.

Keep focused all the time: don't shoot something if you don't know why you need it; on the other hand, make very sure that you do shoot everything that you do need.

Simon: *I think that I could have utilized my time better on the set. I wasn't exactly aware of the set-up time involved for each shot. I wanted to be around the film set most of the time but occasionally found myself at a loose end. This was the time I wasted, time I could have spent with the actors. A director is either accessible or not, the accessible ones were the ones I always enjoyed working with – as an actor they give you confidence. This set-up time is a useful period to make sure that the actors are happy with the up-coming scene. Away from the set you can get their opinion without the whole crew looking on. Actors are often called upon to walk into a room full of strangers and do their best work, which is not always easy, even the best get nervous. I was somewhat prepared for this but could have used my time more constructively.*

As a director or head of department everyone will look to you for a decision. Confidence is your most valuable ally. Confidence comes from the preparation you'll have done on the film throughout its development. One concern I had was with changing my mind, that it would be seen as a sign of weakness. You can visualize your shots all you like but in the end you need to see them in practice. I remember talking to Trevor Coop about this when we'd wrapped at Pinewood. Trevor said that good directors are not afraid to change their mind because they are always open to the creative options. Again, it boils down to confidence, confidence in your own ideas and the confidence to accept input from your creative team.

To coin a phrase, pre-production was all about the script, the script and the script. Production was preparation, preparation, preparation and post-production was organization, organization, organization. As a new director on a big set I felt a little vulnerable. I was an unknown quantity and had yet to prove myself. I was confident with the script, I'd done my preparation and I was happy with my creative team. That was what I kept reminding myself of as I focused on the work.

Unproven directors will all face this challenge. It was an immensely enjoyable experience and my confidence grew as we progressed through each day. I can only take the positive away with me and on to the next production. This project achieved exactly what it set out to achieve – to learn filmmaking from the best in the business. By giving ourselves the greatest challenge possible we had to rise to the occasion. That we came out of it intact is tribute to the spirit of the project and particularly to all the crew involved.

7 The edit

Are you a pessimist or an optimist? During the edit, do you leave out the bad bits, or put together the good bits? It's a layman's question, which starts from the belief that all the real work of movie-making is done on set, in the presence of a camera.

Of course you make a film with a camera. But what you prepare with the aid of a camera is a kind of Lego set. The story still has to be constructed, and there are normally hundreds or thousands of possible variations in the way you put it together, from the tiny to a complete reconstruction.

Any narrative depends largely for its effect on timing – 'it's the way you tell 'em'. The timing on the set might have been perfect or less than perfect. Provided enough material has been shot to cover the scene properly, the edit can radically affect the timing for better and for worse. The most important thing for an editor to have is a good sense of rhythm. And it's the most important thing for a director to have, too. Many people believe that the ideal way for a director to learn his or her craft is to work their way up through the cutting rooms, seeing the way shots do or don't go together; the things that work and the things that don't; the reasons to be cheerful or to curse in the relationship between editor and director. Whatever you believe, this is true: a film is essentially made by three people: Director, Camera-person, Editor. Everyone else is there to help. The script and the performance are the essential material they have to work with; but these three are the people who transmute this material into the Thing that is essentially Film. (I speak generically, not being snobbish about television. Ultimately, there's no significant production difference. The differences are in sales, marketing, exhibition.)

A few very basic examples of the way in which a cut can change a scene:

- The rhythm and feel of a scene where dialogue cuts from CU to CU is quite different from one where the whole scene runs in a single two-shot.
- Where a scene does cut from CU to CU usually the edits are split, so that sound and picture do not cut at exactly the same time. This has the

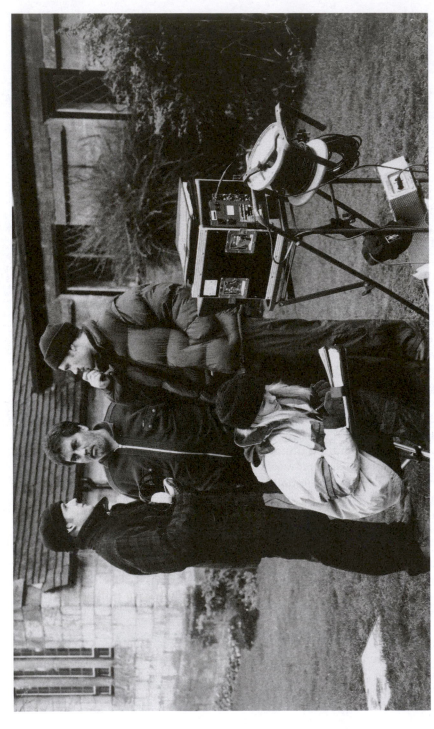

Director, Simon Corris, camera operator, Rodrigo Gutierrez and DoP Gavin Struthers discuss the next shot. Claire Eades, script supervisor, is seated. © Zoë Norfolk 2000

effect of smoothing the cut and making the scene appear less jumpy, but it has an important secondary effect: the direction and timing of the split can radically alter the power structure of the dialogue. For example, if the picture is cut first so the cut is from sync dialogue to a reaction shot, where the listener is waiting for the speaker to finish, the power might appear to be with the speaker. If it were to be cut the other way, with the dialogue response cut very hard on the end of the speech – or overlapping – then the second speaker might appear to be more in control.

- Lots of very fast, short cuts can make things seem much more exciting than they really are. It's often harder to do the opposite, and let things breathe. A lot of films are cut much more nervously than they need to be.
- Another thing to be aware of is the difference between watching something projected on the Big Screen and viewing the same material on the Steenbeck, or monitor that you're cutting on. It's almost literally a physical thing: the kind of fast-cut, sharp-moving, hand-held material that looks really funky in the corner of the living room can make you feel sea-sick when you're looking at it on a screen 6 m across. And (apart from anything else) because the screen is so big, you can't take in the whole picture with one glance as you can with a smaller screen. You simply need more time to keep track of what's going on. You will already have taken account of these differences in the way you shot the film, but it's something worth bearing in mind as you cut, too.
- Not everything happens in picture. The sound is enormously important – not just in obvious ways, like the quality of dialogue, the music, the sound of gunshots; but in the timing, too: in telling the story – in keeping things happening. A sound is an event, just as much as an action, or a cut. In fact, you can get away with some pretty rough edits (should you ever be unlucky enough to be in a situation where your choices are really limited) by creative use of sound. Either by distracting with a spot effect – a gunshot or a dustbin, for instance – or by smoothing over a join with continuous atmosphere.

None of this is terribly difficult or advanced and the list certainly isn't exhaustive. The point is that each tiny detail is just as important during the post-production process as it has been up to this point. Maybe more, because now you're approaching the end. You're making the final decisions. When you finish now, that will be the film. No more changes. No more, 'It'll be good when . . . it'll be great when the music's on.' The music is on. The cut is final. What you show to people is the Thing.

It's all a very concrete, physical, detailed process. Somebody has to make the decision whether to cut *here*. Or cut *here*, two or ten frames further on. And it has to be the right decision for the film.

Processes

It's increasingly likely that you'll end up working on some kind of computer-based equipment, whether the film was shot on 65 mm (for a 70 mm print) or DV.

In contrast to videotape editing, film editing has *always* been a non-linear process. Computer-based editing waited a long time before the equipment was cheap and powerful enough to do what film editors had been doing by hand (originally) on Pic-Syncs, Moviolas and Steenbecks for decades. Finally, the day arrived, and it has been enormously liberating for visual storytellers everywhere. Because now everyone can have the equipment to do most of the work involved in film and TV post-production for little more than the cost of a fast personal computer. Which can be something of a red herring. (You have a red herring on your desktop, madam.) Because, although the drop in the price of equipment has made it available to everyone, it hasn't made the necessary skills available to everyone in equal measure. If you *can* do it, then things are now possible that were completely beyond most people's means less than a decade ago. Go for it. But it's now also possible to foul up big-time at much less expense than previously. If you can't really do it, then get someone in who can – even if it stretches your budget. Better to end with a good product that does justice to everyone involved than to risk throwing it all away and finish up with an unwatchable, disappointing mess.

In the end, with possible variations, you're likely to be going through one of three basic processes in post-production:

- The entire process is completed on film. You shoot 16 mm or 35 mm. The negative is processed and a cutting copy (work-print) made. The film is then cut on Pic-Sync/Steenbeck/Moviola. This is the pre-computer method. You end up with a cutting copy covered in scratches and chinagraph marks to indicate fades, dissolves and wipes, which you see for the first time when the answer print arrives from the lab at the end of the whole process.
- The (probably more likely) hybrid process. You shoot on film. The negative is transferred to tape. Some or all of the tapes are digitized into a computer-based edit system such as Avid. The cut is performed in the computer, and either the tapes or the negative are later matched to the computer cut, depending on whether the final work is to end up on film or tape.
- You shoot on tape – DV or otherwise. In this case you don't have much choice – you edit on computer – unless you want to put yourself through the painful process of linear tape editing.

If you have chosen a digital format, you do still have the choice of whether to treat the edit as an off-line/on-line process, or whether to make the computer-based edit the final thing.

This is almost the other end of the spectrum from the way *Ghosthunter* was produced, but video is being used in this way for all sorts of reasons, and by all sorts of people, from those just beginning (to whom the acceptable quality of DV opens up a whole world of possibilities that were previously too expensive) to highly experienced people such as the Danish Dogme group and British director Mike Figgis, who have chosen DV when they could have chosen 35 mm. I would expect that most readers will have started out from the assumption that they were going to shoot on DV, even if, by now, the project is planned to be produced on 65 mm.

DIY DV

If you are starting with tapes from the DV family of formats (mini-DV, DVCAM, DVCPRO, Digital 8) then you can do a final, on-line edit in your bedroom, to the same quality as a professional edit suite that would have cost around half a million only a few years ago (pounds or dollars, depending on how few years). With the usual caveats about not diving in too deep without knowing what you're doing (after all, most of the success of *Ghosthunter* was down to the fact that the Amulets at every stage asked the experts what they should do for the best), here's what you need:

- A computer that's capable of playing up-to-date games (because games stretch the hardware and lead hardware innovation more than anything else apart from video editing), with at least 128 MB of RAM.
- DV footage needs around 200 MB of disk space for each minute of programme, so you need at least 30 GB of hard disk space available, ideally on a separate drive from the one on which your main programs reside. The hard drive needs to be capable of a continuous transfer rate of at least 3.6 MB per second. Most new EIDE drives can probably keep up with that, but don't take it for granted. To be safe you need a SCSI drive.
- An interface card variously known as FireWire, or IEEE1394, to which you connect the camcorder or video deck. These vary in cost and complexity from the very simple to the very expensive. The difference between the two price bands is in whether the cards contain a DV chip, like the one on the camera or deck, to encode and decode the DV stream or whether they use software drivers and let the computer do the work. It's perfectly possible to do good work with the cheaper cards, but in that case it's particularly important to make sure that you have:
- The right software. There's quite a wide choice of basic DV editing software – some of it bundled with DV editing cards. Most of it shouldn't be touched with a proverbial barge-pole – or any other kind. These are amateur

programs intended for stitching bits of home video together, and it's difficult or impossible to do anything more sophisticated with them.

You might have heard of Avid non-linear editing systems, because, in 1989, they were one of the first computer-based editing tools available. The world has moved on since then and while Avid still produce very capable software, there are now many others to choose from. One of the most common is Adobe's *Premiere*, which is a very mature and powerful editing program. Whichever software you decide to go with, make sure that it's the latest version, since improvements between versions can be enormous and it seems perverse to inflict unnecessary problems on yourself. Making a movie involves quite enough work even when things go well!

What to look for? A way of working that you (or your editor) feels at home with is one of the most important things. It's just as true of editing software as it is of word processing than many programs do basically the same job, but in different ways, and you feel more at home with some approaches than with others.

One thing that distinguishes the amateur or multimedia video editing program from the professional is the way it handles timecode. Make sure you work with an edit program that keeps the original timecode from the tape, and which can generate an Edit Decision List (EDL) from it in a common format used by high-end post-production houses – something like CMX or Sony. You are asking for trouble otherwise. This gives you two advantages. Firstly, you'll be able to batch capture. The edit software will be able to retransfer the DV material from tape, using the timecode; or just re-transfer the shots you eventually used. In this way, your timecode lists are all the backup you need if anything happens. (Keep them safe.) Secondly, you can use DV editing as an off-line edit for a Digi-Beta or High Definition shoot, and take the EDL to a post-production house to auto-conform the program. If you are going to work with a post-production house, talk to them before you start, and find out what they need. Just as you should and would with a film laboratory that you hadn't worked with before. Agree the whole process at as early a stage as possible, and keep each other up to date as you go on. That way nobody will have any nasty surprises later on.

Desktop on-line or off-line?

If the DV stream is simply piped from tape through the FireWire/IEEE1394 port onto disk, edited on disk and piped back again, then you are effectively performing an on-line edit (assuming that the film was shot on DV). There is no generation loss in practical terms between the tape original and the tape copy. The pictures don't get any worse – and they obviously can't get any better, no matter what gear you use. Even though you are effectively performing an on-line edit on DV, it's often still a good idea to take your DV edit master to a 'grown-up' post-production house and tidy it up – dub it to Digi-Beta, make sure the video and audio levels are as they should be, and so on. You can then be confident that you have a master tape that ticks all the boxes the engineers like to tick, too.

Some DV capture cards have analogue inputs as well, and will capture from DV camcorders and other video sources to MJPEG or MPEG. Typically, the video will take up less room than DV, so your hard disk is effectively bigger. But this captured footage can only be used for off-line purposes. You will have to recapture in DV, or match the edit using timecode in an edit suite somewhere else. Clearly, accurate timecode is doubly important in this case. It is, after all, the only reference you have to the original footage. And, in any case, if you have been filming using a higher-quality video format, such as High Definition or Digi-Beta, you will most likely go through the standard off-line/on-line process. There's no reason why you shouldn't do this on your desktop, using DV or not.

It is possible, if you have the hardware, to treat these higher-quality digital formats in the same way as DV, by transferring the datastream to disk, editing on disk and transferring it back. You'll need a faster interface than FireWire/IEEE1394, and a good deal more disk space. It probably isn't worth attempting in the real world, although it is already happening at the expensive end of the market.

DIY editing is most likely to be tempting if you've had a DV shoot. Otherwise, although, as we've seen, it's perfectly possible to edit in your bedroom no matter what the acquisition format you've used, it's most likely that you'll be thinking of finding a professional editor in a professional cutting room. Just remember that his Avid (or whatever) is probably less powerful, in computing terms, than your bedroom computer. Don't be intimidated by the brand names. On the other hand, as with everything in film, generally speaking, the equipment is less important than the skill of the person driving it.

Cutting the picture

However you end up doing it – whether or not you work with an experienced editor – the procedures of editing will be the same.

It's at this point that you discover the importance of accurate and detailed notes taken during filming. On a short film, continuity and technical logs are useful. On anything longer they're essential. Even if you (the director) do remember everything that happened, in the first instance the rushes will be going to a person who wasn't at the shoot – the editor. The editor can always choose not to use information contained in the notes, but if something is

The clapper! © Zoë Norfolk 2000

missing, you can bet your life it'll be something that would have saved hours of looking.

The absolute minimum that the editor needs to begin work is a full shoot log, so that he or she can find where everything is, and a script marked up, shot for shot, with which slates go where, and which ones are the good takes. The editor should really be left alone then to put together a first assembly.

Simon Cozens, *Ghosthunter* Editor: *Let the editor put something together and then come in and discuss it – even if everything's completely wrong. It can be a terribly painful process to sit here with a director deliberating over every single cut; basically you have to have something to discuss, even if everything's wrong and you change it all.*

Another real advantage of having somebody else cut the movie (apart from the personal skills and the fresh look that they bring to the project) is precisely that they weren't there during the filming. They don't know that it took three hours to get that one line right, or that crane shot that you're terribly pleased with. What they do know is whether something works for the story or not. And, in the end, that's all that matters. If it doesn't work, bin it, and that's something a good editor will be the first to point out.

Simon Cozens: *That's a problem I often find with directors – to tell them to stop thinking about the film they have in their head when they shot it or wrote it, and start looking at the film that you've actually got, the footage you've actually shot. It's just frustrating when you want it to be something else – you want it to be faster or slower or whatever – it's difficult to let go of those impressions and deal with the material you actually have. It's almost like a completely separate process, the shooting and the editing – you have to let go of everything you have up to that stage. Often things don't work, or your favourite scenes don't work or you have shots that look great but they serve no purpose. Let them go.*

Ghosthunter

Ghosthunter was unlucky with their editing schedule. The Amulets had expected to go straight into two weeks of editing once the shoot at Pinewood was over. But that didn't happen. They lost two editors to paid work before the second recommended Simon Cozens, who did end up cutting the film. Even that had its drawbacks. Simon was working as Assistant Editor on a feature (a big-budget feature) during the day, so could only give evenings and weekends to *Ghosthunter*. But eventually he was able to start. Simon Corris sent him the rushes (which had been transferred to Beta SP) and the DAT tapes, and he digitized them and synchronized the sound. He then played them off to a VHS tape, which he sent back to the Amulets. They sent him a script marked up with the preferred takes, from which he put together a first assembly of the film.

With a longer feature, the editor would normally already be working during the shoot, synching rushes and cutting sequences and scenes as they were filmed. In the case of a short film, where the production period is so brief, everything waits until the end.

Simon Corris: *Editing was something I was really looking forward to as it's a crucial part of the development of the story. However, it hasn't been as enjoyable as I expected – partly because of editing part-time. It was difficult organizing our time in the Avid suite. I was looking forward to doing it full-time – finishing at Pinewood and going into two solid weeks of editing.*

Simon (Cozens) assembled the shots for a first preview. I was unprepared for the way the film would look, in such a raw state. It sounded awful. In fact, as he was clicking 'play' on the Avid, Simon (Cozens) said 'Are you prepared for this?' I said, 'What do you mean?' He said 'Have you ever seen a film before in this kind of a state?' I said 'Not really.' 'OK, well get used to it', he said.

The film wasn't fully assembled. There were bits missing – and the noise! The background noise and the balance between scenes. When we shot the stuff I had the headphones on and I don't remember noticing any of this, but the bangs, the squeaks and clicks, the noise of the fans on the lights, the noise from the camera, the tracks – everything was highly audible, and it completely ruined it for me. I thought, 'What on earth do we do about all this?' 'It's completely normal', he said. 'This is why you have sound editors.'

Editor Simon's first impression was that the Amulets had nothing to worry about.

Simon Cozens: *It was very slick – looked very good; nicely shot. I think Ghosthunter is probably the most glossy of the shorts I've done. It has great production values. All the money is up there on the screen. A couple of others I've done are different – maybe more exciting, but not very slickly produced, and done with no money.*

Finally, the Simons began work on putting *Ghosthunter* together.

Simon Corris: *I didn't want anyone else in the edit suite – just the editor and me. I didn't want people looking over our shoulders making suggestions. I just wanted us to be left alone to work on the first cut. Lots of people made requests to come in and see it but I said no.*

Finally we had assembled a first cut, which was the cut I had in my mind when we were shooting it; and then we had a viewing with Alison in her producer capacity and Gavin. It was all very dramatic. They arrived that evening, and Simon and I were quite nervous and we gave them comfy seats and a nice warm cup of tea.

Alison: *We didn't get pop corn or ice cream, though.*

Simon Corris: *. . . and we sat them down in front of the monitor and let them watch the film. We'd messed around with the sound mix to make it more even and put a temporary music track on to give it some atmosphere and we watched the film.*
They were both very encouraging. I was conscious of losing my objectivity – seeing the film so many times and working on scenes in minute detail. Having the two of them in at that point was very valuable. We had a long chat afterwards. They were very helpful and confirmed things I was thinking about. We talked about the scene order and the way in which certain shots should cut together.

It was understandable that the Amulets were nervous. Actually, it doesn't matter how experienced you are, everyone is always nervous at the first screening of a new cut or a new stage of a film. Simon, the editor, was quite happy with the way things were going.

Editor Simon: *It's going together very well. There are a couple of problematic scenes, and even they are not really problematic. It's just a couple that Simon's disappointed in. And the ones that he's disappointed with are the ones he had least time to shoot. They covered the scene in an hour or something because that was all the time they had. But I tell him that the coverage is perfectly good, and that's all that matters in the end.*

Once that first, terrifying screening was over, they continued work on the film.

Simon Corris: *We then made three other versions of the film so that we could look at it in different ways – particularly the opening section. So including the first cut we had four different versions of the film each edited to give a different emphasis. We decided one of them was the strongest and we put some temporary music on that and spent a couple of weeks previewing it with people we trust – other filmmakers, friends and people who don't go to the cinema much – trying to get a good cross section . . . just showing it to people to see what their response was. And the response has, thankfully, been very positive. I suppose that was a bonus of having a drawn-out editing process. We can think about it a bit more. If we'd done it as we'd originally planned, in two solid weeks, we might not have had time to assess it properly. So now the thing is to take all the elements from those four versions and get to something that will become a final cut.*

Of course, this is something you can't really do if you're working in the traditional, all-film manner. The cost of all those cutting copies wouldn't be allowed by most production departments. With computer-based editing, it's no more complicated than making a copy of the film and cutting a different version.

There's often a tension in the cutting room between the director and the editor. Very few editors like having hundreds of rolls of rushes dumped on them, and being left alone to make a film out of it. On the other hand, an editor who has grown up in the world of film knows the value of what they can do for a movie. Few film editors like to be supervised on a shot by shot basis, with the director surgically attached to their shoulder all the time. Each relationship has to be worked out on an individual basis – just as each pair of producer–director or director–writer, or director–cameraperson is different; and no two films are the same. However, the editor deserves to be respected – and normally likes to be left alone to play around with things and work without a director between visits – particularly for the all-important first cut, where the editor has to get to know the material, and the story for themselves.

Editor Simon: *I like directors being around. It's good to feel that you're creating something together – not that you're doing something on your own. It's good to feel that you're working together – we're trying to tell a story, what's the best way of telling the story? What am I bringing to it? What is the director bringing to it? Maybe they're too bound up in the shots because they know it too well, or whatever.*

He was impressed, too, with how professional the Amulets were.

Editor Simon: *They'd obviously done a lot of research and done their homework. They were very business-minded. They'd gone away and figured out what they needed to know and contacted people who could tell them what they needed to get the job done. The whole attitude was very professional – everyone treated it as a serious project. Even though people are working for little you have to establish professional grounds in the first place – reasons for people to get involved. The other thing is that they'd scheduled the whole thing out – the process was planned from beginning to end: this is where they want to be on certain dates.*

On other shorts often they shoot the film and then look for money to edit it; or they edit it but they've got no money for optical effects or sound work, or no money for a print so you kind of get stalled at every step of the process. Simon and Alison had gone through the whole thing and scheduled dates for it – cut by this date, sound mixed by then.

This attitude continued throughout the production process. Director Simon was worried by the quality of sound he heard in the cutting room when he went to see the first cut, so he took the sound recordings to the Sound Editors, Mark and Sam Auguste, who had agreed to work on the picture.

Filming one of the flashback scenes in the film. The victim lies dead as director, Simon Corris, watches the shot on the camera's LCD monitor. © Zoë Norfolk 2000

　　Director Simon: *So the first time I went to see the sound editors I went humbly and I said, 'I think we've got problems.' They said, 'What problems?' and I said, 'Well, the noise of the camera and the clicks and the fans cooling the HMIs and the difference in the sound inside the church – the big empty space, the reverb from that. The kick from the footsteps on the wooden floor in the lounge. And so on.' So Mark and Sam looked a bit horrified at the extra work they might have to do. Mark put the tape in the machine, listened and said, 'So you're worried about this? That's nothing. We can get rid of that.' He explained that this was perfectly normal. The dialogue was clean and we had no concerns.*

　　Of course, the point of this is not that your sound recording does not have to be of the best quality, but that your sound recordist needs to know what can and what cannot be handled in post-production. Echoing, reverberant sound, for example, cannot be dried out. You can always add reverb but it's very hard to get rid of it. Brian (the *Ghosthunter* sound recordist) had given them exactly what they needed.

　　Editor Simon has a few other suggestions for things to think about during a shoot that will make editing a creative pleasure rather than a problem-solving exercise.

　　Editor Simon: *Make sure you get things covered, footage-wise. If you lose time in the schedule think about dropping a whole scene rather than trying to do it in fewer shots. If something is important make sure you've got a CU as well as a wide shot. And simple things, such as, if you're covering a particular scene in two halves, overlap the action. Make sure that you cover some of the same action and dialogue in both shots. That way, if you get problems with continuity, or you change your mind about where you'd like to cut, if you have overlapping shots it gives you more places to cut around the problem.*

The promo

It is very difficult after a while to keep any sense of detachment about the work you are doing. 'Always trust your first impression' some editors say. And director Simon did find that he felt they were losing their way a little with all the various cuts they were doing, and the length of time the whole process was taking, since it had to be spread out over evenings and weekends. Rescue came from an unexpected angle. Quantel invited them to the Film Festival in Cannes, and they felt they needed something to take with them to show.

　　Director Simon: *The finish of the film seemed so far away. What really helped us along, and I'd recommend it to anyone involved in a low-budget project, was making a promo. Our post-production team could effectively experiment with what they would carry on into the film – Barrington on the music, Quantel on the effects and Ian Firth on the title design. It became a light at the end of the post-production tunnel and we started to see how our film would ultimately look. It was a much-needed boost. Now we have something that's finished and polished that we can show in Cannes. Prior to that it was all beginning to feel very difficult. It has shown us the way.*

More about the Cannes experience in Alison's diary.

8 Final stages

After what seems like an eternity of cutting and recutting, you eventually realize that you've finished. You can't do any more to the picture. The film isn't yet finished, but the picture is locked off. Time to turn to the sound. It's certainly possible to make further picture changes, but any changes you do make will cause complications for everyone else involved in finishing the film, so it's better to consider the picture untouchable from now on.

Although, in some ways, you probably feel that most of the work is done now – and it is, in terms of the most important editorial decisions – the remaining 10 per cent or so of effort on sound and picture makes a massive difference to the impression that the film makes on its audience. This is not the time to relax. So what remains to be done?

- Any special effects that haven't already been cut in (although you can no longer change the picture length).
- Music.
- Laying and mixing sound tracks.
- The grading and final print if you're working on film; any final picture-processing if you're working on tape.

Special effects

This is not the time to start thinking about special effects. If you are only beginning at this stage, the odds are that anything you do will be horrendously time-consuming and expensive.

Paul Watkins, from Quantel, helped with *Ghosthunter*, and restates Matt Twyford's advice: *Talk to special effects companies as early as you can . . . involve them at the storyboard stage. If you wait until you've finished filming, special effects can become very expensive indeed.*

He also has some general advice about how to use effects.

Paul Watkins: *Good effects support the story. Often they're invisible effects, quite subtle things, maybe a day-for-night shot or adding smoke or sparkle, adding things that aren't in the background – or taking away something that shouldn't be. On* The Dance of Shiva, *I remember we removed a MacDonald's sign that certainly would not have been on the Western Front in 1917.*

Spectacular effects can be fun, but subtle things are very satisfying, too. If you can turn round and show people something that was an effect and they hadn't noticed it, that's very satisfying.

And the special effects man says the same as everyone else: *You must put story first and only use effects where they can really help the story.*

Finally, in technical terms, as with everything else, the eventual quality of the effects depends on the quality of the material you start with. The effect will work well if the footage is well lit, well composed and filmed with thought for the needs of the effects work that's going to be done.

Paul Watson: *Work to the highest quality throughout and you'll be able to do good special effects. It's 'rubbish in, rubbish out' here as everywhere else.*

Music

Music can have a powerful effect on a film – not just on the story-telling, but on the budget, as well. The first thing to say is that you cannot take a piece of music from your personal CD collection and just use it in your film. In order to do this legally, you will need permission from the record company, the composer, the musicians and the music publisher. It's unlikely that permission will be granted without some cost attached. In the case of high-profile or chart recordings, the costs can be considerable or permission denied altogether. If you go ahead anyway and just use the music, then the lawyers employed by the relevant record companies are likely to take you to court, cost you a lot of money and (at the very least) your film will be withdrawn from circulation until you change the music. So it's probably better not to try it.

If you start from the premise that everything is owned by someone from whom you have to ask permission if you want to use it, then you'll be safe. If you're thinking of using classical music, then be careful about dates. The composer's copyright subsists for 70 years from the death of the composer. That means that works by Gershwin, Rachmaninov, Ravel, for example, are still in copyright. In any case, the copyright in the recording lasts for 50 years, so it's unlikely that there will be any 'copyright-free' recordings available.

The figures prepare for their ritual. © Zoë Norfolk 2000

Copyright-free music

There are people who sell so-called 'copyright-free' recordings, but that's not really what they are. Often these are recordings of a composer's own music, which she or he sells to you for a one-off fee, following payment of which you can use the music as many times as you like in as many programmes or films as you like. It's not that there's no copyright in the music, but that you have bought a licence to use the music and the recording. Usually, in these cases, it's a non-exclusive copyright, since the composer obviously wants to sell their on-spec recording and music to as many people as he or she can – so you're quite likely to hear it again in someone else's film.

Library music

A straightforward, but not free, solution is to use music specially composed for film and television and released by libraries such as KPM, De Wolfe and Zomba Music. In this case, the CDs are given away and you pay in units of 30 seconds for the music you use in your film. The amount you pay depends on where your film or programme is going to be shown. A licence for non-paying audiences might cost around £50 per 30 seconds for a European licence. If you need all media world-wide, each unit will cost several hundreds of pounds.

Commissioning music

So commissioning specially written music for your film is quite possibly not only the best idea artistically, but in budget terms as well.

Low-cost technology has changed music, too. In terms of sound quality, a home computer is perfectly capable of producing recordings that are completely professional, using recordings, live music or from sampled sounds. There are, of course, two questions that you, as producer or director, still need to ask. The first thing is to remember that technology is a tool, not a solution. However brilliant the machine is, it's the skills of the operator that you're interested in. This might seem rather reductionist when we're talking about writing music, but it's easy to become seduced by the wonders of technology. You wouldn't choose a scriptwriter for the size of his word processor. So find a composer that you get on with, who understands the film, the story you're telling and whose music you like. The second is to consider whether sampled sounds played on keyboards are an adequate replacement for real instruments.

The music for *Ghosthunter* was composed by Barrington Pheloung, a composer of great skill, talent and reputation. He and the Amulets had worked together in theatre before and it was natural that they should ask him if he would like to help them with the film.

He has a very clear idea of the place of sound samples in music production. Samples enable him to preview a score he has composed and to play it to the director. Once the score is approved, he records it with live musicians who give that indefinable extra richness that keyboard-played samples cannot give, no matter how carefully the samples are recorded or how well the keyboards are played.

Barrington Pheloung: *A very large number of Hollywood movies have some cruddy synthesizer score that sounds dated a year later. As far as I'm concerned, the samples are purely a means to an end – a very helpful tool, but it's against my principles not to record with real musicians. I don't use the samples to put musicians out of work, but the opposite, to show how good a real orchestra can sound.*

In practical terms, however, some very successful scores have been produced using a mixture of sampled and live instruments. As we said, in the end it comes down to the skills of the composer and performer.

Procedures

So how does the music get onto the film? Often the composer is involved at script stage – particularly if music is involved within the action of the film, as it was in two of the films Barrington Pheloung has worked on, *Hilary and Jackie* about the cellist Jacqueline Du Pré, and *Truly, Madly, Deeply*, where Alan Rickman (who is not a cellist) had to play cello in the film. More often, though, the film is already at rough-cut stage before the composer becomes involved. Nonetheless, music works best in a film when it isn't just thought of as a necessary bolt-on to something that is already more or less finished.

Barrington Pheloung: *A clever director – and one with an instinct for music – will purposely leave room for the music to be part of the story-telling rather than have dialogue, dialogue, dialogue. It's those gaps that you leave that can sometimes be the seminal moments in the film. Music can be a very integral part of the story-telling. As well as setting moods, it can also tell you a lot about a character or a situation. So don't butt-up endless dialogue scenes together. I'm not saying you can't underscore dialogue. Sometimes you can have about 5 minutes of dialogue that goes on interminably and you underscore it and it's amazing how it seems to speed up the passage of time. But generally, trust the music. It can be a great support. Think of your choice of the greatest moments in cinema – almost every one of them is going to be scored or underscored.*

In the case of *Ghosthunter*, Barrington Pheloung had already begun developing the basic thematic material for the film while working on the promo. Then, when the fine-cut of the picture was ready, he and Simon went through the whole film, scene by scene.

Barrington Pheloung: *We'll have a spotting session. We'll go through the whole film and say exactly where we want music, why we want it, what it is trying to say. I will get from them a simple adjectival description of exactly what the music is trying to say, the mood it's trying to enhance at each point. Just a simple verbal description is very very helpful. Such as, he's doing that and she's doing that, but why, and which one do you want me to go with? Do you want it happy or sad, or whatever . . .? The collaborative process is very important. Just put what they want the music to be doing into simple English.*

Then I write the whole score, and I'm able to play it to directors in sync with the picture in my studio on my library of orchestral samples. And at that stage we can change things – extend or trim, or change the mood a bit. That's when the tweaking is done. Then the orchestra comes down to the studio and we record it. That's the moment it's worth being a composer for, when my colleagues play the music with care.

Barrington Pheloung is also very clear that his film scores should also be able to stand alone in the concert hall as music in its own right: *I write symphonically, I write from the beginning and go through to the end and I try to make complete symphonic sense of all the strands in the movie, so that if you do join them all up it makes sense. A kind of secondary story-telling.*

Sound editing and mixing

In much of European cinema – possibly partly because of the number of languages often involved in co-productions – there's a tradition of using virtually none of the sound recorded on location at all. All the voices are post-synchronized. All the effects are created or recorded anew. The whole sound picture is artificial. (A reason why it's not always worth being purist about seeing films in their original language. Sometimes there is no original language.) Remember the line in *Day for Night*? The actress can't remember her lines. 'Can't I say numbers?' she asks. 'With Federico I always just say numbers.'

Well, if only for budgetary reasons, you'll want to use as much of the original sound you recorded on location as you can. And you did remember to get an atmosphere track in every location, didn't you? Just the sound of the room for a minute or so?

The principal reason for the sound mix is to even out the sound levels between different scenes and to place music in the right places at the right relative levels. But, of course, there's more to it than that.

Sound can be an important part of story-telling. Sounds can be artificially exaggerated to create a dream-like quality, or to demonstrate the effect that they have on the character – an example might be the insistent ringing of a telephone that becomes louder and louder until it eclipses all other sound. Silence can be important, too – not just in the gaps between words, but (as another example) imagine a character at a heavy metal concert. Suddenly, across the room, he sees the person of his dreams. And all sound is silenced. The band plays on, but you hear nothing. Everything concentrated on the gaze.

Sound can be used as a signature motif of its own, in the same way that a musical theme is often attached to a person or a place. Something quite simple such as the sound of cicadas, or the cry of a peacock can bring back the memory of some time or place through the story. Towards the end of *Once Upon a Time in the West*, as the railroad tycoon lies dying, in the puddle of scarce water next to his head he hears the sound of the ocean he had been so desperate to reach.

Sound post-production is capable of far more than simply tidying up dialogue. Treat sound effects and atmosphere with as much thought and consideration as the music. And don't forget the power of silence.

As with every stage of production, preparation and discussion in advance always save time and energy. Particularly if you are planning to do anything unusual with the sound, talk to the sound editor and dubbing mixer as early as you can. It might even be worth involving them before the shoot, as the Amulets did with *Ghosthunter*, so that you can find out what they would ideally like.

Digital technology has supposedly made life simpler than it used to be, but the reality is that there are now so many different ways in which sound can be recorded, tracks laid and mixed, that if you want to get the best out of the system – not only in terms of quality but in terms of efficiency – you have to know exactly how the sound is going to be treated. For example, are you going to use DAT throughout? Or are you shooting video? In which case, is the sound sampled at 48 kHz or 32 kHz or not digital at all? Are the tracks being laid by the picture editor? How are they going to get from his machine to the dubbing theatre? Or are you going to auto-conform the tapes again just for sound? Although the fundamental process is the same in every case, the technical details can vary considerably depending on the people you're working with, the places you're working and, of course, your budget. So ask before it's too late.

Once the picture edit is complete, the editor will take the sound edits apart again to split them between two or more tracks, so that each track can be balanced separately, and with overlaps to smooth the transition between pieces of sync audio. In a simple dialogue scene, for example, each actor's voice will most likely be laid on a separate track. Another track will have

Hooded figures between exorcisms. © *Zoë Norfolk 2000*

continuous room atmosphere. Further tracks might contain spot effects – door slams, or a car starting up outside, and so on.

Often a specialist sound editor becomes involved at this stage, but it's quite common for the picture editor to lay the tracks. A mistake that's sometimes made by the inexperienced is to try to cram everything into too few tracks. It's actually easier to run as many as you can, because that enables the EQ and level to be set once for each track and allows the dubbing mixer to concentrate on the places where intervention is really needed.

It should be clear by now that it's much easier to add extra noises (the car starting, for example) than it is to get rid of them. The ideal is a dialogue track that sounds natural, but is basically as clean as possible.

Similarly it's helpful if different actors' lines don't overlap during shooting. You can always overlap them in track-laying, but you can't take them apart if they originally spoke at the same time. This isn't always easy to arrange. Particularly in master shots with several actors in frame at the same time it would be foolish to become obsessed with keeping their lines apart. However, it's important to make an effort to avoid overlapping dialogue in close-ups, when you can only see one person in any case.

The dub might go through several stages, depending on the complexity of the sound. You might have created a whole sound-world from nothing in some scenes. Those sections would be pre-mixed separately and the pre-mix laid as one track for the final mix.

It's always a good idea to produce a track containing only music and sound effects (M&E) – everything but the dialogue, mixed as in your film, but without adjustments for dialogue placing. If your film is ever going to be dubbed into another language, this track is essential, and it can either be produced as the penultimate mix – so that the final mix involves only the dialogue and the M&E – or as a separate stage after the final, before the tracks are taken down.

How long does the final mix take? Of course, it depends on the complexity of the sound track and how the dubbing theatre you're working in likes to work, but generally it's reasonable to expect to do a half-hour film in a single day.

If everything is in place and properly planned, the final mix should be a most enjoyable experience. And after all the endless repetition, the going over things again and again, the backwards and forwards, watching the film all the way through without stopping once the final mix is complete is probably the only time you'll ever see the film for the first time. Very satisfying – particularly if the dubbing theatre has a big screen.

9 What next?

You've done it! The film is finished! You've finished the edit, cut the neg, got your answer print, show print, cassette. It's sitting there on your desk or your mantelpiece. You know every frame. You don't need to watch it again, you're happy just to gaze at the box in quiet satisfaction. So we've come full circle. What are you going to do now? How do you go about achieving what you set out to do all those weeks or months ago?

You might already be there. Nothing wrong with that. The satisfaction of having completed the film might be all that you wanted. It might also be the case (be honest) that it hasn't turned out quite as well as you hoped but that you have learned so much from the experience that the next picture is going to be a definite cracker. That short-filmmaking is a training ground is one of the most important reasons that the established film industry supports the activity. Most likely, though, everything is perfect and you're ready for the next step. What options do you have? (One thing to remember is that the expense of producing a film doesn't end with the production. You're still going to need funds available to pay for publicity, the expenses of travelling around selling yourself and the film, the beginning of development work on your next project, and so on.)

Film festivals

Most short films spend their lives travelling from one film festival to another. There's one somewhere in the world at practically any time during the year. The trade paper *Screen International* publishes a list of them, as does the British Film Institute. And a search on the Internet will find lots of sites devoted either to individual festivals or to coverage of the whole festival scene. The British Council is one organization that offers help to filmmakers in getting their work shown at festivals around the world.

Paul Howson, The British Council: *We act as a clearing house for short films. Filmmakers send their work to us on VHS and we look at the film and decide whether it's of adequate quality to promote to festivals. If we think it is then we propose it to a festival – the festival always makes the final decision. If they accept the film we get hold of a print and ship it out and we might pay for the filmmaker to go to the festival, too. We only deal with the finished product – getting it seen by the right audience. We also give some practical help – we might provide a grant for making a print if the film has been accepted in competitions, for instance.*

He is quite clear about why the British Council offers this kind of help: *It's talent spotting, because we believe very strongly that the future of a viable British film industry rests on the constant supply of talent – new producing talent, new directing talent, new technical talent. In short-filmmaking, the debutantes tend to be producer, director and writer, and those are the ones we want to encourage. There aren't many people in a position to offer the kind of practical help that we do.*

The festival circuit is the traditional method of exposure for short films. It exists in a kind of world of its own, related to, but not really part of, the mainstream of film and television, and inhabited largely by people who visit festivals.

Only very rarely do short films appear in the mainstream channels – either as support to full-length features in cinemas, or on television.

Short films used to be very much a part of the cinema-going experience; but some time in the 1970s, cinema-going changed. The main feature increased in length. In order to keep the advertisements and the trailers (both of which earn money for distributors and exhibitors) without losing a showing of the film that was bringing people into the cinema, obviously the short film had to go. A short occasionally does the rounds with a big picture, but it's now very rare.

Similarly, television channels occasionally have brief seasons of short films – either bought in or commissioned by the channel. A television showing certainly provides better exposure than a festival showing; but the licence fees paid by the TV channel are very small. In short, whatever happens, you should think of your film as an investment in your future, not as a way of earning money. It's extremely unlikely to recover even a tiny portion of its cost.

The Internet is fast becoming an important method of distribution for short films and, slowly, broadband access to the Internet is spreading, making the experience of watching moving pictures on the Internet less of an enthusiasts' experience and more something that ordinary people would want to do. At the very least, having your film available on the Internet means that you can give its address to people you meet, instead of carrying tapes around with you everywhere you go. And you never know who might see it. And that's what you want: for the right people to see the film. Ideally you'll win a few awards. Your name will become known. You might even get an offer from someone.

Director, Simon Corris, setting up an effect shot with the 'Ghosts'. First assistant director, Philip Shaw, is seen extreme left.
© *Zoë Norfolk 2000*

What are you going to do next?

If your short is not to be a one-off, you really have to have the next project ready to talk about as soon as you start showing the short. It's possible, but not all that likely, that a producer will be looking for a director, see your short and decide to hire you. What's more likely is that a producer or a distributor is looking for a project. They see your short, they're impressed. 'What's the next project?' they ask, reaching for their cheque-book to finance the five million you need. You need to have something ready to talk about – preferably a script, maybe even a whole package. If you haven't, they might say, 'Shame. Come back to me when you're ready.' They might mean it at the time. But by the time you come back, they'll have put their money somewhere else and won't be able to help you no matter how much they want to. Sorry.

Ghosthunter? The film is only just finished at the time of writing. It will soon be shown at Panavision and at Technicolor to invited audiences. It will be entered for film festivals. Most important of all, it will be sent along with the script as part of the package for the Amulets' next production – a full-length, fully paid-for feature film.

Barrington Pheloung: Ghosthunter *is good because it tells a very strange little story. It's fascinating, just a great little story. It's beautifully performed and beautifully filmed. All the production values are first class. It deserves to do well.*

Watch the web site www.amulet-films.com for news and updates.
And you? Well, if you want to make a film, why not? And if not now, when?

Appendix A – The shooting script

GHOSTHUNTER

By
Alison Reddihough & Simon Corris

Ref: GH999H
Amulet Films Ltd

www.amulet-films.com
E-mail: Mail@amulet-films.com

FADE IN:

1   TITLE SEQUENCE   1

The screen is black. We hear a deep rumbling of thunder and the first title appears, then fades out.

Lightning flashes in the distance. In the flashes we see a church spire against the night sky, rain is falling.

After the flashes we are back to the black screen and the second title appears, intro music starts and the title fades.

Another flash of lightning lights up the exterior of the church as the camera tracks across it.

Black screen and the title of the film 'GHOSTHUNTER'. Title fades. Intro music continues through the opening sequence.

Lightning illuminates a stained glass window, we are now inside the church. We see, in very brief snapshots, a ritual taking place, alternating with the TITLES. The images are quick and rich in colour – hooded figures, a pentacle on the floor, a taper lighting a candle, etc. . . . We also focus on a strange symbol that is used in this practice.

The final image is a close-up of one of the candle flames flickering.

2   INT. LIVING ROOM, AUDREY'S GUEST HOUSE – DAY   2

The camera tracks back from a candle flame as CHARLIE walks into shot. He's a casually dressed, quiet, kindly looking older man. He wanders cautiously around the room. Occasionally he stops for a brief moment, stares into space or listens intently, then moves on. He's watched by AUDREY, an anxious looking lady. Suddenly he stops.

> CHARLIE
> *There's something here.*

3   EXT. ABANDONED CHURCH – DAY   3

We see SARAH as she walks into the overgrown churchyard. SARAH is a tall, quiet young woman in her late twenties. She pauses for a moment to get her breath back. She rummages in her bag, gets out a Dictaphone and talks into it.

> SARAH
> (To the Dictaphone)
> *I'm now at the abandoned church, on the outskirts of the village.*
> *All the stories begin here.*

SARAH walks around the side of the church

> SARAH (CONT'D)
> *You can clearly see the restoration work on the tower.*

4   INT. LIVING ROOM, AUDREY'S GUEST HOUSE – CONTINUOUS 4

CHARLIE is standing where we last left him and is concentrated and still. He shuts his eyes tightly as he tries to focus on something we can't see.

> CHARLIE
> *Gently does it . . . Gently.*

He eases his pace a little.

> AUDREY
> *What . . . who is it?*

> CHARLIE
> *There's an extremely agitated young man here. He's a manservant for a wealthy family. It's 1900. He lived here, on this site. 'Hurry up' he says. He's very impatient to move on, that's why you've had so many disturbances. (Pause) It was a sudden death. He was murdered. He'd seen something he shouldn't have, a meeting. He saw them rape and murder a young woman. He tried to help her. He's been stuck for a long time now, he can't bear it any more.*

There is a loud rap at the door.

5   INT. CHURCH – MAIN BODY – DAY   5

The door swings open and SARAH enters the main body of the church. It's a beautiful, deserted chapel lined with large stain glass windows. SARAH's entrance and the opening and closing of the main doors disturbs the dust, which only serves to thicken the already cold and sinister atmosphere. At the other end of the church three steps lead up to the altar, which is partly covered by dust sheets.

> SARAH
> *Wow.*

Throughout the following SARAH is 'watched' by something inside the church. She wanders slowly down the main body. She climbs the three steps to the huge marble altar.

> SARAH
> *It's beautiful.*

She takes a picture of the altar. She is still being 'watched'.

6   INT. LIVING ROOM, AUDREY'S GUEST HOUSE – CONTINUOUS   6

CHARLIE and AUDREY have been joined by ANNE, AUDREY's daughter. CHARLIE is still very concentrated and tense.

> ANNE
> (Whispering)
> *Is he OK, Mum?*

> AUDREY
> *Shhh.*

CHARLIE continues.

> CHARLIE
> *Someone's coming. It's his wife, he's overjoyed to see her. She's leading him through a gate into a beautiful garden. I can see a light in the distance. She says she's taking care of him now. He's thanking us again and again. He's taking her hand and walking into the light.*

CHARLIE stops, exhausted. AUDREY looks stunned.

> CHARLIE (CONT'D)
> *He's gone.*

7   INT. RETRO-CHAPEL OF THE CHURCH – CONTINUOUS   7

SARAH is examining a faded symbol on the wall (the same one that appeared in the title sequence) and is talking again to the Dictaphone.

> SARAH
> *There's a fine example of the crossed circle, on the wall in the Retro-Chapel.*

She's being 'watched' again. She's about to continue talking when she notices her Dictaphone has stopped working. She shakes it. Nothing.

> SARAH (CONT'D)
> *Damn!*

She opens her bag, and takes out a notebook. She starts sketching the symbol. Behind her, what appear to be natural shadows on the wall, start slowly creeping in.

8   INT. DINING ROOM, AUDREY'S GUEST HOUSE – DAY   8

CHARLIE is now sat having tea with AUDREY and ANNE.

> AUDREY
> *It was remarkable, remarkable. I can't get over it.*

ANNE
How long have you been doing this Mr Fielding?

CHARLIE
About twenty years now. My wife, Emily, encouraged me; we worked together.

AUDREY
Lovely, and does she still accompany you sometimes?

CHARLIE
She passed over two years ago.

AUDREY
Oh, I'm sorry. (beat) *Are you still able to . . . communicate with her?*

ANNE
Mum!

CHARLIE
(Quietly)
No.

He finishes his tea and stands.

CHARLIE (CONT'D)
I really should be going.

ANNE
Are you sure you won't take any money?

CHARLIE
No thank you, no. You won't be bothered again, Mrs Hicks.

AUDREY
I'm so grateful. It's been very frightening.

CHARLIE suddenly stumbles, and clutches at the chair.

9   EXT. OUTSIDE AUDREY'S GUEST HOUSE – DAY   9

SARAH is walking up the path to the front door of AUDREY's guest house. She opens it and goes in.

10   INT. DINING ROOM, AUDREY'S GUEST HOUSE – CONTINUOUS 10

CHARLIE is sitting at the dining room table.

ANNE
Are you all right to drive?

CHARLIE
Yes, thank you, it's quite usual. I'll be fine after a rest.

SARAH enters the room.

SARAH
Oh, I'm sorry.

AUDREY
That's quite all right, Miss Anderson. Mr. Fielding is just leaving. He's a ghostbuster you know.

ANNE
Parapsychologist, Mum.

CHARLIE
(to Sarah)
Nice to meet you. (To Audrey & Anne) *Forgive me but I really must be going.*

ANNE
I'll see you out.

SARAH
(to Audrey)
Could I possibly have some tea?

AUDREY
I'll bring it right up.

11   INT. SARAH'S BEDROOM, AUDREY'S GUEST HOUSE – EVENING   11

It's early evening. We see an empty tea cup. SARAH is sat typing up notes on a laptop from her notebook. She rubs her eyes and pours herself a glass of water. She returns to her laptop to see her work has been replaced by the symbol from the church. She presses a few keys. Nothing happens. She opens her notebook to look at her earlier sketch of the symbol. On the walls behind her, faint images of the symbol glow gently, then fade again.

12   INT. DINING ROOM, AUDREY'S GUEST HOUSE – EVENING   12

AUDREY and ANNE are setting the table for dinner.

ANNE
Will our guest be joining us for dinner, Mum?

AUDREY
I shouldn't think so.

ANNE
How long is she staying?

AUDREY
Until she finishes her research, I suppose.

ANNE
She keeps herself to herself doesn't she.

AUDREY
She doesn't seem to have any family or friends. I think she's rather lonely.

AUDREY and ANNE hear a crash from upstairs.

13   INT. SARAH'S BEDOOM – CONTINUOUS   13

SARAH is standing in the middle of the room, breathing hard. There's a menacing atmosphere. On the floor lies all the items from her desk. She's being 'watched' by something. There's a loud knocking at the door.

ANNE (FILTERED)
(Through the door)
Miss Anderson? Are you all right?

SARAH runs to the door and tries to open it – but the door won't open. The walls again come alive with the glowing symbol, of various sizes, all around the room.

ANNE (FILTERED)
(Through door)
Miss Anderson, open the door!

SARAH
I can't . . . it won't . . .

ANNE (FILTERED)
(Through door)
The key, Mum . . . have you got the key!

A high pitched sound and distorted chanting and whispers fill the room. The symbols glow brighter, piercing the atmosphere. SARAH clutches her ears as the noise reaches its crescendo. The door flies open and ANNE and AUDREY enter the room. As they do everything returns to normal. They look around the room stunned.

AUDREY
Oh my!

14   INT. CHARLIE'S HOUSE – EVENING   14

It is 6.06 p.m. We slowly track and see a close-up of a clock and several different photos of CHARLIE and his wife, EMILY. She is a serene woman. We see their wedding day and pictures of her laughing. The impression is of a loving and caring wife, she and CHARLIE obviously had a close relationship. We end on CHARLIE dozing in a chair. He awakes, as if he's sensed something.

The phone rings.

15   INT. SARAH'S BEDROOM, AUDREY'S GUEST HOUSE – EVENING 15

CHARLIE is wandering slowly around SARAH's bedroom. He is concentrating hard, exactly as he did in the first scene.

AUDREY and ANNE watch him nervously from the doorway. He stops suddenly.

>   CHARLIE
>   *No, there's nothing here.*

He sees SARAH's notebook on the floor and notices the sketch of the symbol.

16   INT. LIVING ROOM, AUDREY'S GUEST HOUSE – EVENING   16

SARAH is sat quietly in the lounge as CHARLIE, AUDREY & ANNE enter.

>   ANNE
>   *I'm sorry if we've wasted your time.*

>   CHARLIE
>   *That's quite all right.*

CHARLIE is still holding the notebook.

>   CHARLIE (CONT'D)
>   *Miss Anderson, what do you know about this symbol?*

17   INT. RETRO-CHAPEL OF THE CHURCH – NIGHT   17

CHARLIE and SARAH are looking at the symbol. It is cold and dark and they carry torches.

>   SARAH
>   *I've come across it several times in the village. This is the clearest*
>   *example.*

> CHARLIE
> *It's an alchemic symbol meaning purification by fire.*

SARAH remains silent, she is wary of CHARLIE.

> CHARLIE (CONT'D)
> *I understand that you're researching the history of this village?*

> SARAH
> *Yes.*

> CHARLIE
> *Are you writing a book?*

> SARAH
> *No. It's just for me, something I needed to do, it's just tricky separating fact from fiction.*

> CHARLIE
> (beat) *You don't trust me do you?*

> SARAH
> *I find all of this psychic stuff hard to swallow.*

> CHARLIE
> *I remember the first time I saw a ghost.*

> SARAH
> *What did you do?*

> CHARLIE
> *Ran like hell – but you get used to it. In fact I don't know what I'd do without them now. There are some spirits I'd give anything to see.* (Beat) *They come for a reason, Sarah, they come for our help.*

Suddenly the whisperings start again from the main body of the church.

18   INT. CHURCH – MAIN BODY – NIGHT   18

CHARLIE and SARAH enter the main chapel. The atmosphere is tense and oppressive. The whisperings continue.

> CHARLIE
> *There's a lot of energy here.*

He moves slowly to the centre of the chapel, looking around him as the whisperings seem to come from everywhere.

> CHARLIE (CONT'D)
> *There's 20, maybe 30 souls. It's an old energy. They're wary of us.*

A shadow crosses across SARAH's back and a sudden breeze blows through her hair. SARAH spins around.

> SARAH
> *I'm going back to the car.*

In the background we see CHARLIE stumble again, SARAH rushes towards him.

> SARAH
> *Are you OK?*

19   INT/EXT. A CAR AT THE ABANDONED CHURCH – NIGHT   19

AUDREY and ANNE are sat waiting in the car.

> ANNE
> *They've been gone a long time.*

> AUDREY
> *I used to come here as a girl every Sunday – it was never a welcoming place. I still remember the day they closed it.*

ANNE looks to AUDREY who stares silently at the silhouette of the church against the night sky.

20   INT. CHURCH – MAIN BODY – CONTINUOUS   20

CHARLIE is sat, recovering. SARAH next to him. The church is quiet again.

> CHARLIE
> *I'm all right. It's a little overwhelming in here.*

He turns to SARAH.

> CHARLIE (CONT'D)
> *Sarah, what do you know about this church?*

> SARAH
> *A lot happened here. The most commonly repeated story talks about the turn of the century, when the tower fell.*

CHARLIE is now very concentrated.

> CHARLIE
> *There's a storm overhead. They're meeting here, they met once a month.*

> SARAH
> *There was a religious group of some kind.*

CHARLIE
The only pure religion they say.

SARAH
It was made up of men from the village.

CHARLIE
They're here to cleanse the area. They have to rid it of the unwanted. They say that they don't deserve to live.

SARAH
They performed some kind of ritual here.

CHARLIE
They have a young woman. Wait! I know this, the young man earlier today, the manservant, this is what he saw.

A menacing hum and distorted whisperings and chanting begins.

SARAH
What's going on?

FLASHBACKS (as in the opening credit sequence, brief snapshots of the ritual): Hooded figures circle the pentacle. A hooded figure, his face in silhouette, turns to look into camera.

CHARLIE
The woman is brought forward.

FLASHBACK: A rope binds the woman's wrists.

CHARLIE (CONT'D)
The ritual begins.

FLASHBACKS: Various items of the ritual are displayed on the altar. A hooded figure drinks from an ornate bowl. The woman's dress is torn.

CHARLIE (CONT'D)
They have to make her see the truth, the purity.

FLASHBACKS: A necklace of the symbol is tied around the woman's neck. A hooded figure blesses an ornate knife. The woman lies dead.

CHARLIE (CONT'D)
The storm is directly overhead.

FLASHBACK: The spire is hit by lightning.

CHARLIE (CONT'D)
They're trapped, they're trying to find a way out.

FLASHBACK: Feet run through frame, smoke and dust.

CHARLIE (CONT'D)
There's a fire.

FLASHBACKS: Panic from the hooded figures. Objects are knocked over. The last hooded figure falls to the floor as flames consume the building.

CHARLIE (CONT'D)
There was nowhere to go. There was no escape.

SARAH
I can see them.

The group of hooded figures appear in the church.

FLASHBACK: The camera pans up from the symbol around the woman's neck and finishes on her face. It is SARAH. We cross-fade onto SARAH'S face in present day. The ghostly figures are now gathered around her.

CHARLIE
They've waited a long time for you, Sarah, they need your forgiveness.

The figures slowly remove their hoods and look towards SARAH.

SARAH
(Quietly)
I know.

SARAH walks away and the hooded figures turn and follow her. CHARLIE watches as they all fade away. The church is now peaceful and calm, moonlight filters in through the windows as CHARLIE stands alone.

21   INT. LOUNGE, AUDREY'S GUEST HOUSE – DAY   21

It is the following day. ANNE is talking to the POLICE.

POLICEWOMAN
I'm sure there's a rational explanation and she'll turn up safe and well . . .

ANNE
If you hear anything please let us know.

POLICEMAN
We will, Miss Hicks.

22 INT. SARAH'S BEDROOM, AUDREY'S GUEST HOUSE – DAY   22

AUDREY is sat quietly in SARAH's room, she is holding SARAH's notebook. She puts the notebook on the table and leaves the room. We focus on SARAH's sketch of the symbol from the church. It slowly fades from the page.

23 INT. CHARLIE'S FRONT ROOM – DAY   23

CHARLIE is sat in his chair, he is lost in thought. We see a photo of him and his wife on a table next to him. Suddenly it shifts slightly, by itself. CHARLIE looks at the picture and straightens it. As he does, the room fills with light and we see the shimmering figure of the woman in the picture, his wife. CHARLIE slowly stands.

> CHARLIE
> *Emily . . .*

EMILY smiles gently as another shimmering figure joins her. It is SARAH. He watches as the two figures smile at him. We end on a close-up of CHARLIE's face as the reflected light on him fades and the room returns to normal.

THE END

ROLL CREDITS

Appendix B – Shot list notes – Simon Corris

Page 7

The following examples are taken from my original shot list. I formatted the script as you see it, to give myself room to write my notes, and spent the weekend working through the script, writing down each shot as I saw the movie unfolding. It seemed the most logical way of communicating my thoughts to the production office. They were then able to break down the script and make the schedule for production.

Having prepared this shot list it slowly developed as I thought more about the film and worked through each location with Gavin (DoP), Rod (camera operator) and the actors on set.

1 This three-shot establishes on the previous page and is a reminder here that the scene is covered.
2 This shot and the single on Audrey was cut in the edit. Focusing so closely on Sarah at this point gave the line much more weight than it needed. The scene is basically Sarah and Charlie meeting for the first time and how they react to each other – Charlie's curiosity and Sarah's awkwardness. Ending the scene with Charlie's reaction shot was right for the scene.
3 I put a note in here as the idea of using a digital camera and downloading images to Sarah's laptop developed through pre-production. I also found in the edit that I could cut Sarah's POV of the church tower in the first scene and use it here in one of her photographs. I liked the idea of keeping some information from the audience and giving it to them at unexpected moments. This is something that was used a couple of times in the film and adds to the mystery.
4 Another change to the script after previewing the film. It was felt more dramatic to delay the appearance of the symbols on the wall until the next bedroom sequence. A shame, really, as it was my favourite shot. Originally I wanted to see the symbols appear behind Sarah, cut away to the exterior shot of her bedroom window, see the light in the window fade slowly as the camera moves away and takes us into the next scene, leaving

the audience wondering what was going on in Sarah's bedroom. In fact if you look closely at the exterior shot of the bedroom window you can still see the action of the light fading – but no one ever notices.

5 We dropped a location close to filming and so the kitchen subsequently became the dining room. What I was most pleased about was that it made this shot much more interesting. Originally the shot was to tilt down from the bedroom window and look into the kitchen window and then cut inside for the rest of the scene. Our new location had a lovely staircase in full view of the window and so I could now get Anne to walk down the stairs and into the dining room during the shot. Sarah's bedroom window is actually the window to a small bathroom of the house we shot at. As it was so small it gave us a few set-up problems and contributed to us losing the night shot of the church because of failing light.

6 A minor blocking change during rehearsal on set. The transfer onto Audrey happens slightly earlier.

Page 12

1 I marked in my script the sound design elements I had in mind. It was also a useful reminder on set when we rehearsed and I tried to convey to the actors just what would be happening around them. It's surprising what you can forget in the heat of the moment.

2 This shot was removed in editing to help move the story along quicker.

3 The crane shot here was the shot we just lost because of failing light. The car was in place, the track and dolly set but we missed the shot by minutes. The shot we use in its place was picked up on the Saturday afternoon after we wrapped. Gavin (DoP), Adam (camera assistant) and myself stayed on to grab a couple of extra shots.

4 This shot changed as Gavin and I walked through each set-up during pre-production and became what you see in the finished film.

5 These lines were cut after the first read-through.

Page 15

1 The flashback sequence (to Sarah in the past) was moved during editing and placed here.

2 After the change in location this scene became the lounge of the guest house. It was also the scene that suffered most in production and was cut from the film after the previews. As you can see, I'd planned to cover the scene from several angles. Owing to lack of time on the day I dropped two

of the shots and covered the scene from the first set-up. The scene always looked rushed and there were no options in the edit to try and make it work. Although it may well have been cut it still would have been nice to have given the scene a chance. I also thought it would have been nice to hear the police exit and walk away over the shot of Audrey alone in Sarah's bedroom.

3 One of the effects shots. We had a total of 22 digital effects in the film, kindly done by CFC (The Computer Film Company) in London. Try and spot them all.

① 3 Shot
Audrey, Charlie e Anne.

GHOSTHUNTER

CHARLIE (CONT'D)
Anne) Forgive me but I really must
be going.

ANNE
I'll see you out.

② MS Sarah

SARAH
(to Audrey)
Could I possibly have some tea?

Single Audrey

AUDREY
I'll bring it right up.

---

11   INT. SARAH'S BEDROOM - EVENING   11

Cu tea, track across room into
overshoulder of Sarah and her laptop
REVERSE: Tilt up from
Keyboard.
Pan with Sarah
as she pours water.

③

* SARAH possibly
transferring digital
Skills onto her laptop.

It's early evening. We see an empty
tea cup. SARAH is sat typing up
notes on a laptop from her
notebook. She rubs her eyes and
gets up and pours herself a glass
of water. She returns to her laptop
to see her work has been replaced
by the symbol from the church. She
presses a few keys. Nothing
happens. Her notebook is open on
her earlier sketch of the symbol.
She picks it up. On the walls
behind her, faint images of the
symbol glow gently, then fade
again.

④

⑤

Exterior Shot of Sarah's bedroom
Window down onto kitchen window.
We See Anne e Audrey inside.

MS Anne, Audrey in background.

12   INT. KITCHEN OF AUDREY'S B&B -
EVENING   12

AUDREY and ANNE are setting the
table for dinner.

ANNE
Will our guest be joining us for
dinner, mum?

AUDREY
I shouldn't think so.

⑥

Track with Anne e
Transfer to Audrey as
Anne leaves frame.

ANNE
How long is she staying?

AUDREY
Until she finishes her research, I
think.

(More)

Page 7

Continued: ①

SARAH
I'm going back to the car.

In the background we see CHARLIE
stumble again, SARAH rushes towards
him.

Background noise.

MCU Charlie, as Sarah enters the frame.

SARAH
Are you OK?

19   INT/EXT. A CAR AT THE ABANDONED
      CHURCH - NIGHT   19

Single Anne in profile in the rear of the car.

AUDREY and ANNE are sat waiting in
the car.

Track with Anne as she leans forward.
Transfer onto Audrey in front passenger seat.
Push into Audrey through her dialogue.

ANNE
They've been gone a long time.

AUDREY
I used to come here as a girl every
Sunday - it was never a welcoming
place. I still remember the day
they closed it.

②
2 shot through front windscreen as Anne sits back
③
Crane up over roof
of car and frame church.

ANNE looks to AUDREY who stares
silently at the silhouette of the
church against the night sky.

20   INT. CHURCH - MAIN BODY -
      CONTINUOUS   20

④
2 shot tracking around
Charlie & Sarah.

CHARLIE is sat, recovering. SARAH
next to him. The church is quiet
again.

CHARLIE
I'm alright. It's a little
overwhelming in here.

He turns to SARAH.

CHARLIE (CONT'D)
Sarah, what do you know about this
church?

MS Sarah

SARAH   ⑤
A lot happened here, ~~but it's~~
~~shrouded in rumour and~~
~~superstition.~~ The most commonly
repeated story talks about the turn

(More)

GHOSTHUNTER

Continued:

figures are now gathered around
her.

cu Charlie.

CHARLIE
They've waited a long time for you,
Sarah, they need your forgiveness.

①

MS Sarah e Ghosts.

The figures slowly remove their
hoods and look towards SARAH.

cu Sarah.
cu Charlie.
MS Sarah e Ghosts.

SARAH
(Quietly)
I know.

SARAH walks away and the hooded
figures turn and follow her.
CHARLIE watches as they all fade
away. The church is now peaceful
and calm, moonlight filters in
through the windows as CHARLIE
stands alone.

WS Charlie.

②

Crossfade into window
pull back as policewoman walks
through frame.
Track with Anne, past policeman.

21   INT. KITCHEN OF AUDREY'S B&B – DAY21

It is the following day. ANNE is
talking to the POLICE.

POLICEWOMAN
I'm sure there's a rational
explanation and she'll turn up safe
and well..

2 shot Anne e policewoman.

ANNE
If you hear anything please let us
know.

Single Policeman. Follow into
3 shot and exit.

POLICEMAN
We will, Miss Hicks.

22   INT. SARAH'S ROOM AT THE B&B – DAY22

WS Audrey e room.

Track with Audrey
and transfer onto notebook.
Slow track and crane up over
notebook as Audrey exits.

AUDREY is standing in SARAH's room,
she is holding SARAH's notebook.
She feels a slight chill, shivers
and closes the window. She puts the
notebook on the table and leaves
the room. A breeze flicks through
the pages revealing the symbol from
the church. It slowly fades from
the page. ③

Page 15

Appendix C – Designer's sketches

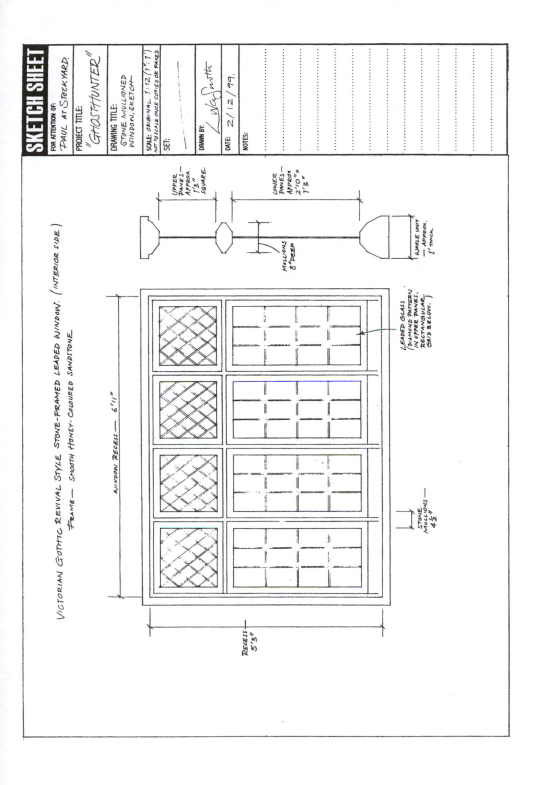

SKETCH SHEET

FOR ATTENTION OF:
PAUL at STOCKYARD.

PROJECT TITLE: "GHOSTHUNTER"

DRAWING TITLE: STONE MULLIONED WINDOW, SKETCH

SCALE: ORIGINAL 1:12 (1":1')
NOT TO SCALE ONCE COPIED OR FAXED

SET: —

DRAWN BY: Luke Smith

DATE: 2/12/99.

NOTES:

VICTORIAN GOTHIC REVIVAL STYLE STONE-FRAMED LEADED WINDOW. (INTERIOR SIDE)
FRAME — SMOOTH HONEY-COLOURED SANDSTONE.

UPPER PANES — APPROX. 1'3" SQUARE

LOWER PANES APPROX 2'10" x 1'3"

MULLIONS 8" DEEP

WHOLE UNIT — APPROX. 1" THICK.

LEADED GLASS (DIAMOND PATTERN IN UPPER PANES, RECTANGULAR GRID BELOW.)

WINDOW RECESS — 6'11"

STONE MULLIONS 4½"

RECESS — 5'3"

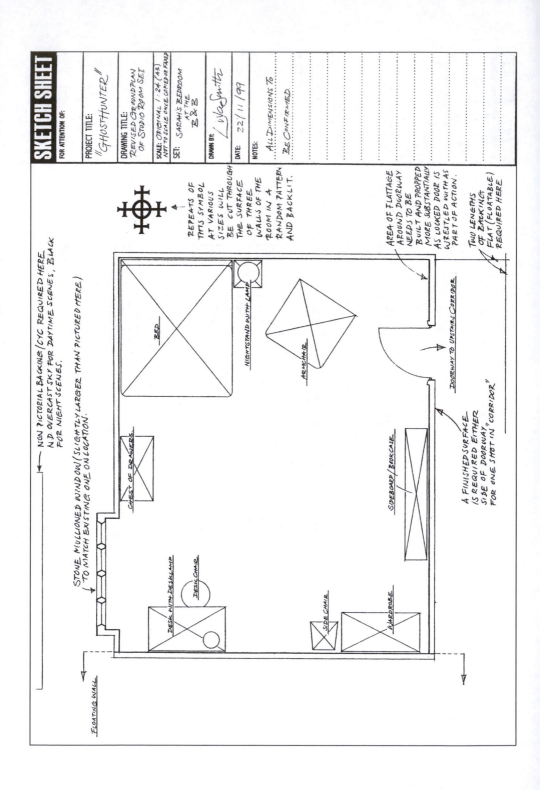

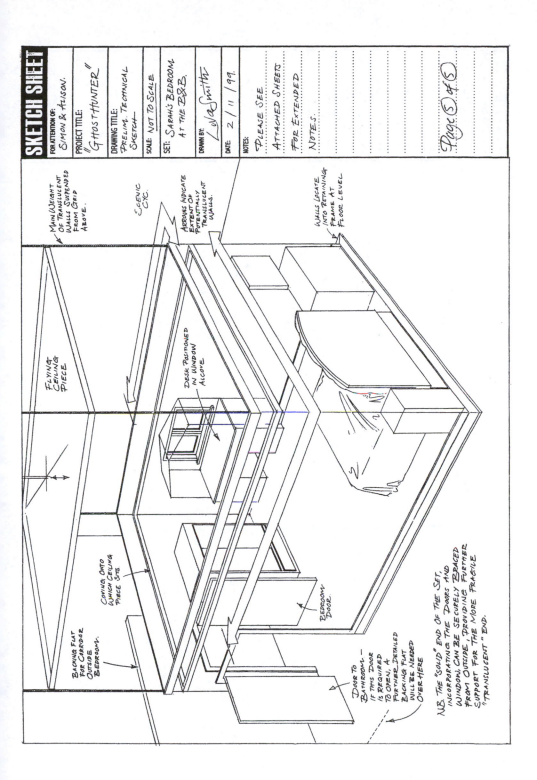

SKETCH SHEET

FOR ATTENTION OF:
Simon & Alison.

PROJECT TITLE:
"Ghosthunter"

DRAWING TITLE:
Prelim. Technical Sketch.

SCALE: *Not to Scale*

SET: *Sarah's Bedroom at the B&B.*

DRAWN BY: *Lola Smith*

DATE: *2 / 11 / 99.*

NOTES:
Please see attached sheets for extended notes.

Page ⑤ of ⑤

Main weight of translucent walls suspended from grid above.

Scenic cyc.

Arrows indicate extent of potentially translucent walls.

Walls locate into retaining frame at floor level.

Flying ceiling piece.

Desk positioned in window alcove.

Coving onto which ceiling piece sits.

Backing flat for corridor outside bedroom.

Bedroom door.

Door to bathroom — if this door is required to open, a further detailed backing flat will be needed over here.

N.B. The "solid" end of the set, incorporating the doors and window, can be securely braced from outside, providing further support for the more fragile "translucent" end.

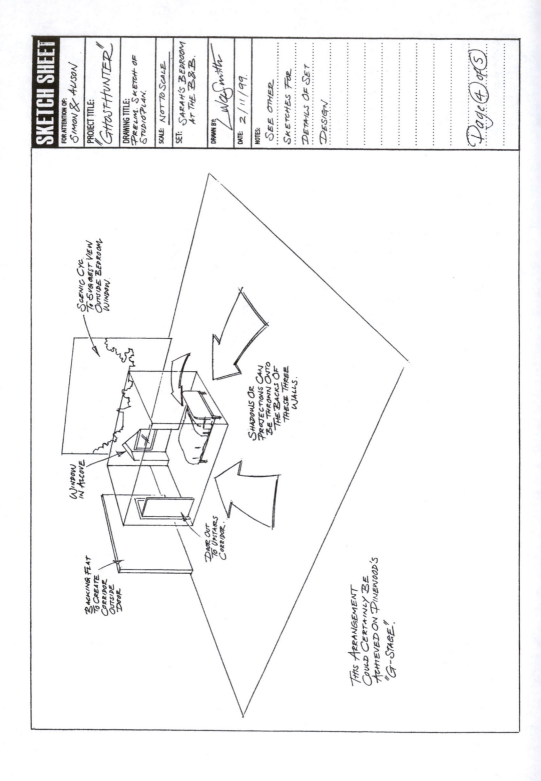

SKETCH SHEET

FOR ATTENTION OF:
SIMON & ALISON

PROJECT TITLE:
"GHOSTHUNTER"

DRAWING TITLE:
PRELIM. SKETCH OF
STUDIO PLAN.

SCALE: NOT TO SCALE

SET: SARAH'S BEDROOM
AT THE B&B.

DRAWN BY: L.W.Smith

DATE: 2/11/99.

NOTES:
SEE OTHER
SKETCHES FOR
DETAILS OF SET
DESIGN

Page 4 of 5

SCENIC CYC.
TO SUGGEST VIEW
OUTSIDE BEDROOM
WINDOW.

WINDOW
IN ALCOVE

BACKING FLAT
TO CREATE
CORRIDOR
OUTSIDE
DOOR.

DOOR OUT
TO UPSTAIRS
CORRIDOR.

SHADOWS OR
PROJECTIONS CAN
BE THROWN ONTO
THE BACKS OF
THESE THREE
WALLS.

THIS ARRANGEMENT
COULD CERTAINLY BE
ACHIEVED ON PINEWOOD'S
"G-STAGE".

Appendix D – Special effects list

Ghosthunter

Shot	Seq	Shot Description	Shot Status	Current	Scan info with cut lengths (scroll for more info)
sc1_vfx1	1	w/s lightning behind tower	cloud plate still from quantel remains to be scanned	action: underexp day for night FX plate: norm exp FX plate: clouds	yes no 10
Slate		scan icl cutters:	–8 to 8		
sc1_vfx2	2	lightning in rose window	2 scanned	action: front lit w' candle flicker FX plate: win backlit w' strobe FX plate –: overexposed flash frame	action_plate/rose_win yes no 123
Slate		scan icl cutters:	–8 to 8		
sc7_vfx3	3	moving shadow on wall	2 more to scan!!!	action: Sarah sketches FX plate: shad 1:1.85 FX plate –: no shad 1:1.85 FX plate – full frame shad	yes no 502
Slate		scan icl cutters:	–8 to 8		
sc13_vfx4	4	symbols on bedroom wall appear	not scanning yet!	action: Sarah @ laptop	
Slate		scan icl cutters:	to		
sc13_vfx6	5	symbols on bedroom wall cut 1		action: Sarah runs to door (scan ghost/sc13_vfx6_7_8/ action_plate/raw shared)	yes no 490
Slate		scan icl cutters:	–8 to 8		

Slate	#	Description	Scan icl cutters	Notes	Action / FX			
sc13_vfx7	6	symbols on bedroom wall cut 1	scan icl cutters:	−8 to 8	action: Sarah falls to knees cut 1 (scan ghost/sc13_vfx6_7_8/ action_plate/raw shared)	yes	no	490
sc13_vfx8	7	symbols on bedroom wall cut 1	scan icl cutters:	−8 to 8	action Sarah falls to knees cut 2 (scan ghost/sc13_vfx6_7_8/ action_plate/raw shared)	yes	no	490
sc18_vfx9	8	ghost crosses in f/g	scan icl cutters:	−8 to 8	action: Sarah spins round FX plate: figure crosses in f/g (clean plate @ head)	yes	no	139
sc20_vfx10	9	m/s lightning hits tower	scan icl cutters:	reuse material from vfx1 −8 to 8	action: underexp day for night FX plate: norm exp FX plate: clouds	no	no	10
sc20_vfx11	10	figure in flames	scan icl cutters:	pending flames video ref due in Friday 26.5.00 morning −8 to 8	action: hooded figure FX: flames	yes	no	30
sc20_vfx12	11	ghosts appear, fading into scene cut 1	scan icl cutters:	look at video – are 12 & 13 the same? smoke beta ref due in Fri 26.5.00 −8 to 8	action: ghosts move into position FX: smoke plate FX: clean pass smoke scan expected to be shared over vfx 12, 13, 14	no	no	126

sc20_vfx13	12	Sarah walks into position cut 2	smoke beta ref due in Fri 26.5.00 grading required at 8-bit lin conv	action: ghosts move into position action: Sarah walks into position FX: smoke plate, FX: clean pass smoke scan expected to be shared over vfx 12, 13, 14	no	no	147
Slate		scan icl cutters:	–8 to 8				
sc20_vfx14	13	Sarah standing in front of ghosts cut 3	smoke beta ref due in Fri 26.5.00 grading required at 8-bit lin conv	action: ghosts move into position action: Sarah walks into position FX: smoke plate, FX: clean pass smoke scan expected to be shared over vfx 12, 13, 14	no	no	147
Slate		scan icl cutters:	–8 to 8				
sc20_vfx15	14	cu Sarah. Ghosts OS cut 1	GHOST PLATE QUERY grading required at 8-bit lin conv	action: Sarah turns cut 1 FX – can use any ghost plate	yes	no	131
Slate		scan icl cutters:	–8 to 8				
sc20_vfx16	15	cu Sarah. Ghosts OS cut 2	GHOST PLATE QUERY grading required at 8-bit lin conv	action: Sarah turns back cut 2 FX – can use any ghost plate	yes	no	51
Slate		scan icl cutters:	–8 to 8				

Appendix D – Special effects list (*Continued*)

Slate	#	Description	action / FX notes	grading			
sc20_vfx17	16	Sarah & ghosts exit	action: ghosts turn & exit action: Sarah turns & exits FX – smoke plate with light FX FX – clean plate with light FX	grading required at 8-bit lin conv	no	no	451
Slate		scan icl cutters:		−8 to 8			
sc20_vfx18	17	CU notepad & symbol	action: with cam move FX clean pad – locked off @ tail	grading required at 8-bit lin conv to			
Slate		scan icl cutters:					
sc23_vfx19	18	Emily's ghost cut 1	action: Emily FX clean pad – locked off @ tail	−8 to 8	yes	no	114
Slate		scan icl cutters:		−8 to 8			
sc23_vfx20	19	Emily fg, Sarah enters bg, cut 2	action: Emily as Sarah enters FX: clean @ tail	check on video	yes	no	10
Slate		scan icl cutters:		−8 to 8			
sc23_vfx21	20	Emily fg, Sarah enters bg, cut 2	action: Emily and Sarah begin to fade away FX: clean plate @ tail		yes	no	10
Slate		scan icl cutters:		−8 to 8			
poss	21	Fishing wire on picture		to			
Slate		scan icl cutters:					

Appendix E – The budget

Acct#	Category Title	Page	Total
006–00	Producer/Director	1	£2,400
007–00	Artists	1	£5,000
	Total Above-The-Line		**£7,400**
009–00	Production Unit Salaries	1	£4,048
010–00	Asst Directors/Continuity	1	£1,918
011–00	Crew – Camera	1	£3,791
012–00	Crew – Sound	1	£1,190
013–00	Crew – Lighting	2	£1,750
014–00	Crew – Art Department	2	£8,177
015–00	Crew – Ward/Make-up/Hair	2	£2,878
016–00	Crew – Editing	2	£1,018
018–00	Stills Photographer	2	£1,000
019–00	Materials – Art Dept	2	£2,700
020–00	Materials – Ward/Up/Hair	2	£950
021–00	Production Equipment	3	£13,683
022–00	Viewing Theatre	3	£700
023–00	Locations	3	£1,500
025–00	Film/Tape Stock	3	£4,700
026–00	Pic/Sound Post-Prod Film	4	£450
027–00	Master Tape	4	£150
028–00	Stills	4	£150
029–00	Rostrum/Graphics	4	£800
030–00	Music	4	£1,000
031–00	Travel/Transport	4	£1,241
032–00	Catering	4	£1,400
034–00	Insurance/Finance/Legal	4	£1,150
035–00	Production Overheads	5	£1,150
	Contingency: 10.00%		£7,622
	Total Production		**£76,444**
	TOTAL ABOVE-THE-LINE		**£7,400**
	TOTAL BELOW-THE-LINE		**£76,444**
	TOTAL ABOVE & BELOW-THE-LINE		**£83,844**
	GRAND TOTAL		**£83,844**

Acct#	Description	Amount	Units	X	Rate	Subtotal	Total
006–00	**Producer/Director**						
006–02	Producer – Expenses Only						
		6	Weeks		200	1,200	£1,200
006–04	Director – Expenses Only						
		6	Weeks		200	1,200	£1,200
					Total For 006–00		**£2,400**
007–00	**Artists**						
007–01	Artists						
	Sarah	5	Days		200	1,000	
	Emily	1	Day		200	200	
	Charlie	5	Days		200	1,000	
	Audrey	5	Days		200	1,000	
	Anne	5	Days		200	1,000	£4,200
007–02	Extras						
	Hooded men	1	Day	8	100	800	£800
					Total For 007–00		**£5,000**
	Total Above-The-Line						**£7,400**
009–00	**Production Unit Salaries**						
009–03	Production Co-ordinator	3	Weeks		509	1,527	£1,527
009–04	Production Assistant						
	Production Assistant 1						
	(BECTU 40 H . . .	3	Weeks		347	1,041	£1,041
009–06	Unit Runner						
	Runners	2	Weeks	3	180	1,080	£1,080
009–07	Production Accountant						
	Flat Fee		Allow		400	400	£400
					Total For 009–00		**£4,048**
010–00	**Asst Directors/Continuity**						
010–01	First Assistant Director						
	1st AD	7	Days		127	889	£889
010–02	Second Assistant Director						
	2nd AD	7	Days		102	714	£714
010–03	Third Assistant Director						
	3rd AD	5	Days		63	315	£315
					Total For 010–00		**£1,918**
011–00	**Crew – Camera**						
	Director of Photography/						
011–01	Camera Ope . . .						
	Set Fee		Allow		1,000	1,000	£1,000
011–02	Supervising DOP –						
	Special advisor		Allow		600	600	£600
011–04	Focus Puller						
	Focus Puller	6	Days		111	666	£666

Acct#	Description	Amount	Units	X	Rate	Subtotal	Total
011–00	**Crew – Camera** (*Cont.*)						
011–05	Clapper Loader						
	Clapper Loader	5	Days		84	420	£420
011–06	Key Grip						
	Grip	7	Days		111	777	£777
011–07	Asst Grip/Crane Operator						
	Assistant grip re extra crane	1	Day		111	111	
	Crane operator	1	8 hrs		217.38	217	£328
					Total For 011–00		**£3,791**
012–00	**Crew – Sound**						
012–01	Sound Recordist						
	Sound Recordist	5	Days		127	635	£635
012–02	Boom Operator						
	Boom	5	Days		111	555	£555
					Total For 012–00		**£1,190**
013–00	**Crew – Lighting**						
013–01	Gaffer						
	Gaffer	5	Days		200	1,000	£1,000
013–02	Electrician 1						
	Electrician	5	Days		150	750	£750
					Total for 013–00		**£1,750**
014–00	**Crew – Art Department**						
	Supervising Designer	1			600	600	£600
014–01	Designer						
	Designer	3	Weeks		800	2,400	£2,400
014–02	Art Director						
	Art Director	3	Weeks		509	1,527	£1,527
014–03	Assistant Art Director						
	Assistant Art Director	2	Weeks		443	886	£886
014–04	Props Master						
	Props	2	Weeks		471	942	£942
014–06	Stand-By Props	7	Days		96	672	£672
014–08	Construction Manager						
	Construction	2	Weeks		575	1,150	£1,150
					Total For 014–00		**£8,177**
015–00	**Crew – Ward/Make-up/Hair**						
015–01	Costume Designer						
	Wardrobe Designer/Mistress	2	Weeks		509	1,018	£1,018
015–03	Wardrobe Assistant 1						
	Wardrobe Assistant	7	Days		96	672	£672
015–07	Make-up Artist						
	Make Up Artist	6	Days		111	666	£666
015–08	Make-up Assistant						
	Make Up Assistant	6	Days		87	522	£522
					Total For 015–00		**£2,878**

Acct#	Description	Amount	Units	X	Rate	Subtotal	Total
016–00	**Crew – Editing**						
016–01	Editor						
	Editor	2	Weeks		509	1,018	£1,018
016–04	Dubbing Editor						
	Included in Studio Price						£0
					Total For 016–00		**£1,018**
018–00	**Stills Photographer**						
018–01	Stills Photographer						
	Stills	5	Days		200	1,000	£1,000
					Total For 018–00		**£1,000**
019–00	**Materials – Art Dept**						
019–01	Sets		Allow		1,500	1,500	£1,500
019–02	Construction Materials		Allow		500	500	£500
019–03	Props Hired		Allow		500	500	£500
019–08	Consumables		Allow		200	200	£200
					Total For 019–00		**£2,700**
020–00	**Materials – Ward/Up/Hair**						
020–01	Costumes Hired						
	Allowance for all costumes		Allow		800	800	£800
020–04	Make-up Materials		Allow		150	150	£150
					Total For 020–00		**£950**
021–00	**Production Equipment**						
021–01	Camera Equipment						
	35mm Camera based on 535						
	Arri	1	Week		2,585	2,585	
	Video Asst	1	Week		763.75	764	
	Lenses		Allow		1,760	1,760	
	Head	1	Week		423	423	
	Short and tall Legs	1	Week		141	141	£5,673
021–02	Camera Consumables						
	Consumables		Allow		50	50	£50
021–03	Grip Equipment						
	Peewee dolly	1	Week		616.88	617	
	30 ft track plus two curves	1	Week		376	376	
	Matt box	1	Week		94	94	
	Paddle Mount	1	Week		29.37	29	£1,116
021–04	Sound Equipment						
	Dat Recorder, SQN, 416,						
	Short and lo . . .		Allow		590	590	£590
021–05	Crane Equipment						
	Crane Marquis 4 ft wide 6.6						
	high 25 ft . . .	1	Day		323	323	
	Remote head	1	Day		470	470	
	Track		Allow		70.50	71	£864

Acct#	Description	Amount	Units	X	Rate	Subtotal	Total
021–00	**Production Equipment** (*Cont.*)						
021–06	Sound Consumables						
	4 DAT tapes	4	tapes		10	40	£40
021–08	Lighting Equipment						
	Allowance for lights		Allow		1,800	1,800	£1,800
021–09	Generator						
	Not sure on size so allowance – possib . . .		Allow		500	500	£500
021–10	Lighting Consumables						
	Allowance		Allow		100	100	£100
021–11	Editing Equipment						
	Avid Edit Suite	2	Weeks		822.50	1,645	£1,645
021–12	Rain making						
	Not sure on size so allowance of		Allow		400	400	£400
021–13	Steadycam						
	Steadycam without operator mk3A	1	Day		705	705	£705
021–14	Radios						
	Radios	1	week		200	200	£200
					Total For 021–00		**£13,683**
022–00	**Viewing Theatre**						
022–01	Allowance for viewing theatre						
	Theatre		Allow		600	600	
	Refreshments		Allow		100	100	£700
					Total For 022–00		**£700**
023–00	**Locations**						
023–01	four locations allowance total						
	location allowance 5 days at £300 per . . .		Allow		1,500	1,500	£1,500
					Total For 023–00		**£1,500**
025–00	**Film/Tape Stock**						
025–01	Shooting Film Stock						
	Kodak 35mm colour stock 1000 ft roll . . .	10	Cans		470	4,700	£4,700
					Total for 025–00		**£4,700**
026–00	**Pic/Sound Post-Prod Film**						
026–01	Negative Developing						
	Neg Developing	9,600	ft		0.20	1,920	
	Mute rushes to Beta SP	9,600	ft		0.22	2,112	£4,032
026–02	Printing						
	Rush print neg cut at 12 mins	1,200	ft		0.64	768	£768

Acct#	Description	Amount	Units	X	Rate	Subtotal	Total
026–00	**Pic/Sound Post-Prod Film** (*Cont.*)						
026–03	Sound Transfer						
	Sound Rushes	1,200	ft		0.11	132	£132
026–04	Opticals						
	Allowance for opticals as depends on . . .		Allow		450	450	£450
026–05	Special Effects on Post Production		Allow		1,500	1,500	£1,500
026–06	Trial and answer prints						
	First Trial Print	1,200	ft		0.69	828	
	Answer Print	1,200	ft		1.13	1,356	£2,184
026–07	Print						
	Print	1,200	ft		0.55	660	
	Allow for extra sound track	1,200	ft		0.11	132	
	Synching charge		Allow		120	120	£912
026–08	Dubbing Theatre						
	Allowance		Allow		1,500	1,500	£1,500
					Total For 026–00		**£11,478**
027–00	**Master Tape**						
027–01	Master Tape grading and tape						
	2 hours allowed plus extra allowance		Allow		450	450	£450
					Total For 027–00		**£450**
028–00	**Stills**						
028–01	Stills stock and processing						
	Stills		Allow		150	150	£150
					Total For 028–00		**£150**
029–00	**Rostrum/Graphics**						
029–01	Rostrum – Credit titles						
	Allow (deal available Howell Opticals f . . .		Allow		800	800	£800
					Total For 029–00		**£800**
030–00	**Music**						
030–01	Composer						
	Allow		Allow		1,000	1,000	£1,000
					Total For 030–00		**£1,000**
031–00	**Travel/Transport**						
031–01	Track re Crane shot						
	Track for large crane as per Grip House	1	Day		141	141	£141

Acct#	Description	Amount	Units	X	Rate	Subtotal	Total
031–00	**Travel/Transport** (*Cont.*)						
031–02	Vans re camera and art department						
	Vans	7	Days	2	50	700	£700
031–03	Travel Allowance reactors/ crew extras		Allow		400	400	£400
					Total For 031–00		**£1,241**
032–00	**Catering**						
032–01	Catering Allow – based on £10 per person		Allow		1,400	1,400	£1,400
					Total For 032–00		**£1,400**
034–00	**Insuarance/Finance/Legal**						
034–01	Insuarance Allowance		Allow		600	600	£600
034–02	Finance – Bank Charges Allow		Allow		50	50	£50
034–03	Legal Fees Allow		Allow		500	500	£500
					Total For 034–00		**£1,150**
035–00	**Production Overheads**						
035–01	Office Equipment and rental Office equipment etc		Allow		500	500	£500
035–02	Telephone Allow		Allow		500	500	£500
035–03	Postage and stationery Allow		Allow		150	150	£150
					Total For 035–00		**£1,150**
	Contingency: 10.00%						£7,622
	Total Production						**£76,444**
	TOTAL ABOVE-THE-LINE						**£7,400**
	TOTAL BELOW-THE-LINE						**£76,444**
	TOTAL ABOVE & BELOW-THE-LINE						**£83,844**
	GRAND TOTAL						**£83,844**

Appendix F – Contracts for cast and crew

ACTORS DEAL MEMORANDUM

N.B. THIS IS A GUIDELINE ONLY AND SHOULD NOT BE RELIED UPON WITHOUT TAKING LEGAL ADVICE.

1.   (a) *the Film Company* ('the Producer')
       (b) *the Actor* ('the Artist')
       (c) *the Agent* ('the Agent')

2.   DATED

3.   FILM

       (*The Film*)

4.   ROLE

       (*The Actor's Character*)

5.   PERIOD OF ENGAGEMENT

       The [Artist] shall provide the Artist's exclusive services:

5.1   During principal photography of the Film which is currently scheduled for _____

5.2   For reasonable periods required for rehearsals, fittings and an interview for the documentary and the like.

5.3   During any period the Artist is providing his services hereunder he/she shall do so to the best of his/her skill and ability at such times for such hours of working and whenever the Producer may require and in accordance with the Producer's instructions provided that the Producer shall not without the Artist's approval (not to be unreasonably withheld) require the Artist to work more than a 12 hour day from arrival on set to release on set.

6.   COMPENSATION

6.1   £_____ (*The Actor's Fee*) to cover the period of engagement and be full consideration for the Artist's services hereunder except as specified in clause 6.2 and 7, and the sum to be payable in 1 instalment within 30 days of completion of filming.

6.2   Previously agreed expenses will be paid at the end of the contract on production of receipts.

7.   OVERAGE

7.1   If the Artist is required to perform services in relation to the shooting of his/her role in excess of the above days chosen by the Producer under clause 5.1 the Producer shall pay the Artist £_____ per day.

7.2   If the Artist is required to perform services in relation to the post-production of the Film (excluding the first post-synchronisation day which shall be free) the Producer shall pay the Artist £_____ per day.

8.   STAND-IN

For any period during which the Artist is providing services the Producer shall provide the Artist with a non-exclusive utility stand-in.

9.   TRAVEL

For any period during which the Artist is providing services the Producer shall provide the Artist with:

9.1   A non-exclusive car between the set and the location to be arranged by the Producer.

10.   CREDIT

Subject to the Artist performing the services hereunder and appearing on screen; the Artist will receive screen credit in the main titles.

11.   PUBLICITY

The Artist shall, subject to his prior approval (not to be unreasonably withheld), provide publicity and promotional services on a second call basis on the same travel basis as set out in this agreement.

12.   <u>VIDEOS</u>

The Artist will be sent one VHS video of the Film as soon as commercially available.

13.   <u>MISCELLANEOUS</u>

13.1   The compensation referred to includes full payment for any overtime and night-shoots and is payable by way of complete buy-out of all rights of whatsoever nature in the Artist's services and no further sums shall be payable by reason of the exploitation of the Film in any and all media throughout the universe.

13.2   All rights in the nature of copyright in the Artist's services are hereby by way of present and future copyright assigned to the Producer absolutely throughout the world for the full period of copyright and all renewals and extensions thereof. The Artist hereby irrevocably grants all necessary Performers Rights under the Copyright Designs and Patents Act 1988 ("the Act") and any subsequent legislation and hereby irrevocably waives all moral rights under the Act subject to the credit provisions hereof. The Artist confirms that the assignment hereunder includes all rental and lending rights under the law of any country whether now or hereinafter and that the consideration hereunder is full and equitable consideration for such rights.

14.   No casual or inadvertent failure by the Producer to accord credit or the failure of a third party to do so shall constitute a breach hereof. The Artist's remedies in the event of a breach of the credit provisions hereof shall be limited to damages and on no account shall the Artist be entitled to enjoin or restrain the exploitation of the Film. The Producer agrees to contractually require third parties to comply with credit provisions set out herein.

15.   All monies shall be paid to the Agent whose receipt shall constitute a full discharge. Any notice to be given hereunder shall be given to the agent and deemed served when delivered if by hand or 48 hours after first class posting or on the day of fax transmission.

16.   The Producer is hereby authorised to use and authorise others to use the Artist's name, approved photograph, approved likeness and voice to promote the Film and in all ancillary exploitation.

17.   The Artist warrants that:

17.1   The Artist is freely able to enter this agreement and comply with its provisions and is not under any obligation to any third party which would conflict or interfere with the services or obligations to be rendered or performed hereunder.

18.   The Artist undertakes to:

18.1   Attend as where and when the Producer may reasonably require for the performance of the Artist's services;

18.2   Render such services as the Producer reasonably requires to the best of the Artist's skill and ability punctuality and willingly as directed by the Producer.

19.   The Producer shall be entitled to assign the benefit of this agreement but shall remain liable for its obligations hereunder.

If you are in agreement with the foregoing, kindly sign the enclosed copy and return it to us at the above address.

Yours sincerely,   Accepted and Agreed

....

For and on behalf of (*The Film Company*)   For and on behalf of (*The Actor*)

GENERAL CREW AGREEMENT

N.B. THIS IS A GUIDELINE ONLY AND SHOULD NOT BE RELIED UPON WITHOUT TAKING LEGAL ADVICE.

FROM: (*Name & Address of Film Company*)

TO: (*Name of Crew Member*)

DATED: _____

Dear (*Name of Crew Member*)

Re (*Name of Film*) **("the Film")**

This is to confirm your engagement by this Company on the following terms and conditions:–

1. We hereby engage and you hereby agree to render your services as (*Crew Member's position*) in connection with the film **("the Film").**

2. Your total fee for all services rendered by you and for all rights granted to us hereunder shall be £_____. The said fee shall constitute full compensation for the exploitation of the products of your services hereunder in all media worldwide. No further pay shall be due. The said fee shall cover all overtime, any no-meal breaks in time, or petty cash in lieu of meal breaks. It will cover all payments for night work, and this fee is inclusive of payment for holiday credits. It will not cover pre-approved expenses, which will be paid at the end of the contract on production of receipts.

3. Your engagement will commence on the ____ day of _____ and terminate on the ____ day of _____.

4. We shall be entitled to your exclusive services throughout the period of your engagement and you agree to render your services to the best of your skill and ability at such times and wherever we may require and in accordance with our instructions.

5. All rights in your services and any products thereof are and shall remain our absolute property and copyright or that of our assignees. You hereby by way of present assignment of both present and future copyright, assign with full guarantee all such products to us to hold throughout the

world for the full period of copyright and all renewals and extensions thereof. You further irrevocably waive the benefits of any rights under Sections 77–85 inclusive of the Copyright Designs and Patents Act 1988 and any provision of law known as "Moral Rights" or any similar laws under any jurisdiction now or hereinafter enacted. You hereby confirm that the above assignment includes an assignment of all rental and lending rights and the compensation payable under this agreement is full and equitable consideration for such rights.

If you are in agreement with the foregoing, kindly sign the enclosed copy of this letter and return it to us at the above address, your payment will then be sent by return of post.

Yours sincerely,   Accepted and Agreed

....

For and on behalf of (*The Film*   For and on behalf of (*the Crew*
Company)   *Member*)

Appendix G – Production forms

Ghosthunter

Movement Order No 1

Locations 1–4: *The Old Convent, Sussex*

Contact: Claire Moore, Unit Manager on 0123 123 456 or the Production Office 01234 567890

Directions: Note for Grips – please get to set for 10:00 a.m. to check equipment

Trains: To Sussex from Central London for Monday morning

Departs:	08:23
Arrives:	09:15
Departs:	09:23
Arrives:	10:15

PLEASE NOTE – THERE IS A TRAIN STRIKE AND THE ONLY TRAINS RUNNING AT THE MOMENT ARE AT 23 MINUTES PAST THE HOUR.

Getting to Neale House: When you come out of the station, turn left and walk up Location Road. Go past the petrol station and at the top of Location Road, where it meets the Location Street, cross over at the lights that are on your left. Take the first road on the left and take St. Mark's Road on the right where there is a sign saying 'To the Old Convent'. You will see a sign for Neale House on the corner of the road here. The entrance to Neale House car park is the first turning on your right. Go to Neale House and find your room.

From Neale House to the Old Convent: Come out of the front door of Neale House and turn left. Walk out of the car park entrance and turn left. Follow this road all the way down. You will be able to see the chapel and the surrounding buildings from there. Go to the chapel.

By car:
To Neale House: From London: Take the A55 from Junction 10 of the M25, south. Location is about 20 miles from the M25. Follow all the signs to location. As you come in to the town, keep an eye out for the Fire Station, which will appear on your left. At the next traffic lights, turn right onto Location Road, and then right on to the old Convent Road; the entrance to Neale House is the first turning on the right on St. Mark's road.

Parking
All cars to be parked in the car park at Neale House, which is where you will be staying for the duration.

Facilities
The crew room for tea, coffee and snacks is in the gym at the chapel, there will be a sign on the door. Toilets are at Neale House. The cast green room is at No 23.

NO SMOKING ON SET PLEASE!!!!!!

<u>Production office</u>　　　　　　**Amulet Films**
PM: Jacqui Wetherill

Ghosthunter

Tel: 01234 56789
Fax: 01234 56789

Date: Monday 10th January 2000
UNIT CALL: 11:00am
Breakfast will be on set at 10:30am

Producer: Alison Reddihough
Director: Simon Corris　　　　　WEATHER: Fine and dry day, frost in
1st A.D. Philip Shaw　　　　　　morning, sunshine, a little cloud in the
Unit Manager: Claire Moore　　　afternoon, light winds

Location 1: Ext of Audrey's B&B, The Old Convent
Location 2: Ext Chapel at the back, side and front
Location 3: Ext of Audrey's B&B, The Old Convent
Location 4: Ext Chapel at front

***NO SMOKING ON ANY SET. THERE ARE CIGARETTE BINS
OUTSIDE THE CHAPEL AND NEALE HOUSE***

Scene No	Script Pg.	Int./ Ext.	Description	Story Day	Day/ Night	Pages	Cast
9	5	Ext	AUDREY'S B&B Sarah walks up the path to Audrey's front door	Day 1	Day	1/8 pgs	3
3	1	Ext	ABANDONED CHURCH Sarah walks nearer church talks into dictaphone	Day 1	Day	2/8 pgs	3
11a	6	Ext	AUDREY'S B&B Shot of Sarah's bedroom window down to kitchen window	Day 1	Night	2/8 pgs	2, 3, 4
1c	1	Ext	ABANDONED CHURCH 3rd shot of church for Quantel with tracking	Day 1	Night	1/8 pgs	
19	10	Int/ Ext	CAR AT ABANDONED CHURCH Audrey & Anne talking in car waiting for Charlie and Sarah	Day 1	Night	3/8 pgs	2, 4

No:	Artiste	Character	Pick-up time	On set to rehearse	M/Up/Cost	Turnover
2	June Watson	Audrey		18:00	18:30	19:00
3	Alison Reddihough	Sarah	N/a	11:00	11:15	11:45
4	Jacquie Phillips	Anne		18:00	18:30	19:00

Supporting Cast/Extras

Requirements

Props:	Dictaphone, laptop, Sarah's bag
Action Vehicles:	Car
Costume	As per Bea
Camera Dept:	As per Gavin
Chaperone:	None
Medical:	Casualty at Queen Victoria Hospital Tel: 01234 123456
Catering:	Lunch at 13:00 at Neale House

Advance Schedule Tuesday 11th January 2000

Scene No	a.o.b	Script Pg.	Int./ Ext.	Description	Story Day	Day/ Night	Pages	Cast
1d		1	Int	ABANDONED CHURCH Montage of ritual for title sequence	Pre-Story	Night	1/8 pgs	5, 6, 7, 8, 9, 10, 11, 12, 13, 14
20a (i)		10	Int	ABANDONED CHURCH Recording of whispering and chanting by hooded figures in the church	Pre-Story	Night	1 2/8 pgs	3, 5, 6, 7, 8, 9, 10, 11, 12, 13, 14
20a (ii)		10	Int	ABANDONED CHURCH Flashbacks in church of the ritual	Pre-Story	Night	1 2/8 pgs	3, 5, 6, 7, 8, 9, 10, 11, 12, 13, 14

ART DEPARTMENT CREW RECORD   CREW

PRODUCTION:

PRODUCTION
COMPANY:

SCREEN CREDIT INFORMATION

FULL NAME:

POSITION:

CONTACT DETAILS

PERMANENT CONTACT NUMBER:

MOBILE / PAGER:

PERMANENT CONTACT ADDRESS:

AGENT / DIARY SERVICE NUMBER / ADDRESS:

INVOLVEMENT

DATES WORKED:

WORK UNDERTAKEN:
(Please detail type of work; e.g. buying/construction/painting/dressing and on which sets/locations.)

Appendix H – Biographies of consultants and key crew

The consultants

Freddie Francis, Consultant Cinematographer

Freddie Francis BSC, one of England's most distinguished Directors of Photography, has been awarded two Oscars for Best Cinematography for *Sons and Lovers* and *Glory* – the only Englishman to have won Oscars for both black & white and colour photography. He has received Lifetime Achievement Awards from the ASC, BSC and *Empire* magazine. Earlier credits include *Room at the Top, Saturday Night and Sunday Morning, The Innocents* and *Night Must Fall*. Between 1962 and 1975 he took time out to direct over twenty features and TV films. He then returned to work as Director of Photography on *The Elephant Man*, followed by *The French Lieutenant's Woman*, winning BAFTA nominations and BSC awards for both. These were followed by, among others, *The Executioner's Son, The Jigsaw Man, Dune, Clara's Heart, The Plot to Kill Hitler, The Man in the Moon, Cape Fear* (which won him a BAFTA nomination for Best Cinematography), *School Ties* and *A Life in the Theatre* for Beacon communications. He also directed the 1985 feature *The Doctor and the Devils*, which co-starred Stephen Rea. Freddie's most recent film, *The Straight Story*, directed by David Lynch, received great acclaim at the 1999 Cannes Film Festival.

Peter Lamont, Production Design Consultant

Peter Lamont, one of the leading Production Designers in the UK, has been awarded an Oscar for his work on *Titanic*, nominated a further three times for *Aliens, The Spy Who Loved Me* and *Fiddler on the Roof*, and nominated for BAFTAs for *Titanic* and *Aliens*. Peter's credits also include *Wing Commander, Top Secret!* and several *Bond* films, including *The World Is Not Enough, Goldeneye, Licence To Kill, The Living Daylights, View To A Kill, Octopussy* and *For Your Eyes Only*. As Art Director, Peter's work includes *Sphinx, Boys From*

Brazil, The Spy Who Loved Me, The Seven-Per-Cent Solution, Inside Out, The Dove, The Man With The Golden Gun, Live and Let Die and *Sleuth.* He also worked as Set Dresser on *Diamonds Are Forever* and *On Her Majesty's Secret Service.*

Barrington Pheloung, Composer

Barrington Pheloung is one of the world's most distinguished and prolific composers. His achievements include being nominated for BAFTAs for Best Television Music for *Inspector Morse* and for the feature film *Hilary and Jackie,* and nominated for Best Original Music in the Ivor Novello Awards for the feature film *Nostradamus.* His enormous body of work includes compositions for film, theatre, television and ballet. His film work includes *Twin Dragons, Hilary and Jackie, Nostradamus, Shopping* and *Truly Madly Deeply.* He is widely known and respected for the music accompanying the very popular long-running television series *Inspector Morse.* The album sales of the series, volumes 1, 2 and 3, have reached platinum, gold and silver, respectively. Other television work includes the music for *Dalziel and Pascoe, The Politician's Wife, The Cinder Path, Boon, The Legends of Treasure Island, The Gift, Mosley* and *Neville's Island.* Barrington has also written scores for several West End plays including *Made in Bangkok, After the Fall, Sweet Bird of Youth* and *The Ride Down Mount Morgan.* He has composed 52 commissioned scores for ballet and dance companies in Britain and Europe. He has also written the scores for the interactive CD-ROM games *Broken Sword* and *Broken Sword 2: The Smoking Mirror.*

Mark Auguste, Sound Editor Consultant

Mark Auguste's sound department filmography includes *Tea with Mussolini* (Sound Effects Editor), *Elizabeth* (Supervising Sound Editor), *The Jackal* (ADR supervisor), *Loch Ness* (Sound Engineer), *Priest* (Sound Editor), *Radio Inside* (Sound Editor) and *Chicago Joe and the Showgirl* (Supervising Sound Editor). Mark worked as a consultant to his son Sam, the Sound Editor for *Ghosthunter.*

The executive crew

Rodrigo Gutierrez, Camera Operator

Rodrigo Gutierrez's credits include *Gladiator, Greenwich Mean Time, The Match, Plunkett & Macleane, The Commissioner, Feast of July, Bliss, The Van, Split Second, The Turn of the Screw, Friendship's Death* and *Out of Africa.*

Trevor Coop, Camera Operator (Pinewood)

Trevor Coop's credits include *Star Wars: Episode I – The Phantom Menace, Anna and the King, Swept from the Sea, Feast of July, Frankenstein, Hamlet, In the Bleak Midwinter, Dealers, Ending Up, American Gothic, Santa Claus* and *Superman.*

Maurice Gillett, Gaffer

Maurice Gillett has over 40 years' experience as a gaffer. His credits include *Princess Caraboo, Superman IV, Return to Oz, White Nights, The Bounty, Witness for the Prosecution, An American Werewolf in London, Flash Gordon, Superman, Revenge of the Pink Panther, Orca the Killer Whale* and *The Innocents.*

Robin O'Donoghue, Sound Re-Recordist

Robin O'Donoghue's credits include *The Man Who Cried, Lost In Space, Shakespeare In Love, Hamlet, Michael Collins, The Madness of King George, We're No Angels, The Fly* and *A Chorus Line.* Robin re-recorded the final mix for *Ghosthunter* in the Korda Theatre, Shepperton Sound, Shepperton.

Key crew

Simon Corris, Director/Producer/Writer

Simon Corris trained at the Bristol Old Vic Theatre School as an actor and has nine years experience of film, television, theatre and numerous commercials. Theatre credits include over 20 plays in repertory including *Salt of the Earth, A Small Family Business, Huis Clos, M. Butterfly, A Man for all Seasons, A Midsummer Night's Dream, Twelfth Night, Privates on Parade, Death of a Salesman, Abigail's Party, Jeffrey Bernard is Unwell, Communicating Doors, The Long and the Short and the Tall, Dead Dogs, Dog Ends* and *The Wizard of Oz.* Television credits include *Young Peter* in *The Old Devils*, a three part adaptation of the Kingsley Amis novel, and two series of *Numbertime* for the BBC. Other credits include *Eastenders, The Bill, Get Real, For Valour, Kiss Me Kate, Just William, Peak Practice, The Upper Hand, Expert Witness, Life and Death, Sam Saturday* and *Then*, a pilot for a new comedy series for Channel 4. *Ghosthunter* is the second short film he has directed. His first, *The Essay*, is five minutes long and was shot on 16mm in 1999. He has acted in several short films including *The Tale, Billy* and *Perfect Day*, and several commercials including B.T., Royal London, Woolworths, Asda, Argos and Cancer Research to name but a few.

Alison Reddihough, Producer/Writer

Alison Reddihough started producing in the theatre with the variety group Sweet Fanny Adams. She then went on to produce and act in a production of *Arms and the Man* for Orpheus Theatre Company and in 1992 she co-founded the Ideal Theatre Company and commissioned, produced and acted in several plays including *These Men* and *Dead Dogs and Englishwomen*. She is also an actress with 11 years of film, television, commercials and theatre experience which includes the short film *The Essay*, two series of the BBC sitcom *Health and Efficiency*, and theatre productions of *Lend Me A Tenor*, *Second From Last in the Sack Race*, *Haven*, *Death of a Salesman*, *Murder at the Vicarage*, *Your Money or Your Wife*, *The Lost Continent* and several pantomimes all over the country. Alison has also appeared in commercials for Utterly Butterly, the Government's Don't Drink and Drive campaign, Oil of Ulay and Sky Digital. She co-wrote *The Essay* and has written a full-length play entitled *The Adventures of a One Bedroomed Flat in Tooting* and had several poems published.

Gavin Struthers, Director of Photography

Gavin completed the three-year cinematography course at the NFTS in December 2000 (supported by the Freddie Francis B.S.C. Scholarship). Prior to this, he shot a dozen short films as Director of Photography, several of which gained entry to the festival circuit. Since *Ghosthunter*, Gavin has photographed three projects outside the NFTS and completed his graduation film.

Luke Smith, Production Designer

Luke Smith has been involved with design and art direction for film and TV since leaving Central Saint Martins College of Art and Design with an MA in Graphic Design. His work has covered a broad spectrum, varying from film-school graduation shorts to full-scale cinema features. His credits as an art director include *Boston Kickout* and *The Palace*, a feature-length 1920s gangster thriller filmed in Los Angeles. As a production designer he has worked on a further two low-budget features, *Time Enough* and *Holding On*; TV pilots *Rough Magik: An Age Of Wonders* and *Small Hotel*; and a variety of ambitious short films. During production of the short-feature *The Dance Of*

Shiva, Luke had the opportunity to work alongside a number of eminent film technicians, including Jack Cardiff, John Mitchell and production designer John Box (*Lawrence of Arabia*, *Oliver*, *Doctor Zhivago*, etc.) who acted as a design consultant.

Jacqui Wetherill, Production Manager

Jacqui began her career in Accounts, but soon realized that her organizational skills were best suited to a profession which fuelled her passion for a challenge. After spending a year travelling and working around Australia, she returned to England to concentrate on a career. After a short film course, she started working for Panico Media Workshop, and played a principal role in developing the charity film school. This gave her invaluable experience of filmmaking, of both full and low-budget productions. Since leaving Panico to freelance as a production manager, she has specialized in creating polished films, often with restricted budgets. She has recently worked on the features *Mumbo Jumbo* and *The Hole*.

Claire Trevor-Roper, Unit Manager

When she was 8 years old her father told her that he had been James Bond in the movie *You Only Live Twice* (he was the naval officer roped in as a Sean Connery look-a-like to sit in the dinghy as the submarine rescues Bond at the end) and she realized that movies were something that people actually made – and became fascinated by the process. Her first job in the UK was working as the production runner on *The Woodlanders* and, since then, she has worked on three short films: *It's Good to Talk* (which was Oscar nominated in 1997), *A Little Faith*, *Ghosthunter*; and two features: *Urban Ghost Story* and *Offending Angels*, mostly in production but also on the unit and location. All films since *The Woodlanders* have been low-budget productions, which put her in a great position to take on the job as Researcher on the second edition of the very successful *The Guerilla Film Maker's Handbook* (Jolliffe, G. and Jones, C., Continuum Publishing, 2000). This book is designed to get young and new filmmakers through the feature-filmmaking process without having to spend a lot of money and without making costly mistakes. Through this, she also ran the Guerilla Filmmakers Advanced Masterclass that Simon and Alison attended as part of their research for making *Ghosthunter*.

Appendix I – Cast and crew list

The cast

Charlie Fielding — Frank Finlay
Sarah Anderson — Alison Reddihough
Audrey Hicks — June Watson
Anne Hicks — Jacqueline Phillips
Emily Fielding — Josie Kidd

Hooded figures

Bill Bostock — Doug Manning
Ben Bower — Richard Perry
Jason Coop — Dugald Scott
Simon Corris — Michael Singleton
Alain Levin — Hannah Smith
Michael Macdonald — Graham Tippet
Paul Watkins

Crew

Producer/Writer — Alison Reddihough
Director/Producer/Writer — Simon Corris
Consultant Director of Photography — Freddie Francis
Consultant Production Designer — Peter Lamont
Consultant Sound Editor — Mark Auguste
Composer — Barrington Pheloung
Director of Photography — Gavin Struthers
Production Designer — Luke Smith
Editor — Simon Cozens
Sound Editor — Sam Auguste
Production Manager — Jacqui Wetherill
Unit Manager — Claire F. Moore
1st Assistant Director — Philip Shaw
Production Assistant — Liesbeth Beeckman
Script Supervisor — Claire Eades
2nd Assistant Director — Sam Jones
3rd Assistant Director — Katia Kogler
Costume Designer — Bea Marx-Logerfo
Make-Up Designer — Julia Laderman
Camera Operator — Rodrigo Gutierrez
Camera Operator (Pinewood) — Trevor Coop
Focus Puller — Dean Thompson

Clapper/Loader	Jason Coop
Camera Assistant	Adam White
Key Grip	Luke Chisholm
Grip	Phil Aylewood
Camera Trainee	Christian Zeidler
Cinejib Operators	John Breedon
	Clive Tocher
Cinejib Grip	Dennis Dillon
2nd Unit Camera Operator	Gavin Struthers
	Jason Coop
Clapper	Adam White
2nd Unit Assistant Director	Harriet Perry
Production Mixer	Brian Greene
Boom Operator	Dugald Scott
Sound Assistant	Jonathan Cousins
Re-Recording Mixers	Robin O'Donoghue
	Richard Street
Recordist	Nigel Bennett
Foley/ADR Mixer	David Tyler
Foley Artist	Rikki Butt
Art Director (Pinewood)	Tracy Ann Baines
Stand-by Art Director	R. Kate Snusher
Assistant Art Director	Michael Singleton
Stand-by Props	Rhian Davies Jones
Prop Makers	Jemma Smith
	Penny Smith
Art Department Assistants	Sharon Hunt
	Danny Jenkins
	Joanna Sangster
	Rachel Williams
Construction Manager	David Flack
Construction Buyer	Lisa Yardley
Construction Assistants	Andy Lee
	Tony Mayor
	Kim Richardson
	Kaimen Stone
Digital Visual Effects by	The Computer Film Company
Visual Effects Producer	Drew Jones
Digital Visual Effects Supervisors	Rob Duncan
	Matt Twyford
Supervising CG Animator	Dominic Parker
Visual Effects Coordinator	Ruth Greenberg
Digital Paint Artists	Sule Bryan-Hurst
	Ian Fellows
Visual Effects Editorial	Roz Lowrie
Digital Lab Producer	Jan Hogevold
Digital Lab	Merrin Jensen
Data	Darrel Griffin
Title Design	Ian Firth at Resource Design
Opening Titles Scanned By	The Film Factory
Executive Gaffer	Maurice Gillett
Gaffer	Michael Vincent
Best Boy	Steve Finburg
Electrician	Doug Manning
Generator Operator	Mark Thornton

Wardrobe Assistant	Alice Lowe
Make-Up Assistant	Natalie Grosberg
Continuity Assistant	Joanne Fairweather
Production Runners	Thomas Freegard
	Eddie Gibson
	Tanya Hazelden
	Vicki Kisner
Mr Finlay's Stand-in	Ron E. Zolkof
Hooded Figure Stunts	Crispy Kev
Person with most credits	Jason Coop
Transport Manager	Alan Ley
Art Department Transport	Tim Wilkins
Catering	Neale House
Stills Photographer	Zoë Norfolk
Computer Consultant	David Flack
Web Design	Jeremy Wells
Company Accountant	Littlejohn Frazer
Legal services	Sean Egan at Bates, Wells & Braithwaite
Insurance services	Aon/Albert G. Ruben
Publicity	Corbett & Keene Ltd
Costumes supplied by	Angels & Bermans
Miss Reddihough's costume by	Joan & David
Lighting equipment	VFG Lighting
Lightning strike	Cirrolite
Colour by	Technicolor Ltd
Lab contact	Ron Taylor
Grader	Phil Ashton
Negative cutter	Professional Negative Cutting Ltd
Opticals	Howell Opticals
Titles	Spectra Titles
Music performed by	Members of the London Metropolitan Orchestra

Sound re-recorded at Shepperton Sound, Shepperton Studios, London
Originated on motion picture film from Kodak

Cameras and grip equipment	Panavision UK

Acknowledgements

The producers would like to thank:

David Parfitt	Kenneth Branagh
Robin O'Donoghue	Jamie Payne
John Rendall	Hugh Whittaker
Kishor Ladwa	Anne Guidera
Paul Watkins	Rod Shelton
Eddie Dias	David Morphy
Ian Firth	Eddie Hamilton
Simon Cox	Chris Dunham
Suzanne Crowley	Focal Press
David Bingham	Dot and Alan Dodd
Albert and Christine Reddihough	Father and Mrs Jeremy Cooper

St. Margaret's Convent and Neale House and all The Old Convent Residents

Appendix J – Alison's *Ghosthunter* diary

July 1999

It's a cold but bright day at Urquhart Castle on the banks of Loch Ness. As I stand high up on the ramparts looking out for the monster, I notice Simon listening intently to his mobile phone. He's checking the answerphone back at home. We're not expecting any messages – we're only away for four days – but you never know. It's important to check. I walk towards him. Any messages? He stares at me, presses the replay button and thrusts the phone next to my ear. I can't believe it. There's a message from Kenneth Branagh's office, apologizing for taking so long to get back to us, but Ken is happy to meet us on Wednesday for half an hour. We'd written to Ken a few weeks previously asking if he could spare the time to meet a couple of aspiring filmmakers to offer some advice. And he'd come up trumps. Little do we realize then, that that meeting will change things for us drastically.

We manage to enjoy the rest of our short break, although a hike in the Scottish hills causes some alarm. There are midges everywhere – tiny little flies that look pretty harmless – and they feast on us. Initially, the bites look pretty harmless (ha!), but by the time the day dawns for our meeting with Ken things have changed somewhat. I look in the mirror to see my face is covered with bright red spots and Simon's arms – well, you can barely see normal skin on them. The truth dawns on us – we're going to meet Kenneth Branagh looking like two plague victims from the Middle Ages. So we arrive at Shepperton Studios in sweltering weather, Simon in a long-sleeved buttoned-up shirt and me with an extra-long fringe and heavy make-up. Only to find Ken has pulled a muscle in his neck and is walking around dosed-up with painkillers, with his head stuck on one side! However, despite all our disabilities, we have a great meeting. Ken is a very nice man who listens carefully to our filmmaking plans, doesn't patronize and offers support and some good advice. We tell him about our plans for a low-low-budget feature that we're working on and a short we're developing called *Ghosthunter*. At this stage we're just thinking about knocking it out quickly and cheaply for experience. The meeting runs for an hour and we're made to feel inspired and optimistic about our plans. Just as we leave, we ask him if he can recommend anyone else for us to talk to. He thinks about it and says he'll get back to us shortly.

A few days later Ken's office calls us with the contact details for Jamie Payne, a director/producer who has made a 30-minute short film called *The Dance of Shiva* that is attracting a lot of attention. We speak to Jamie (who it turns out I was at drama school with) and arrange to meet for lunch. I instantly like and trust Jamie and we have an eye-opening lunch, where he tells us how he made '*Shiva*' with the help of some amazing people. Jack Cardiff was the DoP, John Box was a Production Design Consultant and John W. Mitchell was a Sound Consultant. Wow. How did he get these incredible giants of the film industry? He simply asked them – they were mostly retired and keen to keep busy and help a young filmmaker as much as they could. The result was a film that looks fantastic and has attracted a lot of attention in the industry. The 'buzz' around '*Shiva*' has enabled Jamie to get a couple of features off the ground and further his career enormously. This 'Consultants' route sounds very exciting and gets us thinking. Would it work for *Ghosthunter*? What if we used the money that we'd raised for the low-low-budget feature and made a high-budget short instead? Jamie is very encouraging, and urges us to consider this route. He also offers a few tips for the script and says he can help us build a team for *Ghosthunter*. Simon and I leave the lunch with a lot to think about and a feeling of massive excitement.

August

Before we can approach any potential consultants, we need to have a decent script. Easier said than done. I remember Hitchcock's famous quote about the only three things that make a good film – the script, the script and the script. Writing is not our chosen profession and we're only doing it because we have to. However, we knuckle down and after a month of hard work we finally have a draft (about number 9) of *Ghosthunter* that we're happy to send out. Ibsen it ain't, but it will make an interesting, entertaining and slightly different short. We hope.

September

10th – We've decided to aim to shoot *Ghosthunter* in late autumn so it's time to try approaching some potential consultants. We start with Barrington Pheloung, the renowned composer. This one is fairly easy, as we've met

Barrington a few times before. We know that he's very approachable and it would be fantastic to get a man of his talent and reputation to compose the music for *Ghosthunter*. Barrington is very supportive – 'Yeah, mate, sounds great, I'd love to do it'. Yes! Our first 'name' is on board. We send him the script and arrange to meet up in a couple of weeks.

22nd – We're at a point now where we need to know how much *Ghosthunter* is going to cost us. Jamie puts us in touch with Jacqui Wetherill, an experienced short-filmmaker and Production Manager, who's going to run up a budget for us and possibly come on board as our Production Manager. Jacqui has a calm 'been there done it all' quality and is very reassuring. Then she spoils it by plopping a budget of £85 000 on our laps. We make the reluctant decision to go ahead with the project without paying people – it would take us years to raise that kind of money, and we just want to get on with it. Without pay, the budget drops to a manageable £30 000-ish. Now we're cooking.

27th – This is the Big One. We decide to approach Freddie Francis, twice Oscar-winning cinematographer, as a consultant for *Ghosthunter*. Simon bites the bullet and calls him while I disappear to London on an NLP course for a week. That evening Simon calls me. He's not sure how the conversation went. Freddie has an unnerving ability of leaving long silences on the phone while he digests what you say. 'He was either listening intently . . . or he thinks I'm a complete idiot', Simon tells me. Anyway he's willing to look at the script. Simon also sends a script to *Titanic* Production Designer, Peter Lamont and to Luke Smith (a potential Production Designer who designed *The Dance of Shiva*).

29th – Freddie rings promptly back. He's enthusiastic about the project and keen to help. He feels that he'd like to contribute something to the training of young filmmaking talent. Simon calls me that evening with the news and we whoop at each other down the phone. This is wonderful news for *Ghosthunter*. Freddie's only comment about the script is that it has 'too many words', but that's sort of what you'd expect to hear from a cinematographer. We arrange to meet Freddie for lunch in 10 days' time.

We decide to write to the producer David Parfitt for advice. He's an incredibly successful British Film Producer and it would be invaluable to pick his brains about filmmaking and the industry.

October

5th – We have the opportunity to meet with a Venture Capitalist to get a taste of the sort of feature projects that they look for. It's not the most optimistic meeting we've had so far – he tells us that most British films fail and do not make a profit and out of 400 scripts that they received they only helped to fund six last year. Hmm. What are we getting into??? We hear from David Parfitt's office that he's willing to meet us and we arrange a date.

8th – We meet a potential Production Designer – Luke Smith – a quiet, serious, hard working and honest chap – and marvel at his portfolio. He shows us his work on *The Dance of Shiva*. Jamie said that John Box was particularly impressed with his designs. You can't get a much better reference than that. He's happy to work on *Ghosthunter* but can't commit until a month before. We then move on to our lunch meeting with Freddie. We arrive 15 minutes early. Freddie arrives 1 minute later. A very punctual man – we like that. Over sea bass and white wine we tell him of our hopes for *Ghosthunter* – how we want to achieve the production values of a feature in a short. He's very charming and agrees to help us as much as he can. He suggests that we talk to Gavin Struthers, a young cinematographer who's currently at the National Film School on his scholarship. 'Gavin has the right ideas', he says and, if Freddie Francis says that, who are we to argue? We arrange to meet Gavin the following week.

10th – A quick visit to Barrington's house/studio. He gives us a guided tour and we gawp in amazement. It's an incredible place – it's been completely sound proofed and *every* room can be used for recording. Barrington proudly informs us 'some of the greatest brass players in the country have recorded on this toilet, perfect acoustics for the horn,' he tells us. We talk a bit about *Ghosthunter* and he offers us some good advice. If there are any tricky transitions in the film, make sure that we hold the transition for a few moments and he can help it move more fluently with music. He's keen to help us and we're thrilled to bits.

12th – It's time to start looking for the locations for *Ghosthunter*. We need to find an abandoned church and several interiors for a guesthouse. When we wrote *Ghosthunter* we originally thought of filming it in a converted convent complex in Sussex, which has a huge deserted chapel as its centrepiece. However, Jacqui has advised us to look for a location in London, as it'll be costly to shoot in Sussex and we'll never get unpaid crew to travel there. So, where do we begin? We start at the London Film Commission, who are very helpful and lead us to a room full of files of potential locations. We start to slowly wade through them and it quickly becomes apparent that this is not going to be an easy job. We start to appreciate how valuable location managers and scouts are. However, we manage to find a couple of potential locations near London.

We go on to meet Gavin Struthers in a very noisy pub. Gavin is young, ambitious and very keen to become involved with *Ghosthunter*. We all shout to each other for 2 hours over disco hits of the 1970s. Simon and Gavin bond well – it looks as if we've found our cinematographer.

15th – In an ideal world, it would be fantastic to have a couple of special digital effects in *Ghosthunter*, but they are enormously expensive and we know that we can't afford them. Jamie suggests that we approach Quantel, who helped to support '*Shiva*'. This is the big one. If we can get their support it will make a world of difference to our short. They sound interested and we send the script and a 'package'. The package consists of everything of interest about *Ghosthunter* that we've compiled so far – a synopsis of the story, what we hope to achieve with the film, biographies of Freddie and Barrington, details of Amulet Films, etc. It adds a professional touch, and it's great to see it growing as we add another consultant or sponsor to the project. We also fax a package to Kodak. We really need a good deal from them.

20th – Our meeting with David Parfitt. What a nice man! It's reassuring to meet a highly successful producer who's not a cynical, hard-nosed businessman. He gives us lots of encouragement and several names to contact that might be able to help us with *Ghosthunter*. It's incredible; every day we're learning so much from meeting these people.

21st – Quantel want to meet us, so it's up to the headquarters in Newbury to meet Paul Watkins and Jane Killips. They're very welcoming and Simon starts to describe what special effects we'd like. Trying not to push our luck he mentions a couple of scenes. They seem enthusiastic, Simon starts getting ambitious and by the end of the meeting nearly every scene has some digital effect added to it! Without hesitation, Paul and Jane say that they'd be happy to help us out. Simon nearly falls off his chair. They then take us on a guided tour of Quantel and show us the Domino system (the machine that creates the effects) that is jaw-droppingly amazing. On the drive home Simon is beaming – we can't believe our luck.

25th – Today we meet Robin O'Donoghue, a very established sound re-recordist, recommended by David Parfitt, at the Korda Theatre at Shepperton Studios. It's a fantastic place that has produced the final mix for many great British movies. Dare we hope that *Ghosthunter* is mixed here? Robin is very friendly and we ask him for suggestions for a good sound team (and possibly some sort of a sound consultant). He says he'll try and think of some people who might be interested.

26th – The search for an abandoned church location in London has got nowhere. I've traipsed round a couple of churches, but they've lacked atmosphere (or a roof . . .). We decide to rethink using the empty chapel on the Old Convent in Sussex. So today Gavin and Luke come down to 'do a recce' of it. It's a fantastic building with some amazing features and a great atmosphere, but it's big. Very big. Gavin immediately trebles his lighting requirements and Luke goes very quiet. However, I can tell they're interested. Now we have to think about whether we can afford to film here. Meanwhile we get a fax from Robin giving us some names. Also, the script and an ever-increasing package (now with a section on Quantel) are sent to Panavision. Let's hope they're interested in the project.

29th – I'm manning the office alone today as Simon is away working as an actor. We still have to earn a living somehow, so when the odd day's acting work comes in, we grab it. I begin the day by approaching Focal Press. When we started learning about filmmaking we read every book we could get on the subject, but quickly realized that there were no books on how to make short films, only books on features. This seemed strange, because short-filmmaking is very often the first step for a young filmmaker. Encouraged by Jamie – who had had some interest in a book about '*Shiva*' – I sat down and researched a list of film book publishers. Focal Press has a very good pedigree, so today I ring and pitch the idea of a book about short filmmaking and *Ghosthunter* to Margaret Riley at Focal. She is instantly interested in the idea and I e-mail her the script and package. (I love e-mail, particularly as our post is taking masses of time to get to anywhere. First Class my foot.)

I then contact one of the names on Robin's list – Mark Auguste, a very experienced sound editor. Mark sounds interested in the project and I send him the script.

November

1st – It's time to start casting. We're now aiming to shoot *Ghosthunter* in December, and we want to start tackling this now. However, casting has terrified us more than anything else so far, which is strange considering we're both actors. I suppose we have had first-hand experience of how unremitting agents can be. We are looking for a named actor to play the lead role of 'Charlie', the ghosthunter. We decide to start at the top, with a very prestigious British film actor who, unfortunately for us, is represented by V.B.A. inc. (a Very Big Agent). We've heard mixed tales about this particular V.B.A., mostly saying that they're not interested in short films for their clients and very often they don't even pass the script on. Hence our hesitation. Anyway Simon decides to jump in the deep end and makes the call. I wait, anxiously, in the other room. Simon returns, slightly sweaty, but looking relieved. The actor we have in mind is available and we send the script and 'package' on. Now we have to wait.

2nd – One of those moments that I hate as a low-budget filmmaker. We meet a sound mixer (another recommendation from Robin) – a very experienced and capable man called Brian Greene. He's interested in the project and towards the end of the conversation announces his fee for the film. Horrible silence. We thought he knew. Simon and I then spend the next 10 minutes explaining that there is NO money to pay people, bar a £50 fee for the week (laughable, I know) and expenses. Brian swallows, shrugs and agrees to do it anyway. What a star. However, it leaves a nasty taste in our mouths and we vow that we will only make our feature if we can pay people a proper wage.

4th – We meet Mark Auguste and his son Sam, the Sound Editors. Over a very nice pub lunch we discuss sound and they offer some advice on things to remember when making *Ghosthunter* to make their job easier. For example, if we can get a wild track of all the dialogue that will hopefully save them and us time (and ADR) later on. We promise to try and do that and yet again we leave a meeting enlightened.

5th – A full day and yet another meeting in a crowded pub in London. Our team is slowly coming together. Claire Moore is a highly organized, chatty and bubbly character that we enlist as a Unit Manager. It's so nice to meet people who love doing the jobs we hate. We then go on to a screening of *The Straight Story*, David Lynch's latest film that Freddie was DoP on. It's a wonderful film that really touches the heart. We see Freddie there and meet his lovely wife, Pam. We also see an actor that we were going to approach for 'Charlie' and regret not having a script with us that we could have given him. Our new motto is – Be Prepared.

6th – It's always interesting to see how a film was shot and I love the 'Making of' documentaries that accompany every film and are popping up on DVDs. Although *Ghosthunter* is just a short, we feel that it would be fun to have our own documentary – particularly with the consultants that we have on board. And we know just the man to make it. We approach Charles Sharman-Cox, who is an old friend and an enthusiastic and talented director. He loves the idea and has some good ideas for how to present it.

8th – Simon chases up V.B.A. inc. Nothing. In fact he has yet to talk to the agent herself, instead he's spoken to pretty much every assistant in the building. Very frustrating.

10th – Margaret from Focal Press has got back to me and is very interested in the short-film book idea. I then tell her that we don't want to write it – we're just too busy with the film. So she enlists an established writer and director called Ian Lewis (who had just written *Guerrilla TV: Low Budget Programme Making*, Focal Press, 2000) to write it for us and he cheerfully obliges. Today, Ian comes to meet us and chat about our ideas for the book. We talk about the way to present it and get quite excited. He goes away to draft up a proposal. And finally we get some answers from V.B.A. inc. The artist in question suddenly isn't available any more. They don't even mention the script, which we doubt they even looked at. We look at the next two choices on our list and realize they are also with the Very Big Agent. Very Depressing. Simon has now delegated casting to me (thanks, love), so I plough on and spend the next two days getting nowhere.

11th – A very exciting day. Jacqui (who has now become our Production Manager) and Claire (Unit Manager) come down to sort out Production Management. They breeze in and take away all the jobs that were piling up on us. It's like having a cold flannel placed on your fevered brow. They make a good combination – Jacqui, cool, calm and collected, and Claire, effervescent and chomping at the bit to get started. It feels like we've taken the first big pre-production step. Also Jamie calls and reassures us about casting. Says that the Wednesday before the shoot of *The Dance Of Shiva* he'd only got Kenneth Branagh cast. Feel a little calmer about casting – we've got 4 weeks. A lot can happen in 4 weeks. A lot has to.

12th – Get our website up and running (www.amulet-films.com). It's been designed by Jeremy Wells and we're very pleased with it. Simon will keep it updated and it'll be a quick and easy way of getting information about the project to people. I approach another agent who, thankfully, is friendlier than the last ones. Another script and package is sent off. The script has been through several more drafts and we're pretty happy with it now. But is it going to attract the big star that we want?

In the meantime we've now decided to go for shooting at the Old Convent and the chapel. The location is just perfect and I'm optimistic that we can find a way around the costs of transporting crew down here. We'd like to film 90 per cent of *Ghosthunter* here – not only do we want to use the chapel, but we hope to film the guest house and Charlie's house here too (interiors and exteriors). So today we start the process of talking to the residents of the Old Convent (which consists of 31 'units') as we have to get their approval for filming. If they say no, that's it, we'll have to start looking for a new location from scratch and we've only *4 weeks left*! So we start traipsing around from house to house chatting to residents and delivering a detailed note describing the project. It takes a long time – each resident is very interested in the film, asks lots of questions and plies us with drink. After about the fourth house we are very bored with *Ghosthunter* and very drunk.

13th – Hungover. Only another 27 residents to visit. I hate this film. I feel sick.

14th – Thankfully it was not in vain. The residents are enthusiastic. We can go ahead (liver permitting).

15th – First official day of pre-production. Four weeks to go. This Is It. Time to get serious. Fully recovered from our weekend we head off for a day of meetings in London. First up, Peter Lamont, one of the UK's most prestigious production designers. Peter chats away about working with Jim Cameron on *Aliens* and *Titanic* and tells us tales of all the *Bond* films that he's worked on. Wow. He's interested in the project and happy to come on board as Production Design Consultant. We're thrilled beyond belief, and arrange to meet up the following week with Luke.

We go on to a meeting with the big guns at Panavision, Hugh Whittaker and John Rendall. We're looking for a good deal on camera and grip equipment but will they help us? These guys have been there and seen it all, so none of our assurances of 'how brilliant this film will be' holds much weight with them. They've heard it a thousand times before. They did, however, praise our script and story, which was 'refreshingly different for a short'. They're supportive but non-committal and proceed to give us a lot of advice about making a film. We leave none the wiser about a deal, but much wiser about the film industry.

Dash onto our first official production meeting. Jacqui, Claire and Luke are suitably thrilled by the Peter Lamont news, although Luke looks even more serious than before. The meeting takes a couple of hours, but everyone's been working hard and we leave feeling we've accomplished a lot. And that we've got a cracking team on board.

16th – We now have to sort out how we're going to look after our crew whilst they're in Sussex. We've decided to use our house as a production base with rooms for make-up, wardrobe and green rooms for the actors. However, it's not nearly big enough for our expanding film crew. So we pay a visit to Neale House – a conference centre one minute's walk away from the locations – which we hope to use for catering. Incredibly, we discover that the centre has 43 (cheap) vacant beds, more than enough for our crew. We solve all our travel/location problems in one sweep. The crew can be fed and bedded here, and it's affordable!! Yippee!

Having sorted out the location, we now need studio space. We want to build a set for the scenes in Sarah's bedroom, so that we can add some interesting effects. We approach a couple of studios and Pinewood is the most supportive. We can now sort the schedule to include the final day's filming at Pinewood Studios. It'll be a great way to finish the shoot.

17th – Simon goes off to meet Freddie and his gaffer, Maurice, to go over the lighting and equipment list. I potter around the office getting odd jobs done. Simon returns completely exhausted. The lighting list has been decimated (thankfully – it was getting way too expensive) and simplicity is now the name of the game. Freddie and Maurice go back a long way and tell Simon tale upon tale of jobs they've worked on. After a long afternoon, Simon feels like he's been to 'anecdote heaven'. Meanwhile, back at the ranch, a rejection arrives from our latest actor. Ah well, onto the next.

18th – Another busy day. First a meeting with Quantel, Jacqui, Claire and Luke discussing the digital effects. It goes very smoothly and Paul and Jane from Quantel are even nicer than I remembered. Looks like we can do most of the effects we want with no major problems. The meeting is declared a success and gets everyone quite excited as they now have a clearer picture in their minds of what we hope to achieve.

Onto a costume meeting. Enter stage right, Bea, costume designer, instantly likeable, tall and gorgeous looking, smiley and bright as a button. Asks lots of probing questions about the characters and throws some interesting ideas at us.

Return home, exhausted. Just time to approach another agent and fax another script. We're keeping our fingers crossed – we have a good feeling about this one.

19th – I have a very quiet day in the office, while Simon begins to tackle his shot list. The calm before the storm. Beat the computer at backgammon.

22nd – Three weeks to go. Freddie and Maurice arrive to do a recce of the location and are suitably satisfied. They then sit on our sofa and Maurice's anecdotes begin again – 'well Fred, when I did *Out of Africa* with Robert Redford . . .'. We sit there in awe.

23rd – Up to London for lunch with our lawyer, Sean Egan from Bates, Wells & Braithwaite. We're anxious to get his advice about contracts for *Ghosthunter* – do we need them, if yes, how detailed should they be, etc. He's very helpful and recommends that we use simple contracts with everybody. Not only is it ideal from a legal perspective for Amulet Films, but also it will be good experience for when we come to make a feature. We pick his brains and then move on to a production meeting. Everything's going remarkably well – Jacqui is starting to get some good deals into place, Claire is sorting out the nitty gritty of filming on location and Luke unveils a model for the set of Sarah's bedroom (for Pinewood Studios), which looks very exciting. However, everyone is nervous about not having a cast. Of course we could cast *Ghosthunter* tomorrow if we wanted to – using an unknown actor – but we really want a name. A named actor is going to be a vital part of selling the film later on and, despite our lack of success so far, I'm still optimistic that we can get one. We start to discuss the logistics of postponing until January, which no one really wants to do. Let's hope it doesn't get to that.

24th – Simon goes off to meet Peter Lamont with Luke. They present the model of the Pinewood set to him, which he is very enthusiastic about, they then browse through some of Peter's souvenirs from designing *Titanic*. In the meantime I remain in the office with various e-mails to send and calls to make. Another 'no' from an agent, but I shall not be defeated, and onward to the next I go.

25th – London again, and another meeting with those lovely people from Quantel. Paul has brought along Matt Twyford – a special effects wizard who's worked on some major Hollywood movies – to discuss all our effects and the best way to shoot them. We have a very successful meeting, which solves a lot of problems and gets everyone very enthusiastic. However, the highlight of the meeting is when I manage to talk Paul into a starring role in the film – Hooded Figure No. 4. At least we've got someone cast! We go on to dinner with friends and spend the rest of the evening talking about anything but filmmaking. Bliss.

29th – Two weeks to go. TWO WEEKS TO GO!!! We meet Bea at Angels to have a look at some robes for our hooded figures and some ideas for 'Sarah'. Angels is a fabulous place, with row upon row of costumes ranging from restoration frocks to pyjamas. I feel like a little girl again with the biggest dressing-up box in the world. We find what we want and move on to a meeting with a product placement agency. These guys are great, as they can supply us with lots of free bits and bobs which will make life on and off set a whole lot easier. They're keen to help us and it looks as if they'll be able to get us quite a bit of stuff. We then meet up with Charles, who has assembled a documentary crew and discuss the best way of getting what we want with minimum disruption. Well, miracles do happen. We manage to appease everyone and finish the day with a lengthy production meeting. Jacqui's getting worried about our lack of a cast and says that Friday is Postponement Day. If we don't have a 'Charlie' in place by then, we'll have to postpone or risk losing money. I knuckle down and continue my thankless role as casting director.

30th – Claire comes down to Sussex for the day to chat up the firemen. (Well, OK, she does a *bit* of work too, but we know what her real intentions are . . .) In the opening credit sequence Simon wants rain falling on the church as the storm brews. Rain machines are expensive – firemen are not. So Claire has bravely volunteered to approach the local fire station to see if they can help us. She manages to charm them and the firemen agree to come and spray down our chapel, as long as there are no fires in Sussex that day. Claire also pays a visit to Neale House, who couldn't be more accommodating (forgive the unintended pun) whilst I continue casting, casting, casting. Some good news comes through though – Illumina TV have got wind of the project and are interested in doing a documentary on the making of *Ghosthunter* for Film Four. Very exciting!

December

1st – Casting. Again. However, I think I'm getting better at it, and I am learning a lot about it.

2nd – I meet Bea and Julia, our make-up and hair ladies in London. Julia is lovely, very sweet and friendly and we have a great girly chat about Sarah's make-up and hair over a creamy cup of hot chocolate. Much as I'm enjoying producing, it's really nice to have moments where I can immerse myself in the acting side of *Ghosthunter*. I return home with bad news on the casting front. It's looking increasingly difficult to get an actor who's willing to work so close to Christmas. They're all going away or are involved with carol concerts. I've never known so many carol concerts going on! Postponement is imminent. But I manage to fax another script through to a very jolly agent at 7 p.m. I pray hard, but realize that time is running out for a December shoot.

3rd – Reluctantly, we decide to postpone to January. Simon and I have been defeated by 'casting against the clock' and time is running out. If we want to make this film with a 'named' actor it's best to cut our losses and spend a little longer aiming for that. It's a stressful day, and not a decision that we wanted to make. However, all is not doom and gloom and, as the day progresses, we learn that actually most of our crew are relieved by the delay as it gives them more time and breathing space. Jacqui is optimistic that most of our crew will still be available for the January dates. So January it is then.

6th – Refreshed after the weekend, a production meeting is called and we all discuss where we go from here. Everyone is very positive about the changed dates and we now have the luxury of 3 weeks' extra pre-production and an unhurried Christmas. We set the new shoot dates for 10–14 January, with a day at Pinewood on 18 January.

8th – Simon is in a foul mood today and I'm just about ready to strangle him when the phone rings. It's an agent and . . . Yes . . . I don't believe it but . . . WE HAVE AN ACTOR!!! And not just any old actor but the amazing FRANK FINLAY!!! He loves the script, he's really keen to do it and he's so perfect for the part! Simon's mood changes instantly and we beam at each other. It's a huge relief and we feel very excited and honoured to have such a great actor in our film. It couldn't be better.

More good news comes in. Focal Press have approved and confirmed the book and it's all systems go for *How To Make Great Short Feature Films – The Making of* Ghosthunter (surely the longest title in history . . .).

The only slightly sour note of the day is that we lose a location on the Old Convent. Once we had got the residents approval for filming, we then looked for a house that would serve as the interior locations for the guest house scenes. We thought we'd found somewhere, but were having problems with it and so decided to cut our losses and pull out. It's not an easy decision – finding another suitable location isn't a job we relish – but we're confident we'll be able to get somewhere else as good, or better. At least we've got some time – thank God we're not filming next week.

10th – I start searching for a new location and start casting for 'Audrey', the owner of the guest house. Now we've got Frank Finlay I feel very confident ringing agents. The project is sounding pretty impressive – Freddie, Peter, Barrington, Frank, Quantel, Pinewood, book, documentary, T-shirt . . .

13th – Just as I've got the hang of casting, the next worse job looms up in front of me. Contracts. I feebly try to dump this job on Simon, but he's too busy preparing shot lists and schedules. Grimly, I start getting them together with the assistance of our lawyer, Sean. We need a respectable contract to send out to the actors, and something simple but effective for the crew. I hate contracts. However, Simon's not having a great day either. He's decided that he definitely needs to film on the Saturday – time will be too tight otherwise – however, our crew have already been told 5 days on location and Jacqui anticipates that they won't be happy with an extra day. Eventually, they compromise with a half-day.

14th – Camera, film and make-up tests at Panavision. A very exciting day. Gavin gets to play with the camera for the first time and experiment with the Varicon and various effects. Julia gets to try out some make-up and hair ideas on me and I get my first go at being filmed on 35 mm film. It all starts to feel very real.

16th – After a few days of increasing anxiety, we finally secure a new (and better) location for the guest house scenes on the Convent from a very generous resident. It's a beautiful house and it will really add to the production values of the film. We tell the good news to our team at a production meeting. Everyone seems to be on top of everything and the meeting goes well. We hear that the camera tests are ready to be viewed . . . however, the only time they can fit us in is 8 a.m. tomorrow.

17th – Up at the crack of dawn. It's still dark as we zoom to Technicolor for the screening of the camera tests from Panavision. The varicon/bleach bypass technique has produced some interesting results. Including the fact that I look 108 (a combination of some unforgiving lighting on the day, some 'ghostly' make up and the bleaching effect). Apart from that it's been an essential tool for getting the look of the film right, and Gavin and Simon seem confident that they're on the right tracks. We then zip home and are taken out for a very nice lunch with Margaret from Focal Press and Ian, the writer.

20th – Despite my super-confident casting approach we are no nearer to getting our 'Audrey'. However, I persevere – with Frank on board I know we'll eventually get someone good.

21st – Simon and I throw a festive production meeting and our team grows with the addition of our First Assistant Director, a big, confident Aussie called Philip Shaw. Much mulled wine and mince pies are consumed and the schedule is tackled seriously for the first time. Luke stays on to start building a dais for the flashback chapel scenes. The chapel is near freezing, but Luke keeps beavering away and defrosts occasionally for tea and toast.

23rd – Bea has come up trumps and has managed to persuade the Bond Street designer Joan and David to loan some clothes for my 'Sarah' costume. We enter the world of the super-rich and are treated impeccably for an hour as I try on various different, beautifully made clothes. Eventually we find an outfit that we both agree is 'Sarah' – practical and comfortable, yet chic and elegant too.

24–28th – We collapse for Christmas.

29th – 'Audrey' still hasn't been cast and we're getting worried. We've only 10 days to go before filming starts. We fax the script out to some distant repertory theatre where a potential 'Audrey' is in pantomime.

30th – The actress is interested . . . we hold our breath . . . and then at 5.55 p.m. we get a call from her agent saying that she's just been offered another job with the RSC. Aargh! Why is casting so difficult???!!!

31st – We ring an old friend, Christopher Dunham, to pick his brains about casting and he suggests his wife June Watson for the part. We had previously thought of her but had heard she was working on *102 Dalmatians*. However, she is available for our shoot dates, she reads a hastily faxed script and agrees to do it. We're delighted – June is a very experienced, prestigious actress and a good friend – it will be lovely working with her. We celebrate the New Year relieved and raring to go.

January 2000

3rd – Only a week to go. ONE WEEK!!!!! And So Much To Do! But everywhere is closed! It's an extra bank holiday. Apart from a few phone calls and a bit of paperwork the day is wasted. We chomp at the bit.

4th – ALL SYSTEMS GO, GO, GO!!! First we get a script out to Jacqueline Phillips, who we hope will play 'Anne', Audrey's daughter. We've held off casting Anne until we had cast Audrey, her mum. Jacqueline was at drama school with Simon and looks remarkably like June. She is available and accepts. Yippee! In the meantime we have a hot lunch date with the almighty Frank Finlay. He's lovely – a real gentleman – and I can't wait to start working with him. We then drag him off to a costume fitting, and I meet up with Claire and race back to Sussex. Claire's Unit Manager job is now really kicking into action and she can't wait!

5th – Claire knuckles down with glee and effortlessly manages to charm Neale House as well as the firemen (again!). We've changed the date for the firemen's hose down of the chapel, so she tirelessly dashes off to tell them! We then hurry back to a London pub for a final production meeting and the chance to meet some more of our crew. The production meeting unfortunately never happens, as Simon, Gavin and Jacqui are all stuck in traffic and can't get there on time. They eventually arrive having spent the day meeting the camera crew at Panavision. Simon is elated with his camera team – all experienced professionals – and can't wait to get going. The rest of the evening goes well – we meet most of our crew, who are all very enthusiastic and lovely people – and we drive home exhausted but happy.

6th – Busy, busy, busy. Busy. The phone never stops and is a constant distraction as Claire and I try to tackle the hundred and one things that need doing. I'm trying to cast 'Emily' and turn again to Chris Dunham, who comes up trumps, and the lovely Josie Kidd is cast. Josie is with Simon's agent, so there are no problems there. I also thrash through more contracts trying to get them all sorted before we start filming (have I said how much I HATE that job?!!), but finally get on top of it. I really feel like a Producer today – thoroughly stressed, agonized, panicked and having a really good time!

7th – I'm a little less stressed today. The product placement stuff arrives and Simon and I gleefully dive into boxes of Monster Munch and gorge ourselves on Iced Gems (not recommended . . .). Not quite sure what we're going to do with the bumper box of KY Jelly though. I have a blissfully quiet evening going through the script with Simon and discussing 'Sarah'. I start to get to grips with how I'm going to present this intense and private character.

8th – Cast read-through at Ealing Studios. After all the weeks of agonized casting, there's a real sense of satisfaction seeing such a talented group of actors sitting around the table. Simon gives the customary welcome speech and we launch into the read-through. The script has been extensively rewritten since we first sent it out. Will it work? How will it sound? Are the characters believable? Are there still too many words???!!! Our fears are unfounded as everyone reads beautifully and Simon and I sneak an excited glance at each other. This is it!! One day to go! We return home to find our lounge is full of camera gear and the chapel is full of grip equipment. Our house has been taken over. It's begun.

9th – A tense day as Simon and Gavin try and juggle the shots they want into an already packed schedule. Deciding to postpone a lock-off shot that was scheduled for today does not help this. However, we have to get round it with slightly longer days, and hopefully our crew will be flexible.

This is it.

Production week

10th – First day's shoot on location in Sussex – A day from Heaven and a day from Hell. The crew arrives through the morning and the set-up for the first shots begins – it's all exteriors today and, thankfully, the weather's perfect. It's so exciting seeing everyone arrive and slot into place. Julia (make-up) and Bea (costume) are the last to arrive, having been stuck in bad traffic, so it's late morning by the time I get into costume and make-up and am called to set. The first shots filmed are of Sarah walking through the grounds to the abandoned chapel talking into her Dictaphone. I manage to rehearse without a) tripping up, b) forgetting my lines or c) dribbling profusely. Simon's satisfied and we go for a take. Philip screams 'Action!' and we're off.

The morning goes well, bar a few technical problems, and I love every minute of it. I feel excited, relaxed and confident in front of the camera. Rodrigo Gutierrez, the camera operator, contributes to this, as this big bear of a man goes out of his way to put you at your ease. This is something that I truly appreciate throughout the week, and I grow very fond of Rod. Simon has a great morning too and, over a very tasty lunch at Neale House, we can't help but notice a really good atmosphere developing throughout the crew.

However, in the afternoon things go slightly sour. The schedule changes, longer hours have upset some of our key crew and Simon and I have to placate them. There's no way around it, we feel rotten because the last thing we want to do is upset our team and tempers are short. We're all tired and stressed. Matters are not helped by a confrontation with a very angry resident threatening to force us off the Convent because of a minor parking incident. I'm at the end of my tether and swearing that I'll never produce again. We reluctantly decide to cancel the fire brigade hose down (much to Claire's disappointment) to avoid disrupting the residents any further.

However, eventually everyone starts to calm down, we talk to the crew and realize that things aren't so bad after all. They've quickly adapted to the changes and are bonding well with each other. After a few drinks in the pub the atmosphere has returned to one of good will and enthusiasm. I collapse into bed thinking that maybe I'll give producing a couple more days . . .

11th – Second day's shoot – I wake up with renewed energy and excitement. Start the day being filmed in the Retro-Chapel, closely watched by our documentary crew, who are here for some 'behind the scenes' footage for the day. Simon spends the afternoon filming flashback sequences with hooded figures (and yes, Paul from Quantel gives a 'stunning' performance as hooded figure number 4), while I'm getting made up and sewn into the costume for the Flashback Sarah scenes. Julia gleefully makes me look 'dead' (which, alas, wasn't too challenging for her) and I lie in the icy chapel having 'blood' poured all over my neck trying to keep a glazed glassy eyed 'dead' look and trying not to shiver. It's amazing how badly your eyes want to blink when they're not supposed to. However, I survive and manage to sneak a look at the rushes from the first day. They look great. A much better day, and I sleep like a baby.

12th – Third day's shoot – I'm dog-tired today and thankfully I only have one small scene to do at the end of the day. So I put my 'producers' hat on and watch some of the scenes being shot at the guest house location. It's Frank's first day and I'm anxious to see that he's treated well. I needn't have worried; everyone treats all the actors with the utmost respect and friendliness. June and Jacqui are working really well together and they uncannily look like mother and daughter. They're also great fun to have around, and they stay over at our house to save the long drive home. We spend the evening relaxing with red wine and more product placement Monster Munch. Perfect!

13th – Fourth day's shoot – The atmosphere amongst the cast and crew has grown into a really good, positive feeling. It is a joy walking onto the set – everyone seems very comfortable with their jobs and I can honestly say there isn't a 'bad apple' amongst them. I spend as much time as I can throughout the week trying to get to know some of the crew and thanking them for their hard work. When you're not paying a crew I think it's essential to treat them with respect. I'm especially grateful to Maurice, our executive gaffer, who has worked tirelessly throughout the week (no mean feat when you're in your 80s). Our only concern now is time. Will we get everything shot on this very tight schedule? Simon's starting to regret not getting the extra time he wanted.

We work on more scenes in the guest house today. Frank is settling nicely and giving the perfect, understated film performance. I learn an enormous amount just watching him. I'm really looking forward to our scenes together.

Lunchtime, as usual at Neale House. The food here has been excellent – much to our relief – and our crew seems happy with the accommodation. In fact there have been reports of some great midnight toast parties, the highlight of which appear to be our gaffer Mike Vincent's filthy stories!

The afternoon brings visits from Anne Guidera from Kodak and John Rendall from Panavision. I've grown particularly fond of John, a kindly, gentle man, who has been incredibly supportive of the project from the beginning. It's lovely to have him and Anne on set – to show them some rushes and to be able to thank them personally for their support.

As the day goes on, it becomes clear that we're not going to be able to fit everything in and a scene is postponed until tomorrow. We end the day shooting in the Retro-Chapel, but time is running out and both Simon and I feel that the scene ends up rushed. We end the evening with a late-night production meeting working out how we're going to fit everything in tomorrow. Simon and Gavin huddle together, exhausted, and manage to reduce the shot list a little. It's going to be a tight fit.

14th – Fifth day's shoot – A long, long day. The morning goes well and we finish on schedule. We use the Cinejib for the first time. More visitors – Peter Lamont arrives on set, much to the delight of our art department – and my mum and dad stop by to gawp (and meet Frank Finlay). Focal Press arrives and are given the guided tour (I'm getting very good at it) and are suitably impressed by the organized chaos of a film set.

The afternoon drags a little. We get stuck on a couple of scenes and little gets done. The clock keeps ticking. Despite this, I'm enjoying my scenes with Frank and relishing the experience. We eventually get onto the final chapel scene – a special effects shot involving eight disappearing ghostly hooded figures – and it takes forever. Eventually we wrap for the day at 11 p.m. – way over schedule. Jacqui and Claire have thoughtfully organized some drinks at Neale House, and we somehow conjure up the energy to roll over there and party until 3 a.m. A long, long day.

15th – Sixth day's shoot and the final day on location – There's a 9 a.m. call, but miraculously everyone's on time. There's a slightly muted (hungover) atmosphere though. Everyone's tired and looking forward to going home (and besides, they've now heard all of Mike's stories . . .). We have to finish with the bulk of the crew at midday today. We're filming the scenes at Charlie's house. They go smoothly and we manage to squeeze in the postponed scene from the guest house and wrap at 12.20 p.m. A big sigh of relief.

The crew slowly disbands, leaving a skeleton crew to film a few pickups in the afternoon. We slowly get them done, surviving on tea and Monster Munch (which we're heartily sick of now) and collapse in the evening. The house looks as if a bomb has hit it and we're exhausted. But we've got the bulk of our film and it's been a fantastic week.

16th – No rest for the low-budget filmmaker. Up to London to drop off some costumes and chat over the shoot's progress with Jacqui. Jacqui and her production assistant, the super calm Liesbeth, have been fantastic throughout the shoot, handling all the production management with aplomb. We discuss the day's shoot at Pinewood. There have been problems – the set building is very behind and they've only one day to finish it. We return home wondering if we'll have a set on Tuesday.

17th – I never want to see another mop again. I spend the day cleaning the filthy chapel with Claire and Tanya Hazelden (one of our excellent production runners). Also the big Panavision vans arrive and we (the producers, director and unit manager! – oh the joys of low-budget filming!) spend an hour loading all the camera and grip equipment. Simon then dashes off to Pinewood. The news there is not great – the set is taking a long time.

18th – Seventh day's shoot at Pinewood Studios – After very little sleep we get up at the crack of dawn and drive to Pinewood, unsure of what will greet us there. Surprisingly, everything is fine, thanks mainly to our hard-working art department and Philip (our First AD, who mucked in with the construction as well) and Luke (who has been there all night and looks completely shell shocked). So we can relax and we begin to enjoy the day and the fact that we are filming at Pinewood Studios. Pinewood Studios! Right next to the *007 Bond* Sound Stage! And the day goes beautifully. The atmosphere on set is calm and happy. We had to find another camera operator for today and were thrilled to get Trevor Coop. Trevor Coop! How lucky are we!?! We have a lot of visitors throughout the day – Freddie Francis, Peter Lamont, Quantel and Focal Press all show their support, whilst our documentary crew and the Film Four documentary crew capture plenty of behind the scenes footage and interviews. The studio is a hive of activity. The filming goes very smoothly and the effects look great. It's a fantastic day and a fantastic way to end the shoot of *Ghosthunter*.

22nd – The house is finally back in order and we getting ready to go up to the wrap party in London. We've spent the rest of the week tidying up the locations and starting to get on top of the accounts. Simon has thankfully taken on that job and is slowly wading through the receipts handed over from Jacqui. One problem has arisen. Our editor, Eddie Hamilton, has been editing the feature film *Dead Babies*. He should have finished in December, but it's dragging on, and he's now unsure of when he'll be ready to edit *Ghosthunter*. Hopefully it'll only be a couple of weeks.

The wrap party takes place in a bar in Notting Hill, and it's lovely to see Freddie and Maurice there and the majority of our crew. It's good to relax with them all, and very gratifying to hear about the contacts they've made whilst working on *Ghosthunter*.

24th – Bad news about Eddie. He's going to be busy for quite a while on *Dead Babies* so it looks as if we're going to have to find another editor. Our post-production period, which we were hoping to launch straight into, is now on hold. The search is on to find an available editor.

February

The month is chiefly spent wading through paperwork – receipts and contracts and bills – and looking for an available editor. It's not been an easy job but we are helped enormously by Robin O'Donoghue to whom we turn again and again for suggestions. Eventually, we get to meet Simon Cozens, who is currently Assistant Editor on *The Man Who Cried* but who is keen to edit *Ghosthunter* in his spare time. He has a lot of experience, he's been highly recommended and he's a very nice guy. He starts to digitalize and sound synch the rushes.

We also spend the month looking for writers and reading screenplays. We're anxious to start getting some feature ideas together, so that when *Ghosthunter* is released and we're asked 'what next?' we have something to show people. Interest in *Ghosthunter* starts growing and a couple of interviews crop up. Simon and I man the office daily and prepare ourselves as best we can for the future months ahead.

March

Post-production begins in earnest. However, the edit is going slowly. Simon (editor) is very busy with his feature and the *Ghosthunter* edit is squeezed into his spare time – which is limited. We're not too worried – we don't have a deadline for the film – but we would like to get on with it. I keep away from the edit suite and let the Simons battle it out.

7th – Whilst the edit has been plodding along, I have continued my quest for a scriptwriter. I've been wading through over 20 scripts and the standard is very mixed. However, one script stands head and shoulders above the rest and I eagerly handed it to Simon to read. We both agree that the writer, Clifton Stewart, has the kind of qualities that we're looking for and today we arrange to meet him. Clifton is a friendly, easygoing guy and we all click together pretty easily. We discuss the sort of films we're interested in and he seems very happy to work with us.

We also meet up with Luke and Gavin. It's good to see them both again and we fill them in on the progress with *Ghosthunter*. Gavin is positively chomping at the bit to see a first cut – he'll have to be patient for now. Meanwhile Luke is working on a poster design for the film (and a cover design for this book) and we discuss various ideas with him.

17th – The Simons have had a few good editing sessions together and at last, Simon comes home with a rough cut to show me. I'm quite nervous. I've seen all the mute rushes, but this is the first time I've seen the film, in order, with sound. What's it going to be like? Will it make sense? Is the acting good? IS IT GOING TO WORK???!!!

The first shock is the sound. It's very rough and ready, and everything has been picked up. And I mean everything. The whirr of the camera sounds as if a helicopter is in the room, the hum of the lights sounds as if half the crew is blow-drying their hair. We crack up at one of the most serious scenes in the film because Frank has a very squeaky shoe. It initially looks like a huge problem. However, Simon (editor) has assured us that it's quite normal and most of it can be cleaned up without any problems. We hope. Apart from the heightened sound, I'm pleasantly surprised. The edit is rough but the acting is fine, we've got the shots we need and it's coming together well. What I can't judge is whether the story makes sense. We'll have to have some sort of test screenings to determine that. But it's getting there.

Back at the office, we continue to work with Clifton and develop ideas with him. He's now in the process of writing up some treatment ideas that we had discussed. Also, we're debating whether to go to the Cannes film festival in May. *Ghosthunter* won't be ready to show there, but it could be a great experience and a good way to extend our list of contacts. Our minds are made up for us when Quantel tell us that they have a boat in Cannes and some screens in the British Pavilion and that we could screen an extract from the film there. We decide that even though the film won't be ready for Cannes it would be great – and feasible – to take a short promo of the film out there. It would also be an invaluable opportunity to start pitching our feature treatments and see what sort of response we get. We click into overdrive. We've now got a lot to get done and a deadline to meet.

21st – Time for another lunch with Sam and Mark Auguste, our sound editor and consultant. We discuss our concerns about the sound. Mark pops our rough cut into the machine, listens carefully to our blow-drying crew, fiddles with a few controls and, hey presto! – it's miraculously gone. 'You're worried about that!' he exclaims. 'That's nothing.' We both sigh with relief and thank our lucky stars that our sound edit is in very capable hands. Sam will be doing the bulk of our sound edit while Mark consults. He seems to be looking forward to it and his eyes glisten at the prospect of all the sound effects needed for *Ghosthunter*.

Simon spends the evening editing whilst I go to a Cannes Survival Seminar run by the NPA (New Producers Alliance). It's an informative evening, and I feel a little more prepared for the trip to come.

25th – Gavin and I go into the edit suite to watch the first cut and it's great to see that the film is starting to shape together well. Simon (editor) has levelled out the sound a bit and added some temporary music and a few basic effects. It makes a world of difference. The music immediately grabs your emotions and I'm struck by how scary the film is. It's getting exciting.

Our excitement is heightened today when we take the first cut to show Barrington, our composer. He's the first person outside of the Simons and myself to see a cut of the film. We wait anxiously for his verdict. We needn't have worried – he loves it, fully understands the story and says all the right things. He's very supportive of us both and it's just the boost we need after 2 months of frustratingly slow progress. We leave his house walking on air.

28th – One of the most important things about making a film is publicity. Without it, no one's going to know about or see your film. As yet we have no money to spend on it. However, we approached Jessica Churchill of Churchill Kirsch during filming and she has agreed to help us out if she can. Today she has managed to arrange a meeting with the organizers of the British Short Film Festival. They're interested in having a *Ghosthunter* event at the forthcoming festival in September. The meeting goes well and we arrange to put together some ideas for filling a 90-minute evening. It would be a good start for getting *Ghosthunter* seen and publicized.

29th – It's been an incredible 6 months since we first met Jamie Payne, our Short Film Guru. And here we are again, ready to pick his brains about the next step to take on the rocky road of Distribution and Completion Funding. Although we've spoken to him on the phone many times during those months, it's good to see him again and be spurred on by his support and enthusiasm. He gives us a few names to contact and warns us of some potential pitfalls – it has been invaluable having someone who's been there and done it offering a guiding hand. We leave, promising to show him a cut of the film soon.

April

The edit continues. The second cut is faster and neater and we prepare to show it to a select few. Meanwhile, the Simons begin working on the promo in earnest. It's a tiring process – suddenly we seem to be spending long days in the car travelling to and from Barrington, Sam, Simon and Quantel with their various requirements. They're all very busy people, and we start to get anxious about whether we're asking too much of them or whether we'll get it ready in time. It's getting tense.

11th – Time for another meeting with Sean, our lawyer – yet another invaluable member of our team. We cannot recommend strongly enough getting a good and friendly lawyer – not only has Sean helped us with the nasty job of contracts, he's also provided some excellent advice. We pick his brains about distribution, Cannes, copyright and more contracts (yes, they're never-ending).

18th – Today, we take a trip to Quantel to start on our first digital effects for the promo. Matt Twyford, our digital effects supervisor, sits in front of the Domino system and our mouths drop in awe as he whizzes through its technicalities with the greatest of ease. Also we get to see the real resolution of the film for the first time – in all its 35 mm glory – you feel that you could almost step into it, it's so rich and deep. We've brought along two effects for the promo and Simon discusses with Matt how he'd like these to take shape. Matt continues playing the Domino like a master musician and the effects start to take shape.

We return home to an e-mail from Jacqui. She's drawn up a post-production budget for us and the news is not good. We've already spent the £30 000 that we budgeted for the whole film (gulp) and we need at least another £5000 to finish it. Actually we really need about £10 000, if we want to employ Jessica (publicity) and use some live musicians for the recording of Barrington's music. Over the next few days I start to make some tentative approaches for some completion funding, but the response is not encouraging. Try again in a month is the best response I get. I start to get concerned about whether we're going to find the funds to finish this film.

20th – We've spent the week starting to show the second cut of the film to a few friends. Today we show *Ghosthunter* to Jamie, and I'm surprised at how nervous I feel before we show it. However, Jamie is as supportive as ever – his advice on the cut is very useful and he genuinely seems impressed with what we've achieved so far.

21st – The pressure builds, as we strive to get the promo finished and our poster and postcards printed. We have a deadline of 3 May to have everything done and, at the moment, things are frustratingly slow. Simon is also working later and later in the office trying to get on top of the accounts and VAT, and the long drives here, there and everywhere continue. We're tired and stressed. Was this promo really such a good idea??

However, after a week of 'test' screenings of the film, the news is encouraging. The story seems to be coming across and the comments have been overwhelmingly positive and constructive. It's very reassuring, and we start to feel that we really are getting somewhere . . . with the film at least.

26th – Our last meeting with Clifton before we go to Cannes. We've worked together well and come up with some excellent ideas, and we're really pleased with the way the treatments are progressing. It feels very refreshing to start focusing on something other than *Ghosthunter*, and it gives us a sense of purpose.

28th – More driving, rushing, stress, promo, aargh! Fed up.

May

2nd – Hooray!! Yippee! IT'S FINISHED! The promo is ready on time! And we've got the postcards and posters printed and they look fabulous. Luke has done a fantastic job (ably assisted by Ian Firth, our titles designer). However, no time to sit on our backsides and we spend the day racing around sending copies of the promo out to Quantel (for their stand in the British Pavilion), to the British Short Film Festival (so they can see how the film is progressing) to Ian Lewis (our writer who's offered to transfer it to our website) and to FilmFour for their documentary (which is due to be shown on 12 May). We also send out 65 postcards informing our cast, crew and contacts of the FilmFour documentary. I don't think I ever want to lick another stamp again. And then we pack. Because tomorrow, we go on holiday . . . and I CAN'T WAIT!! We'll return in 10 days and then it's straight off to Cannes for 5 days. Up until now, we've sort of sat on the fringes of the film industry, quietly doing things our own way. However, Cannes will be a baptism of fire. Now we're looking for some completion funding for *Ghosthunter* and some development money for our treatments, along with several hundred other hungry filmmakers. All we've got is a promo, some classy postcards, some interesting film ideas and oodles of optimism. It's going to be very interesting.

Cannes 15–20 May

We arrive in Cannes mid-afternoon, dressed in our best, ready for an evening drinks do at the Kodak pavilion and clutching our postcards, packages and treatments. We've got an hour to kill beforehand. OK. Where now? Time to get a feel for the place.

First, we register. To be able to walk around the pavilions and hotels you need a Unifrance pass. This you apply for way back in March, or you can get it on the day (but be prepared to spend half the day doing it). They're very strict registering and you have to be able to prove very thoroughly that you are in the industry, stopping short of providing your blood group. We have registered in advance; however, we nearly get turned away because we left our passports at the hotel. After much sweet talking (even offering to supply our blood group . . .) the very nice French girl processing our registration relents and we get our badges (with the obligatory dreadful passport photo on them).

We wander around, soaking up the atmosphere (and the sun!). Our first impression is that Cannes is crowded. Hundreds of hopeful filmmakers mingling with stars mingling with tourists from all over the world. We bump into the All Saints (or rather their very burly 7 foot bodyguards) leaving a press conference. We start to explore further. The film festival stretches along the whole of the Croisette. The core of it centres around the Palais (a rather depressing concrete bunker-shaped building) where all the competition films are screened. An assortment of pavilions are grouped around this area and most of these you can freely wander into. We tended to gravitate towards the British Pavilion and the Kodak Pavilion, although the American one looked quite fun. The Marche (the main film market) is actually in the Palais building; however, you need another pass to get in there that costs a few hundred pounds. Having said that, towards the end of the festival they let us in with our Unifrance pass. The rest of the festival is dotted in the hotels along the Croisette, which are completely taken over by different film companies. This is where you go if you want to do business.

It can be a little intimidating at first. There are groups of filmmakers huddled wherever you go, who glance briefly at you when you enter, then resume chatting when they see you're not famous or important to them. However, we keep a positive attitude and confidently proceed to our drinks do. Once inside the pavilion, we discover another reason why the film industry flock to Cannes. Free booze. And lots of it. The wine flows freely and as the week goes on we meet several people who spend their whole days drifting from one cocktail party to another, in a constant alcoholic daze. The drinks do is interesting – we meet a few other filmmakers and compare experiences – but uneventful. We collapse back at our hotel and plan our strategy for the next few days. And that is one of the most important things about going to Cannes: knowing what you're going to do when you're out there, and preferably having a lot of appointments and parties lined up *before you go*. Otherwise, it's easy to wander around rather aimlessly, with a sinking sense that you're missing out on something good.

So, clasping our plan of action, we successfully spend the next few days renewing some old contacts and making some new ones, as well as squeezing in a couple of parties. We spend a lot of time with Paul Watkins on a luxurious yacht, which has been jointly hired for Cannes by Quantel, Fuji, Panavision and Lee Lighting and, as promised, he shows our promo. He also introduces us to a few people who could be useful for *Ghosthunter* towards the end of post-production. We then bump into Hugh Whittaker from Panavision and finally meet our contact at Technicolour, Kishor Ladwa, who is instantly likeable and very friendly. He promises us a screening of *Ghosthunter* sometime in the future

Amongst others, we have a good chat with David Webb at Kodak and discuss our films in development and the plans that Kodak have for helping to finance films. We meet Paul Howson from the British Council and discuss the possibility of their help with a print grant and distributing *Ghosthunter* when it's finished. We introduce ourselves to FilmFour. We suss out all the various 'dot.com' Internet companies that are vying to show your short on their site. We meet up with some other filmmakers and actors who are in the same boat as us and swap experiences and business cards. And, OK, we have the occasional drink.

One night we wangle an invitation to the screening and party of a new British film called *Dead Babies*. It's a popular event, so popular in fact that the club where the party is held is jam-packed so tightly that no one can move in or out. Simon and I last 5 minutes and then decide to move onto the Quantel boat, where another party is in full swing. There's plenty of room on the boat; however, there's some surprise entertainment. The boat next to Quantel's has been hired by an American billionaire who is throwing a live strip show on the open deck! Only in Cannes! I try and have a serious conversation with Simon and Paul, only to see their eyes keep wandering over to two skinny, naked girls doing strange things with a bottle of champagne. It was the most popular boat in the harbour and even the policemen ended up lined up on the dockside cheering them on. Needless to say the party was one of the most talked about the next day.

Eventually, we've had enough of Cannes. Also, as the festival nears the end of it's second week, there's a feeling that everything is winding down, and that everyone is heading home. It's been a worthwhile trip. We haven't raised any more funds (yet), but we've done some valuable networking, and spread the word about *Ghosthunter*. And importantly, we now know how Cannes works and the best way to navigate it – firstly, make sure you're going with a strong purpose or, even better, a finished film to show; secondly, try and arrange meetings and parties before you go; and thirdly, be bold, be confident and be prepared to sell your project in a positive way at anytime. So, until next year, we scoot off into the sunset in our hired Fiat Punto, and spend the last day and half exploring the beautiful Cote D'Azur, before returning to cold, damp England.

23rd – Back in the office with renewed energy and determination to finish the film, we face our next hurdle. Whilst we were away we heard that Quantel can no longer handle our special effects owing to a lack of personnel. We now have to find a special effects house that will take on all the effects for us. It's a bit of a blow to say the least; however, Paul Watkins has busted a gut for us and arranged meetings with various different effects companies in London. We meet Drew Jones of the Computer Film Company (CFC) today and, after talking through the work involved, they very generously offer to take on all the effects. We're very relieved – we now fully turn our attention to locking off the film. We can't wait!

That concludes my diary. However, I have a few last tips that I'd like to pass on. Hope they're useful.

1 Present yourself and your company as professionally as possible. There's a lot of competition out there and you'll be taken more seriously if you have decent headed paper, a well-put-together package and a polite and friendly approach.
2 If something goes wrong, don't panic. There is always a solution and very often the solution is better than the original plan.
3 Be prepared. Make sure you have all the information you need at your fingertips for important meetings and phone calls.
4 Write everything down. Carry a notepad around with you constantly. There is so much to remember when working on a film, and writing everything down is the only way to keep on top of it.

5 If you don't know something, don't be afraid to ask. If possible, get yourself a contact that you can call anytime who is experienced in filmmaking and whom you can ask about absolutely anything.

6 If you're doing two or more jobs at once (producing/acting, producing/directing/writing), then make sure that you have some strong and able crew to help you with/take over one of the jobs whilst you're concentrating on the other. It was essential for me to know that I could trust Jacqui and Claire to handle the production side of things whilst I was on set acting and Simon was directing. It would have been a nightmare otherwise.

7 Take the time in pre-production to find a crew who are enthusiastic, good natured and (if possible) experienced. Don't have anyone on your crew who acts as if they're doing you a huge favour because they're working for nothing. It's your film, and if you have a shoddy, argumentative crew, the film will suffer. And last but not least . . .

8 Go for it! Just go out there, believe in yourself and your film, be respectful to those who deserve it, and honest and true to yourself, and sock it to 'em!! (And may the force be with you.) Good luck!!

Appendix K – Useful addresses and websites

Amulet Films – for the latest news on *Ghosthunter* and future projects, visit the Amulet Films' website and join the 'E-mailing list'
www.amulet-films.com

Computer Film Company (CFC) – a leading visual effects house, working on feature films and commercials at the very highest level
www.cfc.co.uk

Farnham Film Company – Ian Lewis, writer of this book, set up the The Farnham Film Company in 1985 to produce international television programming
www.farnfilm.com

Fb Films – for affordable, user-friendly Movie Budgeting software and the innovative CD-CV
www.fbfilms.co.uk

The Global Film School – professional training on the Internet from three of the most prestigious film and television schools in the world
www.globalfilmschool.com

Internet Movie Database – the place to find any information on films
www.imdb.com

Kodak
www.kodak.co.uk

The Lux Centre – offers affordable equipment hire and edit facilities, and some great courses
2–4 Hoxton Square
London N1 6NU
Tel: 020 7684 0202
www.lea.org.uk

Netribution – a website offering a comprehensive database for British filmmakers
www.netribution.co.uk

New Producers Alliance
9 Bourlet Close
London W1P 7PJ
Tel: 020 7580 2480
www.npa.org.uk

Panavision – for information on equipment, sales and all the latest news
www.panavision.co.uk

Quantel – a world leader in the development and manufacture of digital graphics, effects, editing and server systems for broadcast, post-production and film applications
www.quantel.com

Screen International – trade paper with a daily news update (by e-mail if you prefer)
www.screendaily.com

Shooting People – a UK mailing list where you can recruit cast and crew and research absolutely anything about filmmaking
www.shootingpeople.org

Appendix L – Join Amulet Films' e-mailing list

FOR ALL THE LATEST NEWS ON

AND FUTURE PROJECTS VISIT

WWW.AMULET-FILMS.COM

JOIN OUR E-MAILING LIST

AND BE THE FIRST TO RECEIVE
UPDATES OF PRODUCTION NEWS AND
INFORMATION ON SCREENINGS

TO JOIN, VISIT THE WEBSITE AND CLICK ON

'E-MAILING LIST'

Appendix M – Who does what on a film set

Art Director
Has slightly more nuts and bolts responsibilities, although this may be the same person as, or another name for, the Production Designer.

Assistant Art Director
Design department assistants.

Associate Producer
Most often an honorary title given to someone involved with the getting the project off the ground, but whom you wouldn't want to trust with any important decisions.

Boom-swinger/Sound Assistant
Often balletic individuals who are able to squeeze themselves into unbelievably small spaces in order to hold the microphone in exactly the right place. Unsung heroes!

Camera Operator
The person who actually looks through the camera, frames the shots and photographs the action.

Cinematographer
See Lighting Cameraman/woman.

Clapper-loader
The person who operates the clapper board and who loads the film into the magazines.

On smaller shoots the camera team often consists of two people: the Lighting Cameraperson, who also operates the clapper board, and a Camera Assistant, who does everything else.

Continuity
Takes notes of everything as it is filmed and makes sure that people are wearing the clothes they should be wearing, walking in the right direction, facing the right way, and so on.

Director
Has direct responsibility for what appears on the screen: directs the film's action and how the camera looks at it.

Director of Photography (DoP/DP)
See Lighting Cameraman/woman.

Dubbing Editor/Sound Editor
Once the picture is complete, a specialist sound editor will often prepare the sound tracks ready for mixing by the Dubbing Mixer.

Dubbing Mixer
In charge of mixing the various dialogue, music and effects sound tracks to produce the film's final mixed sound track. (Dubbing is known as 're-recording' in the USA.)

Editor
Takes the rushes and turns them into a film. The Editor is one of the three most important people working on a picture (together with the Director and the DoP). The Editor often has an Assistant Editor to help with the routine parts of the job.

Executive Producer
Has to do with finance. This is sometimes a Head of Department of a TV Station or a Distributor which has put money into the picture. Sometimes it is a financier who has no active production role.

First Assistant Director
In charge of the set itself – wherever filming is taking place. Attempts to keep everything moving along on behalf of the Director. If you ever visit a film location, the First is the person whose permission you ask to be on the set.

Focus Puller
Operating a camera needs at least three hands. Operators without a third arm work with a focus puller – special people who can keep a shot in focus without being able to see through the camera.

Gaffer
The Head Electrician, who will work with one or several other (qualified) electricians.

Grip
The person who moves the camera around, with the help of tracks, cranes and other expensive equipment. The Grip's sense of timing in moves is crucial to the success of a shot.

Hair and Make-up
Self-explanatory, really. Includes wigs.

Lighting Cameraman/woman, Director of Photography(DOP/DP), Cinematographer
All the same person. This is the head of the camera team and is normally said to have 'lit' a picture. Responsible (in conjunction with the Director) for the overall look of the film. Some DoPs operate the camera themselves. Many don't.

Line Producer
On bigger pictures there may be a Line Producer who basically has the management responsibilities of a Producer without the creative control.

Location Manager
Often finds locations and persuades people to let the Unit in to their home or street; have taken down television aerials for the period film, and so on. Will normally be with the Unit solving the thousands of daily problems that always crop up.

Producer
Usually the driving force behind making a project happen. Arranges finance, hires key personnel (Writer, Director, cast), or persuades them to become involved. Is responsible for the overall schedule and budget, and for selling and promoting the film once complete.

Production Assistant (PA)
This role exists mainly in television. The PA combines the roles of First Assistant Director and the Continuity.

Production Designer
Defines the overall look of sets and locations, and has the responsibility for making it all happen – from a grand design to the right teaspoons.

Production Manager
Makes sure that everything and everybody are in the right place and at the right time. Will often negotiate the production's deals with facilities and crew, and make sure that the relevant trade union agreements are adhered to.

Props Buyer
Good Props Buyers have encyclopaedic knowledge and an instinct for finding exactly the right thing, even from unsuspecting attics.

Runners
Fetch, carry and drive as they are told and are very important to the smooth running of the film.

Second Assistant Director
Helps the First Assistant Director. Often has primary responsibility for managing Extras.

Second Unit
On bigger projects there is often a second, smaller production unit to shoot material not requiring the principal cast, for example background shots of cities the main unit never actually visits; aerial or stunt sequences, and so on.

Sound Recordist/Mixer
Sits in a corner on a camp-stool with headphones on, oblivious to everything except the sound coming from the microphone wielded by the Boom-swinger/Sound Assistant.

Standby Carpenters and Painters
'Standby' because they are on set ready to make alterations or repairs while filming is going on.

Third Assistant Director
Assistant to the Second Assistant Director. Second and Third Assistant Directors basically allow the First Assistant Director to be all over the location (not just on the set) at the same time.

Wardrobe Designer
Head of the Wardrobe Department – makes, hires, buys exactly the right clothes and associated accessories (sporrans, swords, hats) for the film. Will usually work with several assistants, especially on days involving a lot of Extras.

Writer

The person who provides the reason for everyone being there in the first place.

Note: Larger productions may well have an Executive Producer, Producer, Associate Producer, Line Producer, Director, Writer, Production Manager and Location Manager. At the other extreme, one person might be doing everything. In any case, the boundaries between the functions are very fluid, and vary with the individuals involved.

Index

Note: Page numbers given in italic refer to illustrations.

Films for Filmmakers

Kodak Vision 800T film 7289/5289

Tungsten-800 EI Daylight-500* EI

The world's fastest tungsten-balanced stock. Offers the sharpness and grain structure you would expect only in slower products.
Allows for increased creative flexibility in low light, fast action, anamorphic, super 35mm and other filming conditions, where systems speed is vitally important.

Kodak Vision 500T film 7279/5279

Tungsten-500 EI Daylight-320* EI

With improved grain and sharpness, this high speed tungsten balanced stock offers rich colours and excellent detail in low and very low light conditions.

Kodak Vision 320T film 7277/5277

Tungsten-320 EI Daylight-200* EI

This unique tungsten balanced stock offers a less saturated look with slightly lower contrast whilst providing superb shadow detail and clean white highlights.

Kodak Vision 250D film 7246/5246

Daylight-250 EI Tungsten-64**EI

A high speed daylight balanced film stock providing the highest image quality for its speed. It delivers a rich reproduction of blacks in natural and mixed lighting conditions.

Kodak Vision 200T film 7274/5274

Tungsten-200 EI Daylight-125* EI

A higher speed tungsten balanced stock with fine grain and outstanding sharpness, offering a wide exposure latitude and excellent colour reproduction. A very good all round stock that works very well in almost any lighting condition.

Eastman EXR 100T film 7248/5248

Tungsten-100 EI Daylight-64*EI

A medium speed tungsten balanced stock with wide exposure latitude. Very good grain and saturation producing excellent highlights and shadow detail.

Eastman EXR 50D film 7245/5245

Daylight-50 EI Tungsten-12**EI

A daylight balanced stock, extremely sharp and virtually grain free. This film offers a wide exposure latitude with rich, natural colours. An excellent choice for bright exteriors.

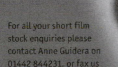

For all your short film stock enquiries please contact Anne Guidera on 01442 844231, or fax us on 01442 844987.

The Kodak Professional Motion Imaging web address:
http://www.Kodak.com/go/motion

Kodak
Entertainment Imaging

Interactive CD-CVs

FB Films

Multimedia Designs

Showreel Editing

CD-CV

A new, interactive way for Film and T.V professionals to present their showreel, music, CV and details of production experience to prospective employers. Choose from a number of CD-CV templates or we can produce customized designs.

All CD-ROM designs are stand alone programs, which do not require the user to install any software. Showreel playback direct from CD is high quality with no frame drop.

Prices start at £70 for the standard CD-CV templates. This price includes transfer of up to 4 minutes of video into MPEG format, 5 copies of the CD-CV with designed CD inlay and back, and storage of all files and video required for later up-date. For an additional cost we can provide customized designs for individuals or companies. Please contact us a for a quotation and further details.

Showreel Editing

A good showreel is essential in promoting your work and we have two alternatives to create a stylish presentation. Choose from a full version using music, dialogue and video or a basic version using titles in between selected clips.

Other Services available
* Personalized design service
* Conversion to a website format
* Video/CD packaging designs
* Postcard and poster designs
* Short films and pilots transferred to CD-ROM

FB Films
Tele/Fax - 020 7916 0365
e-mail: mail@fbfilms.co.uk
Web: http:\\www.fbfilms.co.uk

 **Focal Press**   **www.focalpress.com**

Join Focal Press online
As a member you will enjoy the following benefits:

- browse our full list of books available
- view sample chapters
- order securely online

Focal eNews
Register for eNews, the regular email service from Focal Press, to receive:

- advance news of our latest publications
- exclusive articles written by our authors
- related event information
- free sample chapters
- information about special offers

Go to www.focalpress.com to register and the eNews bulletin will soon be arriving on your desktop!

If you require any further information about the eNews or www.focalpress.com please contact:

USA
Tricia Geswell
Email: t.geswell@elsevier.com
Tel: +1 781 313 4739

Europe and rest of world
Lucy Lomas-Walker
Email: l.lomas@elsevier.com
Tel: +44 (0) 1865 314438

Catalogue
For information on all Focal Press titles, our full catalogue is available online at www.focalpress.com, alternatively you can contact us for a free printed version:

USA
Email: c.degon@elsevier.com
Tel: +1 781 313 4721

Europe and rest of world
Email: j.blackford@elsevier.com
Tel: +44 (0) 1865 314220

Potential authors
If you have an idea for a book, please get in touch:

USA
editors@focalpress.com

Europe and rest of world
ge.kennedy@elsevier.com

Contents:

DVD-VIDEO

- 'Ghosthunter'
- 'The Making Of Ghosthunter'
- Dolby 5.1 soundtrack for 'Ghosthunter'
- 'Sound on Film - with Robin O'Donoghue'
- 'Special Effects Show and Tell by CFC - Audio Commentary by Director Simon Corris'
- 'The Cannes Promo'
- Kodak

DVD-ROM

- Contracts - Crew
- Actors
- Release Form
- Budget and Contact Database software demo
- Useful addresses and websites
- Production forms
- Scriptwriting software and tutorial
- 'Ghosthunter' production stills
- 'Ghosthunter' poster